Baylor University Medical Center:
Yesterday, Today and Tomorrow

Baylor University Medical Center: Yesterday, Today and Tomorrow

by
Lana Henderson

Baylor University Press • 1978 • Waco, Texas

Acknowledgments

No book—least of all a history—is the effort of any single individual. The preparation of this account of the first 75 years of Baylor University Medical Center, which began in May 1977, involved an all-out effort by many people and the invaluable assistance of scores of others in order to have the book ready in time for the anniversary.

The author acknowledges with deep gratitude the reference material obtained from other authors, especially the Rev. Powhatan W. James, whose *Fifty Years of Baylor University Hospital* was published in 1953 on the occasion of Baylor's golden anniversary. The Rev. James preserved a great deal of priceless information, gathered from people connected with the hospital in its early days, that otherwise would have been totally lost by 1977. He spent six months in research, interviewing oldtimers and painstakingly studying volumes of minutes kept by the Board of Trustees, financial records and other documents. Other vital reference works for this 75-year history included *Doctors and Doctors—Wise and Otherwise* by Dr. Charles M. Rosser; *A History of Baylor College of Medicine* by Dr. W. H. Moursund; *The University of Texas Southwestern Medical School, Medical Education in Dallas, 1900-1975* by Dr. John S. Chapman; *The Oral Memoirs of Milford O. Rouse,* published in 1972 by Baylor University; *The Story of the 56th Evac,* edited by Dr. Ben A. Merrick, and *The Early History of Medicine in Dallas, 1841-1900,* a master's thesis prepared by Marie Louise Giles.

To list the names of everyone without whose help this book might never have happened is out of the question in this limited space, but there are a few who must be singled out in particular: Robert L. Heath, executive officer of the Dallas County Medical Society, and Laurine Abernethy, the medical society's executive assistant, who opened their library and research files to me to help establish a starting point for the project; the researchers in the Texas Collection of the Dallas Public Library, who offered immediate assistance each time I called with a question; the Public Relations Department at the Medical Center, whose files and photographs all were made available to me; my advisory committee, composed of Dr. George J. Race, Dr. Ben A. Merrick, Dr. Oran V. Prejean, Dr. James Cantrell, Dr. Travis S. Berry and C. T. Beckham; Boone Powell and David Hitt, who spent innumerable hours working with me.

In addition, four Baylor secretaries helped me in countless ways through dozens of crises. Judy Williams, Lola McKinney, Lisa Polansky and Marilyn Hulse served as capable research assistants, set up interviews, typed, Xeroxed material, delivered messages, etc. You name it and they did it—not because it was a requirement of their jobs or because they were being paid extra, but because they wanted to.

And, finally, I appreciatively acknowledge the professional assistance and moral support of my husband, freelance writer Bill Sloan, who came to the rescue every time a deadline neared, editing my material and generally helping me shape the book into its final form, while also tolerating the piles of books, photos, manuscripts and memorabilia I had strewn from one end of our house to the other.

Lana Henderson
Dallas, Texas

Foreword

The story of Baylor University Medical Center from 1903 to 1978 chronicles the growth and development of a small "sanitarium" into one of the world's finest medical centers with the most modern equipment and a highly specialized staff offering advanced medical services for all human disorders. It is also the story of the progress of the rather primitive medical science of 75 years ago to the complex procedures, dramatic breakthroughs and exciting research of today.

This story exemplifies how American free enterprise has given rise to the finest health care system in the world, and offers a most persuasive argument against the nationalization of our health care institutions and for the continuation of the unparalleled progress we have attained under private enterprise.

In many ways, the history of Baylor University Medical Center parallels the phenomenal growth and progress of the great City of Dallas. Both the Medical Center and Dallas are tributes to the energy, imagination and dedication of a special breed of men who have wrought so much here—and done it so wondrously well.

Abner V. McCall
President
Baylor University
Waco, Texas

Contents

Introduction

This record of the 75-year history of Baylor University Medical Center is remarkable in many respects. It vividly documents the events and accomplishments of this important institution, from its earliest days in 1903 when it began as the Texas Baptist Memorial Sanitarium, housed in a renovated 14-room house costing $22,500, to the present far-flung and thriving Medical Center, which includes five separate hospitals, covers nine city blocks and has facilities valued in excess of $100 million.

The Medical Center commands high regard among the nation's major health care facilities, and this historical account makes clear how this envied position evolved. For not only has the center kept pace with developing patterns of patient care, but it has also taken the lead in many prime areas of medical services. These innovations, widely copied by other hospitals, include procedures developed at Baylor in hematology and blood banking, critical review of surgical procedures and heart disease diagnosis. And, most significantly, the concept of hospitalization insurance had its origin there, in the form of the "Baylor Plan"—a system born during Depression days to cover hospital costs for financially hard-pressed Dallas school teachers.

This volume, together with Dr. John Chapman's book, *Southwestern Medical School: Medical Education in Dallas, 1900-1975*, provides a rich documentary source for anyone interested in the growth of medicine in Dallas during the first three-quarters of the Twentieth Century—a time of tumultuous change. In tandem, these two sources supply the most complete record available of the rupture of relationships that occurred in the early 1940s, leading to the decision by Baylor University to move its medical school from Dallas to Houston in 1943.

Perhaps most importantly, the history records in considerable detail the vital role played by relatively few dedicated and talented persons who, in turn, influenced many others who made valuable contributions in one way or another to the development of the Medical Center. Any list is apt to omit someone, but special note should be made of the contributions of Dr. Charles Rosser, in the very beginning; Colonel C. C. Slaughter; Dr. George Truett; Dr. E. H. Cary; Mr. Boone Powell, and Mr. Dewey Presley. Mr. Powell, in particular, should be recognized for his leadership, his vision, his organizational ability, and his dedication of purpose which have sparked the remarkable growth of the Medical Center over the last 30 years. To an extraordinary degree, the growth of the Medical Center can be likened to the growth of the City of Dallas itself. From the outset, both have enjoyed leadership and support from among the most enlightened and public-spirited citizens in the community. The several successful fund drives conducted by Baylor, most notably those for the George W. Truett Memorial Hospital and the Erik and Margaret Jonsson Medical and Surgical Hospital, have demonstrated the broad, flint-hard base of support that exists, cutting across denominational lines, a pattern which has become characteristic of Dallas philanthropy in support of worthwhile projects intended to improve the quality of life for its people. The extent to which Baylor Medical Center has benefited from this enlightened community consensus testifies not only to the generosity of the citizenry but to the evident quality of the institution and its programs.

In addition to the constantly expanding and improving services its hospitals and related facilities have provided their patients, Baylor has been a vital force in the fight against threatened and once seemingly irreversible deterioration of the homes and business establishments of the geographic area surrounding the center. Between the mid-1950s and 1970, there was a substantial and progressive deterioration of property in the heart of old East Dallas, but during the 1970s this trend has been halted and now appears permanently reversed—and Baylor, demonstrating a strong ongoing commitment to the revitalization of a sizable sector, can take considerable credit for this accomplishment.

Thus we have documented in this useful history the mutually shared benefits derived from interaction between a worthy service institution and the community which it serves and from which it draws life-giving support. In countless ways, the community is indebted to all those individuals who, through the years, have had a part in shaping the once diminutive Good Samaritan Hospital on Junius Street into the model health-care mecca that it is today, rising to its present recognized position as one of the truly outstanding hospital complexes in the nation. It has been a pacesetter in the past, and there is every reason to believe it will continue to be that in the future.

Charles C. Sprague, M.D.
President
University of Texas Health Science Center
Dallas, Texas

Baylor University Medical Center: Yesterday, Today and Tomorrow

I

Today and Yesterday

A Medical Giant

The story of Baylor University Medical Center is inseparably linked to the same pioneer spirit that has built Dallas from a prairie crossroads into one of the great cities of the world, and Texas from a vast, empty wilderness into the rich agri-industrial empire it is today. It is the story of tireless frontier doctors who traveled countless miles by horse and buggy to aid the sick, the newborn and the dying, and of modern researchers who fight disease with space-age technological miracles in sparkling laboratories. It is the story of outmanned physicians of another era grappling with killer diseases, such as typhoid, malaria and tuberculosis, and of today's medical experts, seeking new breakthroughs against cancer and heart disease. It is a dynamic story of conflict, courage and accomplishment, written by people with the wisdom to profit from the past, the energy to serve the present and the vision to face the future. Along the way, an incredible cast of characters has played key roles in the dramatic story of Baylor's progress—cattle barons and college presidents, ministers and manufacturers, bankers and lawyers, judges and hospital administrators, physicians and community leaders. All in all, it is, in many respects, a story as big as Texas itself.

Today, 75 years after its founding in a converted residence on Junius Street, the Baylor University Medical Center campus stretches out to encompass nine full city blocks around that original site in old

1

East Dallas. With a total of 1,275 beds, the Medical Center includes five separate hospitals, each with its own administration. It has grown from the $22,500 two-story brick house in which it began as the Texas Baptist Memorial Sanitarium into a massive health-care complex, consisting of a network of corporations, with a physical plant valued at $100 million.

As it observes three-quarters of a century of expansion, medical advancement and service to mankind, the Medical Center, a unit of Baylor University at Waco, has a medical staff of 750, an employe staff of 4,000 and more than 800 students in medical, paramedical and nursing education programs. Nationally, Baylor ranks as the second largest church-related hospital entity and the sixth largest among all non-governmental general hospitals. In the number of patients admitted, Baylor ranks fifth among all non-governmental general hospitals in the United States with more than 45,000 admissions annually. And yet, as big as it has become, there are still a few physical evidences of Baylor's proud past. The columned building on Junius Street, which was opened in 1909 to replace the original two-story residence housing the hospital, is one example. It still faces Junius, although the main portion of the Medical Center now fronts on Gaston Avenue, East Dallas' major thoroughfare, and it still bears the inscription of the "Texas Baptist Memorial Sanitarium." Now, however, it is officially known as the Minnie S. Veal Teaching and Research Hospital and adjoins the four other hospitals comprising the Baylor complex: The George W. Truett Memorial Hospital, completed in 1950; the Karl and Esther Hoblitzelle Memorial Hospital, added in 1959; the Erik and Margaret Jonsson Medical and Surgical Hospital, finished in 1970, and the Carr P. Collins Hospital, dedicated in 1972. Other major facilities on the Baylor campus include the Charles A. Sammons Cancer Center, the H. L. and Ruth Ray Hunt Heart Center, the A. Webb

Roberts Center for Continuing Education, the Wilma Bass Memorial Residency Hall, the Harry W. Bass Education Center, the Grady H. Vaughn Department of Physical Medicine, the W. W. Caruth Surgical Research Laboratory and the Baylor Medical Plaza physicians' office building, consisting of twin towers named in honor of James K. and Susie L. Wadley and Albert S. and Velma Barnett and a base building containing diagnostic and therapeutic units, restaurants, hotel, post office and other businesses. The Baylor University School of Nursing and the Baylor College of Dentistry are also located on the campus.

With its broad range of services, Baylor's patients come from all over Texas and across the Southwest. It is nationally recognized as a regional medical referral center, and, in many published rankings of the best hospitals in recent years, it has been cited as one of the top 10 centers in the country.

Since its humble beginning in 1903 as the Texas Baptist Memorial Sanitarium, the Medical Center has drawn nationally recognized medical talent to its staff and to Dallas, including many of the first specialists in Texas. Among those pioneer physicians who aligned themselves with Baylor were J. B. "Daddy" Shelmire, the city' first dermatologist (he is also said to have been the first Dallas physician to have a microscope in his office); J. M. Martin, the first x-ray specialist; Curtice Rosser, the city's first colon and rectal surgeon; Robert Shaw, the first thoracic surgeon; James T. Mills, the first plastic surgeon; Albert P. D'Errico, the first formally-trained neurosurgeon; J. H. Black, the first pathologist and allergist and the first physician to perform a blood transfusion in Dallas; W. B. Carrell, the first orthopedic surgeon; A. I. Folsom, the first urologist; Ruth Jackson, the first woman in the United States to be certified by the American Board of Orthopedic Surgery; H. Frank Carman, Dallas' first pulmonary disease specialist; and E. M. Krusen, the first specialist in physical medicine in North Texas. It was also the home hospital of the only two Texans ever to serve as president of the American Medical Association, Drs. Edward H. Cary and Milford O. Rouse.

Throughout the years, Baylor has been recognized as an innovator in the hospital world. It was the birthplace in 1929 of the Blue Cross hospitalization prepayment concept, which now finances health care coverage for almost 90 million Americans. Later, in the 1940s, the American Association of Blood Banks and the International Society of Hematology got their starts at Baylor. Baylor has also remained a national pacesetter in its administrative concepts, many of which are in use in hospitals across the country. For example, Baylor employed the idea of organizationally dividing a large medical center complex into separate hospitals to offer patients the personalized care of a small hospital, while providing the specialized services available only in a very large medical facility. And the Medical Center's organizational system for long-range planning, in effect since 1962, allows Baylor to keep astride of today's developments while contemplating and preparing for advancements that may still be years away.

Clearly, the "team" concept of management and the close exchange of ideas among hospital administration, the Board of Trustees and the medical staff have been vital forces in shaping the destiny of the Medical Center. But every team needs strong leadership, and it is provided at Baylor by Boone Powell, chairman of the Medical Center's Executive Committee and a vice president of Baylor University, and David H. Hitt, the Medical Center's executive director.

Through his farsightedness and his determination never to settle for less than the best in either facilities or personnel, Boone Powell has been a part of Baylor's march to greatness for more than 30 years. Since being named administrator and chief executive officer in

4

1948, he has been a key figure in every expansion of the Medical Center since that time. He was named Baylor's director in January 1975 and continues today, as chairman of the Executive Committee, to lead Baylor toward even greater accomplishments and to lend personal daily meaning to one of his favorite axioms: "The future belongs to those who prepare for it."

Looking ahead has always been a characteristic of Baylor. But no matter how easy it might sound, none of the progress has come easily. Throughout its colorful history, Baylor has repeatedly overcome what seemed insurmountable obstacles at the time. Only in this way has it become one of the largest and most respected medical facilities in the United States.

From its infancy up until the founding of the George W. Truett Hospital in 1950, the Medical Center faced an almost constant problem of insufficient funding, a problem that since has been lessened by growth with careful management and with the generosity of Texas Baptists in particular and Dallas citizens in general. It survived the temporary loss of many members of its medical and nursing staffs who answered the calls for front-line duty in two World Wars. It lived through the Great Depression and the moving of the Baylor University College of Medicine to Houston in July 1943, an acute blow to the status and role of Baylor University Hospital for several years. It witnessed at close range the deterioration in the "silk stocking district" of East Dallas with the population migration to the suburbs that began in the 1950s. But despite these changes, the Medical Center engaged in an aggressive program of urban renewal and continued to build and to serve as a steadying influence and a growing landmark of hope and prosperity in its neighborhood. Today, Baylor's faith in old East Dallas is joined by other groups in a surge of revival and redevelopment occurring in this historic section of the city.

As one decade has dissolved into the next, new challenges have constantly arisen. The mid-60s brought Medicare and a growing tide of government regulation and intervention in the hospital industry and an angry outcry from both government and citizens for rigid steps to contain rising hospital costs in the face of multiplying demand for services and inflation. The mid-70s saw the development of a nationwide malpractice insurance crisis, which sent Baylor's insurance costs soaring by more than 1,000 per cent within a four-year span. And, as Baylor moves to the threshold of the 1980s, still other challenges lie ahead.

But Baylor is not afraid of challenge. Indeed, challenge has been its trademark from the very beginning.

Birth of an Idea

The official charter for the institution now known as Baylor University Medical Center was granted by the State of Texas on October 16, 1903, to a small medical facility then called the Texas Baptist Memorial Sanitarium. The events that led to the establishment of the sanitarium actually began in the summer of 1900—long before Texas Baptists had ever considered undertaking a hospital project in Dallas. That summer, the University of Dallas Medical Department, which was to later become Baylor College of Medicine, began to take shape, although that shape was at first nebulous and ill-defined. It was the creation of the medical department that called attention to the need for another hospital in town. Because the long and complicated history of the medical school's birth pangs and the eventual beginnings of Baylor University Medical Center are inextricably entwined, it is impossible to separate one story from the other.

The driving force behind the medical school idea

was tall, plain-spoken Dr. Charles McDaniel Rosser, a native of Cuthbert, Georgia, who had come to Texas in 1865 at the age of four, settling with his parents in Camp County, near the town of Pittsburg. Dr. Rosser obtained his early education at the East Texas Academic Institute at Leesburg, and as was then customary for a young man who wanted to become a physician, later served a preceptorship under Dr. E. P. Becton of Sulphur Springs. In 1884, he entered the Medical Department of the University of Louisville, but since no college education was required for Texas physicians in those days, he left after a year, obtained his medical certificate and returned to begin his practice in the small Texas communities of Donaldson, Lone Oak, Emory and Reagor Springs. But in 1887, he went back to Louisville to complete his second year of medical school. He graduated with honors and then set up a practice at Waxahachie. By 1889, he had caught the attention of the medical community by delivering a paper on yellow fever control before a meeting of the Texas State Medical Association in San Antonio. As a result, he was named associate editor of the *Texas Courier Record of Medicine* published in Dallas, where he moved that same year.

Dr. Rosser was a man of limitless drive and energy. By 1891, he had been appointed health officer for the City of Dallas, a position in which he witnessed at firsthand the appalling conditions at chaotic, overcrowded City Hospital. An 1891 report by a municipal hospital committee painted a graphic picture of the hospital at the time Dr. Rosser took office:

"The premises, especially the privy, were in filthy sodden condition—there being no sewer connection. The hospital was crowded to the doors with patients, most of them old chronics and incurables. The doors and windows of the main building, including the kitchen and dining room were without screens, an encouragement to disease and infection. And, above all, the steward, who was utterly ignorant of drugs and their effects on human beings, was filling prescriptions, which was not only a danger to patients, but a violation of state pharmacy laws."

At the time, Dallas was far from being the sparkling, modern city it is today. Residents were still complaining about lax laws that allowed hogs to run loose and create "stinking mudholes" in the town's main thoroughfares. The dumping of refuse and animal carcasses in piles along the sidewalks was a common practice. Sanitary sewer systems were rare. Even the purity of drinking water could not always be taken for granted.

Dr. Rosser was appalled at some of the conditions he found and became a major force in seeking reforms at City Hospital and in the enactment of public health ordinances. Although he resigned his municipal post in 1892 to become surgeon for the Houston and Texas Central Railway and chairman of the state medicine section of the Texas Medical Association, he helped set the stage for the construction of the city's new Parkland Hospital in 1894. In 1895, Dr. Rosser was appointed superintendent of the North Texas Hospital for the Insane at Terrell, but resigned two years later to join Dr. S. E. Milliken of Dallas as a partner in private practice. By this time, Dr. Rosser was convinced that Dallas not only needed, but deserved, its own medical college. As a new century began, he and several other local physicians approached the city fathers to enlist their support in a drive to build such a school.

To obtain an accurate perspective on the times in which the medical college was conceived, let's look back to the hot summer day of August 14, 1900, when physicians supporting the concept met at the office of Dr. J. B. Titterington to announce their formal agreement that the school should be built.

Dallas had come a long way since its "hog wallow" days of the early 1890s. It was now a prosperous city of 42,638 persons with a rapidly spreading reputation as a cotton, railroad and financial center. Worley's City Directory listed the names of 146 practicing physicians in Dallas, and there were two hospitals: Parkland, the tax-supported public facility on Oak Lawn Avenue, and the privately owned St. Paul Sanitarium, which had been completed just two years earlier on Bryan Street. The doctors attending the meeting were dressed in top hats and tails, the unofficial uniform of the well-dressed physician of the period. Among them were Drs. Rosser, Milliken, A. F. Beddoe, V. P. Armstrong, L. Ashton and B. E. Hadra, all of Dallas; J. E. Gilcreest of Gainesville and Joe Becton of Greenville. They arrived in elegant glass-windowed coaches drawn by teams of sleek horses. Most of the doctors wore beards, perhaps to add dignity and age to their appearances.

The day after the meeting, an announcement appeared in the newspapers inviting "all reputable physicians" throughout the community to attend a special meeting the following day. The announcement, signed by Dallas Mayor Ben E. Cabell, Chamber of Commerce President Charles Steinman and attorney W. J. Moroney, read in part:

"At the request of a large number of the physicians of Dallas and Oak Cliff, we respectfully announce that a meeting of physicians will be held in the Council Chamber of the City Hall on Thursday, August 16, at 8:30 p.m. for the purpose of taking the necessary preliminary steps to establish a medical college in Dallas. All regular physicians in good standing are invited to be present and to aid in organizing a college. . . . If for any reason some of the physicians cannot now be of active assistance in the work, it is hoped that they will at least maintain a friendly attitude toward the institution, and become identified with its success at a later period. . . ."

From the beginning, though, there was opposition to the idea from within the local medical community.

In fact, the meeting that followed deteriorated into little more than a shouting match. Of the approximately 55 physicians who attended the gathering, about 40 opposed the medical school concept and only about 15 favored the proposal. The opposition was led by Dr. Stephen D. Thruston, who was supported by St. Paul Sanitarium, the strongest medical influence in Dallas at that time. St. Paul physicians and administrators cited three reasons for their opposition: (1) There were already too many medical colleges operating in the country; (2) Dallas was not large enough to support such a facility; and (3) the physicians of Dallas were not capable of instructing medical students.

As the debate raged on, Dr. Rosser, a stalwart but mild-mannered and statesman-like man, finally walked to the front of the room and faced the audience. "I can understand why a possible majority of the profession might not want personal connection with the enterprise," he said, "but why are you here? Not every man who has a dollar that he does not need for his daily bread wants to run a bank, but would gentlemen not so disposed go to a place of meeting to disturb and make organization difficult for those who do? Not every politely educated man wants to teach literature, but would others not so qualified or inclined go to a place of meeting for the purpose of embarrassing and making difficult such conclusion? No! Never on earth, gentlemen, did a set of gentlemen assemble for a purpose such as you gentlemen have assembled tonight."

After thus chastising the dissident physicians, he added matter-of-factly: "There may be some here who, if left to themselves, would not want to organize a medical college, but if there is going to be one they would like to be in it. I tell you now, not as a threat but as a matter of information—there is going to be one . . . ."

Not surprisingly, a charter for the University of

Dr. Charles M. Rosser was the founder of the University of Dallas
Medical Department and the Good Samaritan Hospital. The medical department
later became the Baylor College of Medicine, and the Good Samaritan Hospital
evolved into the institution we know today as Baylor University
Medical Center.

Dallas Medical Department was filed with the Secretary of State's office on September 15, 1900, with the stated purpose of teaching the theory and practice of medicine and surgery and allied sciences, and the formation and operation of a polyclinic for instruction and separate departments for dentistry and pharmacy. Capital stock was listed as $3,000 and incorporators as Drs. Milliken, Titterington and Ashton.

The medical college officially opened its doors on November 19, 1900, in a leased building in what is now the 1300 block of Commerce Street, across from the present site of the Adolphus Hotel. The first faculty included Dr. Gilcreest, an 1876 graduate of the University of Missouri Medical School, as president of the college and teacher of gynecology; German-born Dr. Hadra, a graduate of the University of Berlin who had come to Texas in 1870 and who was the current president of the Texas Medical Association, as vice president and teacher of surgery, and Dr. Titterington, an 1897 graduate of New York's Bellevue Hospital Medical College, as dean of the faculty, acting secretary and teacher of anatomy and diseases of eye, ear, nose and throat.

Dr. Rosser taught clinical medicine and mental and nervous diseases; Dr. Becton, an 1890 graduate of Vanderbilt University School of Medicine, taught physiology; Dr. Beddoe, who received his M. D. degree from Memphis Hospital Medical College in 1894, taught diseases of children; Dr. David Davidson, an 1898 graduate of Long Island College Hospital Medical School, taught histology and physiology; and Dr. Elbert Dunlap, who received the M. D. degree from the Beaumont Hospital Medical College in St. Louis in 1896, was appointed to teach materia medica.

Prior to the actual opening, however, school officials began to worry about the "calamitous embarrassment" that would result if no students showed up for classes. But the enterprising Dr. Rosser put an end

12

to these worries, too. He had learned that one William T. Dunn of Greenville was preparing to leave his hometown to attend medical school in Memphis, Tennessee, and was planning to board a Cotton Belt Railway train for the trip. As Dunn was about to step aboard the train, Dr. Rosser intercepted him and made him the following proposition: If Dunn would turn in his train ticket and use the refund to buy a horse and saddlebags and come to Dallas, he could have the newly created position of registrar at the Dallas medical school. In return for his service as registrar, his fees ($75 per session, $5 for matriculation and $25 for graduation) would be paid by the school. As Dr. Rosser would recall later: "When the engine was through switching and the train was going north, the 'bird in the bush' was in the hand . . . ." Thus did it come to pass that Registrar William T. Dunn signed himself up as the first student—and, for a time, the entire student body—at the fledgling Dallas medical college.

Almost simultaneously, though, a controversy erupted at the neighboring Fort Worth School of Medicine and another 20 students were suddenly added to the Dallas school's enrollment. By the time the first course of lectures began, Registrar Dunn had earned his keep by enrolling no less than 80 other students.

Medical Education Circa 1900

From all available records, it appears that lectures were the principal method of instruction at the new school. Reports indicate that facilities and materials for anatomical dissection and chemical laboratory teaching were made available during the first session. In such all-important courses as human anatomy, the only cadavers available for dissection were unclaimed bodies snatched on the sly, either before or immediately after burial in paupers' graves.

13

There is no better illustration of the grisly, clandestine and sometimes nerve-wracking manner in which medical students had to obtain bodies for anatomical study than the following excerpt from Dr. Rosser's book, *Doctors and Doctors, Wise and Otherwise*, in which he tells of two medical students who were working their way through school by transporting bodies to the school's dissecting room. Usually, the trips were made discreetly late at night when the streets were deserted. Once in a while, though, they weren't quite deserted enough. On this particular night, one of the students had a body in his wagon and was hurrying toward the medical school when a slight mishap took place. "The specimen, already in rigor mortis (and) bent to the shape of a half-closed jack knife, sat beside the student in an open piano-box buggy," Dr. Rosser wrote, "(and was) fully clothed. Down Main Street, a quick turn to the left on Akard en route to the college, and a hat from the lifeless companion went with the winds, to be overtaken by a late straggler on the streets. 'Hello, you've lost your hat,' the straggler cried. 'All right,' said the student, 'he says you can have it.' "

As Dr. Dunlap, a member of the first faculty, would recall in a brief history written in 1931: "The equipment was 'meager and inadequate.' "

But no matter how inadequate its facilities may have appeared in retrospect, the University of Dallas Medical Department was progressive and forward-looking in comparison to other schools of its time. The education of the doctor of the late Nineteenth Century was primitive at best, and, prior to July 1901, Texas medical laws were among the most lax in the United States. Virtually any medical diploma entitled a practitioner to treat the sick, and even in the absence of a diploma, obtaining a certificate to practice medicine involved little more than a formality and the payment of a $15 fee.

The would-be physician usually began his train-

First faculty and class
of the University of Dallas
Medical Department—1900

ing by reading medicine as a sort of apprentice under a qualified preceptor. He could then apply for admission to medical school, the only prerequisites for which were a high school diploma or equivalent and a certificate "signed by any reputable doctor (stating) that the student had, under his directions as a preceptor, given reasonable study to fundamental branches of the sciences."

After just two years of medical school, a new doctor was ready for practice, with none of the modern internship or residency requirements to delay him. With any type of medical degree, he had only to register his diploma with the county clerk and hang out his shingle.

But perhaps the most important difference between early and modern medical education requirements is that a doctor could practice for a lifetime without ever having attended a medical college. The aspiring physician choosing this route had only to pass an examination before a district board composed of three doctors appointed by a district judge to receive a certificate for practice. A set of ethical standards was observed by most physicians who held membership in national, state, city or county medical associations, partly because other society members watched them closely for unbecoming words or deeds and violations of the accepted behavior code. One Dallas physician of the period, for example, was severely reprimanded for attempting an operation on a horse.

Part of a physician's practical education was in learning what fees were appropriate. An office visit usually cost the patient $1, while a home visit fee was $2. For a case of confinement, in which a doctor might have to bathe and dress babies of ailing mothers, he might charge $10. And it was normal procedure to add a fee of 50 cents for every mile traveled out of the corporate limits of the city.

Because of the lax laws, cults and pseudo-scientific systems of practice grew up in many areas. But because the cultists did not assume the obligations placed on physicians by the code of ethics, they were able to practice freely and lucratively for many years. And actually these pseudo-scientific practitioners were no more poorly trained than any other physician. They were merely general practitioners who supported a different system of cures than those supported by regular doctors. Many were graduates of medical schools which, however disreputable they may have been, still enjoyed the same degree of legal recognition as all the rest.

II

Birth of a Hospital

Good Samaritan Founded

One of the main obstacles in producing fully qualified physicians was the lack of hospitals in which medical students could receive clinical training. In Dallas, municipal authorities readily agreed to allow the local students to attend patients at city-operated Parkland Hospital. But there was no street car service to Parkland at the time, and it was too far to walk from the school's downtown Commerce Street location. Nevertheless, because senior students needed bedside and operating room training, they made the trip three times a week in a "rough-riding" wagonette drawn by two bay ponies—except in wet weather, when the roads became impassable.

After a short while, though, Dr. Rosser decided to make other arrangements. The only private general hospital in Dallas was St. Paul, which had opposed creation of the medical school in the first place, but Dr. Rosser sought permission to let his students train there, anyway. The ensuing conversation between Dr. Rosser and St. Paul's sister superior, Sister Mary Bernard, reportedly went like this:

Sister Mary Bernard: "Dr. Rosser, I will be glad for you to bring your patients here and your students as you would any other visitors, but we cannot officially recognize your college. Our staff opposes it."

Dr. Rosser (with hat in hand): "Sister, I want to be polite, but I must tell you that the college refuses to die. In order to live, it must have hospital facilities, and if St. Paul can't furnish them or will not furnish them, we must make other arrangements. I bid you good morning, madam."

Disheartened, Dr. Rosser decided to ask his friend and confidante, Dr. J. B. Gambrell, a leader of the Baptist denomination, for his advice. Dr. Gambrell told Dr. Rosser he should try to start a hospital of his own and attempt to win support for the project among the city's influential Baptists. "We will come to you, but I don't know when," Dr. Gambrell said. "Colonel C. C. Slaughter (the famed cattle baron who made his home in Dallas) is a good man who is worth millions. He has done a great deal for our denomination, and some day he will do something worthy for his city. It might just as well be a hospital."

His enthusiasm thus bolstered by the glowing prophecy of his friend, Dr. Rosser plunged ahead, as usual. He purchased a two-story, 14-room brick mansion located in a grove of native oaks on Junius Street and known as "The Hopkins Place," after obtaining advance approval of the site by Dr. Gambrell and two other leading Baptists, Dr. R. C. Buckner, founder and president of Buckner Orphans Home, and publicist J. B. Cranfill. The house had been built by Colonel W. B. Wright, an early-day pioneer, in 1880, and was owned by Judge M. L. Crawford at the time Dr. Rosser decided to purchase it for the hospital. Dr. Rosser felt the site was well suited to his purposes, since it was as near to the center of town as he could afford and far enough away from surrounding residential areas to avoid community protest. The purchase price was $22,500, to be paid out over an extended period.

The house, once owned by Captain William H. Gaston, the man for whom Gaston Avenue was named, was remodeled to provide space for a ward, an admitting area and operating rooms, and by 1901 the erstwhile mansion was ready to begin functioning in its new role as the city's second privately operated general hospital. Advertisements for the formal opening ceremonies of the Good Samaritan Hospital brought people from all walks of life to the site on Junius Street. At the moment that evening when Dr. Rosser rose to address the crowd, no one had ever heard of Baylor University Medical Center, but Dr. Rosser's words were amazingly prophetic. He said that he believed the ultimate success of the medical college enterprise "might finally depend upon the support of a hospital of great importance," and expressed the conviction that "history would record this occasion (as) the initial step in the promotion of a great general hospital of the future."

A Momentous Visit

By the late spring of 1903, Dallas was a restless young city in ferment. No longer just another frontier town, it was flexing the growing muscles that would someday catapult it to a place of prominence among the nation's municipalities. Perhaps it took its cue from Teddy Roosevelt, the bombastic "Bullmoose" with the "Big Stick" who occupied the White House. Its population had swelled to a record 50,000 people and it seemed to be shouting flamboyantly: "Hey, look at me!" The fact that Dallas was going some place in a hurry was noisily attested to by an "automobile fad" that had brought no less than 40 motorcars to Dallas owners. No city of comparable size in the entire South could boast so many "horseless carriages."

Into this climate of ambition and prosperity and competitiveness came an international celebrity whose brief presence was to have lasting impact on the populace of Dallas and convince it that such a dynamic city needed and deserved a new hospital. The visitor's name was Dr. Adolf Lorenz, and he had won fame in the nation's press as the "Bloodless Surgeon of Vienna." He had come to the United States from his native Austria at the request of Philip Armour, wealthy head of the Chicago meat-packing

20

firm, who had heard of Dr. Lorenz' revolutionary treatment of congenital joint and bone deformities and who wanted him to correct a prenatal hip dislocation affecting one of the Armour children. Dr. Lorenz was known as the "Bloodless Surgeon" because he scorned the use of the scalpel and treated his patients by manual manipulation. His fee for the Armour case— huge by any standards, but especially for that era— was $30,000. That, plus his controversial and spectacular method of treatment, garnered him headlines from coast to coast.

Dr. Rosser had originally met Dr. Lorenz in Chicago while the latter was conducting demonstrations at Mercy Hospital there. Six months later, Dr. Rosser again encountered Dr. Lorenz at the American Medical Association's convention in New Orleans, where he invited the famous Austrian physician to come to Dallas as a guest of the medical school faculty.

During the convention, Dr. Lorenz held a series of treatment clinics at New Orleans' Charity Hospital, which were attended by delegates from all parts of the country. One news report gives the following account of one such clinic: "The operations were on two particularly aggravated cases of clubfoot, and the subjects were children. The amphitheatre was thronged, many delegates being present. The operations each took more than an hour and appeared to restore the deformed feet to a normal condition. He (Dr. Lorenz) said cures would become permanent after four months. His demonstrations made a strong impression. It is reported that they attracted a large number of children, but he was too fatigued after two operations to do more."

But before Dr. Lorenz left the convention site, he accepted Dr. Rosser's invitation to come to Dallas, which was, in itself, irrefutable evidence that Dallas was "coming of age" among America's cities—even if it currently had only about 100 hospital beds for its

50,000 inhabitants. Texas newspapers made front-page news of Dr. Lorenz' arrival in Dallas, and requests for seat reservations for his public appearances poured in from medical professionals in every part of the state.

He arrived on May 20, 1903, and after a welcoming breakfast at his hotel and a hurried drive around the city, he went directly to the Good Samaritan Hospital to examine prospective patients who had registered there from across Texas. An assigned assistant, Dr. E. E. Wrightman, noted the names of those selected for treatment. Finding the demand for his services so great and his time strictly limited, Dr. Lorenz agreed to hold two clinics daily, alternating locations between the hospital and the medical school building, instead of the one clinic per day he had originally planned. He also agreed to stay in Dallas for two additional days. In all, he stayed more than a week. By the time he departed, half a dozen former Texas Medical Association presidents, the chief surgeons of several Texas railroads, nearly all the state's high-ranking officials and a large percentage of its leading medical and surgical practitioners had come to see Dr. Lorenz in action. As Dr. Rosser recalled later: "The brilliant and splendid operative work, which centered attention and drew crowds, more than met every expectation. Hopeless cripples were cured, the man and his methods better understood, and science was advanced to broader usefulness."

But, as great as these achievements were, Dr. Lorenz made an even greater contribution to the welfare of Dallas, a contribution that would outlive any of the patients he treated during that momentous week. On the eve of his departure, a group of prominent Dallas citizens gathered at the six-story Oriental Hotel on Commerce Street, the largest and most prestigious hotel in town, to pay tribute to Dr. Lorenz. The program included addresses by Mayor Cabell; Dr. Rosser; the Right Reverend A. C. Garrett, bishop of the

Dr. Adolf Lorenz, the famed "Bloodless Surgeon of Vienna" focused worldwide attention on the Good Samaritan Hospital, below, when he visited Dallas in 1903. His visit was the catalyst that caused Texas Baptists to assume control of the hospital.

Episcopal Diocese of Dallas; Texas Attorney General M. M. Crane and Judges George N. Aldredge and Edward Gray, all of whom heaped glowing praise upon "the stranger within our gates."

But perhaps the most important speech of all, from an historic standpoint, was the final address of the evening. The speaker was Dr. George W. Truett, the forceful and eloquent young pastor of the First Baptist Church of Dallas. All eyes were fixed on the 36-year-old minister as he issued a resounding challenge to Dallas citizens. "Is it not now time," he asked, "to begin the erection of a great humanitarian hospital, one to which men of all creeds and those of none may come with equal confidence?" The audience signaled its affirmation by rising to its feet in a storm of applause.

For a fleeting moment out of time, Dr. Lorenz had focused the attention of the entire medical world on Dallas. But the legacy he left in the hands of men like Dr. Truett and Dr. Rosser would cause that attention to return again and again in years to come.

The memorable Lorenz visit, which culminated in Texas Baptists assuming responsibility for the development of a new hospital, was recalled in a letter written 30 years later to Dr. Rosser. The writer was Dr. Lorenz himself, and the letter read in part: "I remember the old Good Samaritan Hospital . . . and often wondered by what magnificent steel and concrete structure it might have been substituted in the meantime. I remember the big hotel dinner, not overwhelmingly good, but richly spiced with lengthy speeches praising the bounty and the riches of glorious Texas. And I remember you—a dark boy with brown, touseled hair; very energetic and promising a lot of good work, which you have achieved, as I see by the papers. I congratulate the founder of Baylor Hospital and its medical school. I remember Main Street, which was so short that you could see from one end to the other. Cities grow faster in America than men grow old . . . ."

Although Dr. Lorenz expressed the desire to come back to Dallas in the letter, he never got the chance. But his predictions were as accurate as his memories. The day after the Lorenz banquet, Colonel C. C. Slaughter, a devout Baptist, noted philanthropist and a millionaire many times over in the cattle business, pledged $25,000 to Dr. Truett to get the new hospital going. But the sage Dr. Gambrell, the same one who had advised Dr. Rosser so well over the years, urged Dr. Truett not to accept the money. "Don't take it," he said. "You can't begin a million dollar hospital with $25,000 from a millionaire. Go, sit with him. He'll give you $50,000 just as easy."

Further conferences proved Dr. Gambrell correct. Colonel Slaughter not only contributed $50,000 outright; he also agreed to give two dollars for every one dollar contributed by other sources. The colonel's generosity, which progressively aggregated to about $200,000, not only made it possible to build a hospital, but guaranteed the continuation of the medical school as well. (It should be noted that Dallas businessman J. B. Wilson, builder of the historic downtown Wilson Building, also gave $50,000 to match Colonel Slaughter's original gift.)

In June 1903, less than a month after the drive for the hospital began, the medical school succeeded in consummating sponsorship by Baylor University, and soon thereafter came a directive that Texas Baptists assume responsibility for the construction of the "great humanitarian hospital" Dr. Truett had envisioned in his speech.

The hospital project was undertaken by the Baptist General Convention in a meeting in Dallas on a recommendation from an authorized committee composed of Dr. Gambrell, Dr. Truett and Colonel Slaughter. At the meeting, the Baptist General Convention of Texas also named the men who were to serve on the first Board of Directors. Dr. Buckner, a

Dallas resident who had advocated the hospital's creation in church journals two years before it became a reality, was selected to serve as president. Other members of the board were Dr. Truett, secretary; Colonel Slaughter, treasurer; E. T. Lewis of Dallas, who was to become the hospital's first superintendent; Dr. Gambrell of Dallas, a South Carolina Confederate veteran who came to Texas in 1896 and later became general secretary of the Baptist Convention's executive board; A. B. Flanary, G. W. McDaniel and A. N. Hall, all of Dallas; George W. Carroll of Beaumont; G. H. Connell of Fort Worth; F. W. Johnson of Pecos; F. L. Carroll of Waco; and J. P. Crouch of McKinney. According to the records, "all were brethren most active in promotion of the enterprise."

The first Board of Directors meeting was held on October 23, 1903, at which time the state charter for Texas Baptist Memorial Sanitarium was officially adopted.* Dr. Buckner had personally written the original charter, and filed it in Austin at his own expense.

At a subsequent meeting on October 26, the board discussed an offer by Dr. Rosser to allow the Baptists to purchase the Good Samaritan Hospital at the same price he had paid for it. "Gentlemen," he told the board, "you can have my hospital, the Good Samaritan, at what I paid for it, or, if you choose another site and build, the day you open for business I will close mine and move into yours and start practicing. Moreover, I will make you a present of my equipment."

A committee composed of Dr. Buckner, Colonel Slaughter and A. B. Flanary was appointed to report on the property. When the committee arrived at the Good Samaritan location for an on-site inspection, Colonel Slaughter was delighted. "The ideal site," the crusty cattle king exulted. "I bedded cattle down un-

*See Appendix A.

26

der these oak trees forty years ago. Let's buy it."

When the board met again on October 30, Dr. Rosser's offer was unanimously accepted. The seeds from which Baylor University Medical Center would later sprout had been successfully sown.

III

Triumph and Turmoil

Construction Begins

The Texas Baptist Memorial Sanitarium officially opened in the building formerly called the Good Samaritan Hospital on March 11, 1904. Five days later, on March 16, a group of twenty-two physicians was named to the hospital's medical staff, most of whom were also members of the medical school faculty. Dr. Pierre Wilson was designated as the hospital's first chief of staff. Originally from Denison, he had joined the faculty of Baylor University College of Medicine in 1903 as a professor of pathology and clinical surgery, and was serving in that position at the time of his hospital appointment. Other physicians named to the staff included Drs. Rosser, S. E. Milliken, J. M. Pace, R. W. Allen, V. P. Armstrong, Elbert Dunlap, S. W. Leeman, A. F. Beddoe, A. C. Graham, J. R. Bragg, J. H. Florence, W. W. Samuell, W. E. Crowe, F. J. Hall, A. M. Elmore, T. B. Fisher, P. L. Campbell, W. M. McRee, J. T. Wells, Lindsey Smith and S. D. Thruston. It is interesting to note, in passing, that Dr. Thruston was the same physician who had led opposition to Dr. Rosser's plan to start a medical school, an event that eventually led to establishment of the very hospital on whose staff Dr. Thruston was now serving, and that Dr. Milliken was one of the leaders of a faculty revolt that almost wrecked the medical school in its infancy.

Within six months of its opening, Texas Baptists had decided that the old hospital building did not fit in with their expansion plans, and so, on September

28

25, 1904, a building committee composed of Colonel Slaughter, Hospital Superintendent Lewis and Dr. Buckner was appointed to consider and report on plans for a new and adequate hospital. Less than a month later, the committee reported a tentative agreement with Dallas architect C. W. Bulger to draw up the plans for a new hospital, providing the Baptists could come to terms with Bulger on a fee. The Baptists moved with characteristic speed in approving the arrangement and a fee, and on Saturday, November 5, 1904, groundbreaking ceremonies for the new hospital were held at a site adjacent to the old building. Colonel Slaughter turned the first spade of dirt to symbolize the beginning of a new era of private philanthropy and civic responsibility in Dallas.

One week later, on November 12, the Texas Baptist Memorial Sanitarium made its first annual report to the Baptist General Convention of Texas, meeting in Waco. The report was prepared by Dr. Truett, who was serving at the time as secretary of the hospital board, and was read to the convention by him in behalf of the Board of Directors. The following is an excerpt from that report:

This convention will recall that one year ago the following action was taken:

Resolved (1), That it is the sense of this convention that the Baptists of Texas have too long neglected a proper and practical emphasis on the healing work in the life and ministry of Jesus Christ. Hospitals are the natural product of Christian religion and are becoming, more and more, the urgent need of our modern civilization.

Resolved (2), That we most heartily approve the timely movement recently inaugurated to establish in the City of Dallas, The Texas Baptist Memorial Sanitarium, and we pledge to the movement our cordial sympathy and substantial support. We believe the completion of this momentous movement will work a distinct advance in the denominational life and growth of our people.

Resolved (3), That this convention unreservedly commends this broadly humanitarian and Christian enterprise to the prayerful consideration and unstinted cooperation of all the pastors and churches within our bounds and to the goodwill and generous help of the general public.

Resolved (4), That this convention accepts the privilege of selecting the directors of the sanitarium in the way and manner prescribed in its by-laws. (The by-laws asked that the directors be selected by the convention at its regular annual meeting, with no more than three directors appointed each year, except to fill vacancies caused by resignation, death or removal from the state.)

In the speech accompanying his report, Dr. Truett called the birth of the Texas Baptist Memorial Sanitarium "the beginning of a new movement, looking to the rounding out of denominational agency to take in the full meaning of the Great Commission." He added that the directors were very fortunate to have secured the plot of ground for the hospital, near the heart of the city, and that "the experiment has more than justified our most sanguine hopes. The building has usually been overtaxed, and already the good results of the work are manifest in many ways. The sick from various parts of the Southwest are even now seeking and receiving its benefits."

In seeking the convention's blessing for the proposed new hospital, Dr. Truett spoke glowingly of a large central building with more than 100 "choice" rooms, a beautiful chapel and several large wards. The anticipated cost: $125,000. "This enterprise is a most persuasive appeal to practical philanthropy," he said in closing. "It will be God's instrument for the healing and saving of human life in all classes and conditions. It will contribute directly and immediately to the advancement of the healing idea, as specially represented by the competent physician and the trained nurse, and this institution must come to be the direct helper of every home, and a most potential factor in the progress of Christian civilization. . . ."

But as is the case with most great expansion projects, there was to be a great deal of sacrifice and inconvenience before the dream outlined to the conven-

30

tion by Dr. Truett could become a reality. On February 25, 1905, the sanitarium's Board of Directors voted unanimously to shut down the building they had bought from Dr. Rosser, at least insofar as the treatment of patients was concerned, because they felt it would be "unsafe for the best interests of patients to be closely contiguous to the work and noise incident to the erection of the new building." During the remaining years of its existence, the old Good Samaritan building would serve various functions, as a temporary home for the medical school and as a nurses' quarters, but it would never again be utilized as a treatment facility for the sick. In fact, as a result of the board's action on that winter day, not a single patient would be treated on the site of the Texas Baptist Memorial Sanitarium for more than four and one-half years. The sanitarium closed its doors on March 11, 1905, and would not reopen until mid-October, 1909.

In the interim, however, officials and directors of the hospital stayed constantly busy. One of their principal efforts was soliciting funds to help pay for the new construction and to begin a modest endowment fund. In October 1906, directors Slaughter, Buckner and Truett were appointed to a fund-raising committee, but the campaign they waged was only moderately successful. It is not known exactly how much money they actually raised, but in April 1907, the sanitarium increased a note for $50,000 to Colonel Slaughter to $100,000 and reduced the interest rate from eight to seven per cent. Prior to the execution of the larger note, work on the new building had come to a standstill because of a shortage of funds.

(To help the modern reader grasp the difference between $100,000 in the early 1900s and the same amount today, in relation to its purchasing power, consider a typical hospital bill issued by the Texas Baptist Memorial Sanitarium in 1904 to D. L. Riley, whose mother was discharged on May 8 of that year.

The younger Riley's total bill for his mother's hospital stay of two weeks and two days came to $36.20, of which $34.20 was for her room, $1.80 for "Gibson water," and 20 cents for laundry. By contrast, the average cost per day per patient in Dallas area hospitals in 1978 was $180.)

But financial woes failed to cloud the board's enthusiasm or to delay for very long the hospital's expansion. In July 1907, the directors authorized construction of a separate science building on the hospital grounds, and by the following November, the money for the project materialized in the form of a gift from Mrs. P. S. Ramseur of Paris, Texas. Mrs. Ramseur's donation included some 9,000 acres of Texas land and $15,000 in cash, its overall value exceeding $100,000. In recognition of her impressive contribution, the science building was formally named the Ramseur Science Hall. During the same period, numerous other gifts of real and other properties were made to the sanitarium. In fact, the hospital became the owner of so much land that it became necessary to appoint Dr. J. B. Cranfill, a new member of the Board of Directors, as "land agent" for the corporation.

The Slaughter Legend

On November 21, 1908, Dr. Buckner resigned as president of the Board of Directors, and Colonel Slaughter was elected to that position. In a historical sense, it was only fitting that this great soldier-rancher-humanitarian should occupy the hospital board's top office at the time of the opening of the new hospital he had made possible. The scion of a pioneer family with roots in both the Texas and American Revolutions, C. C. Slaughter was not only a financial godsend to what we know today as Baylor University Medical Center; he was also a true giant among giants in the annals of Texas history.

He was born in Sabine County, Texas, on February 9, 1837, when the Lone Star State was still a fledgling republic. His father was George Webb Slaughter, who served as Sam Houston's chief of scouts during the Texas Revolution and who was the last Texan to see the defenders of the Alamo alive. The elder Slaughter was present at the Battle of San Jacinto, where Houston's tattered army surprised and defeated Santa Ana and secured Texas' independence from Mexico. Soon after that stunning turn of events, General Houston gave his faithful aide permission to go home to Sabine County and marry Sara Anne Mason, a direct descendant of George Y. Mason of Virginia, who had served with Thomas Jefferson on the committee that wrote the Declaration of Independence in 1776. Christopher Columbus Slaughter was not only the first-born son of this union, but was said to have been the first white boy born in the Republic of Texas.

Following the Mexican War, in which the elder Slaughter served as a brevet colonel, the family moved to Palo Pinto County, where George Webb Slaughter launched a dual career as a successful cattle rancher and freelance Baptist preacher. He built his own church on his own land and preached the gospel as he believed it. Subservient to none, beloved by many, and described as "a man big in brains and courage," the elder Slaughter became a close friend and co-worker of Dr. Rufus C. Burleson, a former president of Baylor University.

In addition to a legacy of strength, wisdom and courage, George Webb Slaughter also gave his son a start in the cattle business—in the form of ninety-two "dogies" or motherless calves. Through hard work, keen management ability and sheer perseverance, C. C. Slaughter soon established himself as a leader among the cattlemen of the Southwest. He moved from Palo Pinto County to Jack County in 1869, and his business continued to thrive until raiding bands of

Comanches began to deplete his herds. He left his ranch to become a noted Indian fighter, serving as a captain in the Texas Rangers for several years. At the time of his election as president of the hospital board—and, indeed, until the day he died—Colonel Slaughter carried a rifle ball in his chest as a reminder of a violent frontier episode in which he was accidentally shot by one of his own Rangers while trailing a band of hostiles along the Devil's River in Southwest Texas. In critical condition, he was strapped to a blanket between two mules and carried to his Palo Pinto County home some three hundred miles north, where he eventually recovered.

In 1877, Colonel Slaughter moved his cattle to the headwaters of the Colorado River and established the Lazy S Ranch. At one time, he claimed a chunk of West Texas measuring two hundred miles square— not square miles—and encompassing a total of 24,000,000 acres of public domain. Later he owned in fee simple more than a million acres of fenced, improved ranch land, and was for many years the largest individual taxpayer in Texas. During this time, there were probably more cattle marketed under the Lazy S brand than any other brand in the world. Colonel Slaughter played a major role in converting the Texas livestock industry from the legendary Longhorn, which was less desirable as a beef animal, to the Hereford and other improved breeds. He was one of the organizers of both the Texas Cattle Raisers Association and the National Beef Producers' and Consumers' Association.

Colonel Slaughter moved to Dallas in 1875 and became prominently identified with almost every major community endeavor for the next 40 years. He also became a leading figure in the city's developing banking industry, serving as an organizer or key officer of four early-day Dallas banks, including the American Exchange National Bank, one of the forerunners of the First National Bank in Dallas.

34

In the early days of the Texas Baptist Memorial Sanitarium, Colonel C. C. Slaughter, the famed Texas cattle baron, was the primary benefactor for the hospital. In 1904, it was Colonel Slaughter, who turned the first spade of dirt at groundbreaking ceremonies for a new hospital to replace the old Good Samaritan building.

In all, Colonel Slaughter had nine children, five by his first wife, the former Cynthia Anne Jowell, whom he married in 1861 and who died in 1876, and four by his second wife, the former Carrie Aberill, whom he married in 1878. One of his children, the late Mrs. Minnie Slaughter Veal, also became one of Baylor's greatest financial benefactors. The present-day Veal Hospital, located in the building constructed largely with her father's financial gifts, is named in her honor.

Colonel Slaughter would remain president of the hospital board until May 1, 1911, when he stepped down because of an injury to his hip. But for all the remaining years of his life, he continued to be a vital guiding force for the new hospital he had done so much to make a reality. Late in his life, he summed up his philanthropic sentiments in simple, straightforward terms, saying: "I have prayed the Master to endow me with a hand to get and a heart to give." And, truly, he had seen his prayers answered in both respects as few men have before or since.

Realizing a Dream

When the Texas Baptist Memorial Sanitarium opened again on October 14, 1909, it marked one of the most important medical milestones in Dallas history up to that time. The opening of one of the most modern medical facilities in the Southwest was "the talk of the city," and justifiably so. The ornate new hospital boasted a total of 250 beds in six large wards and 114 private rooms, with every room and ward having outside ventilation. Based on a foundation of solid rock, the building faced 171 feet on Junius Street and was 134 feet in depth. It was described as "absolutely fireproof throughout." The central unit had five stories, including a basement, and two wings had four stories, also including basements.

The first patient admitted to the new hospital was

36

Mrs. J. K. Garner of Cisco, Texas. Although no records remain to show her exact ailment, her physician was Dr. Sydney S. Baird, a specialist in kidney diseases. It is also known that only medical patients were admitted during the first few days after the re-opening, because the operating rooms for surgical patients—a large amphitheatre where spectators, including family members of the patient, could watch the operation— was not quite ready. Although records do not show the date, the first surgical procedure at the new hospital was an eye operation performed by Dr. Edward H. Cary, one of the nation's outstanding eye, ear, nose and throat surgeons, and the man who succeeded Dr. Rosser in 1902 as dean of the medical college.

A graphic picture of what the new hospital was like when it first opened was obtained, nearly six decades later, from Mrs. Joe L. Harrell of Dallas, who was an 11-year-old patient named Edyth Brown when she entered the hospital with a knee injury on a November day in 1909, just a few weeks after the opening. In an October, 1968, article in the Medical Center employe magazine *Baylor Progress*, Mrs. Harrell remembered herself as a small, hurt, lonely child away from home for the first time and knowing no one in this seemingly vast city.

"On my first afternoon there," she recalled, "I was sitting in the corridor near the elevator when Mr. B. J. Roberts (who was named to succeed E. T. Lewis as hospital superintendent in 1909) came and sat with me for a while. Then he said, 'Let's take a walk back to the ward, for it's almost time for supper to be served.' I wasn't familiar with hospital terms, and I wondered just where we were going. I don't think I even felt worried or fearful in the hospital atmosphere; at that early age, it was interesting to me.

"I remember Dr. George W. Truett's frequent visits and concern for me. On Christmas morning, I found on my bedside table a beautiful plant with his card

The new Texas Baptist Memorial Sanitarium, above, was completed in 1904, and its facilities, such as the private patient room, below, were the most modern in the city. At left, the first class of nurses at the hospital poses on the front steps of the newly-completed building.

Hospital bills weren't what they are today, but then facilities didn't compare to today's either, as witnessed by the ward in a sanitarium clinic building, below. A private room, complete with the luxuries of a telephone and earphones to listen to a radio devotional, below, was a rarity.

Baptist Memorial Sanitarium

Dallas, Texas, 5-8 _____ 190_

two weeks & two days at 15⁰⁰ per week _____ 34.2

Gibson water   1.8

Laundry   2

34.2

Paid   Mrs Estelle Sharp

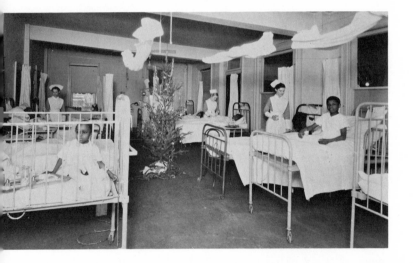

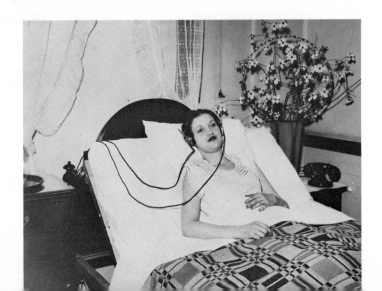

reading, 'To Edyth, the little girl who is over 300 miles away from home and her family at Christmas time. With love, George Truett.'

"Another highlight of my stay was Christmas dinner with Dr. J. B. Gambrell's family. As they lived only a short distance from the hospital, an orderly took me over in a wheelchair and a member of the family returned me to the hospital late that afternoon.

"I was given two dolls; one I dressed as a nurse, the other as a baby doll. I did this in the hospital sewing room where the nurses' uniforms were made. After this, I went regularly to the sewing room and learned to sew, helping with the uniforms. I could slip out of the wheelchair and sit at the machine. This helped me to pass the three months . . . ."

Whether it was viewed through the eyes of a small child or a full-grown adult, however, the new hospital of 1910—modern though it was by the standards of the day—couldn't compare with today's gleaming, computerized Medical Center. In a prospectus published that year by the Texas Baptist Memorial Sanitarium, some of the facilities were described as follows:

"The main floor back of the administration department is to be used for doctors' offices, waiting rooms and examining rooms. This department is connected with the ambulance entrance, which is located in the rear of the building. The balance of the space is to be used for linen and drug storerooms.

"The two wings on each side of the administration department are typical ward departments and this arrangement prevails on each of the three floors.

"The space over the main building on the second, third and fourth floors is taken up wholly by private bedrooms. These are neatly but plainly furnished . . . .

"The entire building is heated and ventilated by a system known as the 'blower system.' When it is desired to heat the building, fresh air is drawn from the outside by a fan eight feet in diameter and driven over a large steam coil, which is supplied with steam direct from the power plant. In passing over this steam coil, the air is heated and driven to the various rooms of the building by means of galvanized ducts.

"The Johnston system of temperature regulation has been installed. This consists of compressed air tubes, with openings in each room where the temperature is to be regulated. At these openings instruments known as thermostats are installed . . . .

"In each of the ward wings are located push button elevators, just large enough for one person with a basket or tray, which are to be used exclusively by the nurses or attendants. The main elevator for general hospital use is seven feet square, and is located in the center of the building . . . .

"A system of twenty-five house telephones connects all the offices, nurses' rooms and doctors' rooms in the building, independent of the city service, and in addition to this there is a complete system of 'buzzers' with annunciators in the nurses' rooms . . . .

"The institution has its own complete power plant for generating electricity and furnishing steam for heating and sterilizing. It is of 300 horsepower and furnishes also steam and power for the laundry . . . .

"A deep artesian well has been sunk and equipped with pump and tanks. The water is pumped directly from the well into storage pressure tanks located in the basement of the main building. These tanks are so arranged that the water can be forced into them under pressure and the entire building be supplied with water from them . . . .

"The entire roof of the building has been arranged for the use of a roof garden for convalescents. The parapet walls are lined with electric lights, and plants and seats make the place beautiful and comfortable. One physician has announced his intention to have all his pneumonia patients nursed on the roof garden . . . . The view from this spot is pleasing. Buckner Orphans' Home, six miles away, is plainly visible and

Oak Cliff can be seen across the river . . . ."

Even in such opulent surroundings, there were some complaints, of course. Mrs. Edna Bateman Vandervort, a nurse who was present at the delivery of the first baby born at the new hospital, recalled some forty years later that many doctors did not like the door sills over which wheelchairs had difficulty passing. They were also critical of the location of the elevators in the center of the building.

Presumably, the hospital's physicians, nurses and other staff personnel, and even patients, may also have had some complaints about the lengthy list of rules that governed their conduct and the day-to-day operation of the sanitarium. Some of these rules included the following stipulations: "Physicians and surgeons will not be allowed to solicit patients, unless requested to do so by the attending physician. All physicians and surgeons, as far as possible, will visit their patients during the day. Physicians and surgeons must not visit socially with the nurses on duty."

Surgeons who wished to use a hospital operating room were required to make the necessary arrangements at the business office, and were warned bluntly that any surgeon who was not prompt would forfeit his turn, that visiting doctors or medical students must apply to the operating room nurse for a sterile gown, and that instruments and apparatus could not be loaned for use outside the sanitarium. Furthermore, unnecessary noises, smoking and profane language were strictly prohibited, "with the one exception that smoking may be allowed on the grounds."

Nurses were regulated even more stringently. Loud talking and laughing were forbidden. Those on the evening shift were admonished that "no part of the uniform is to be removed at night." Sleeping on duty was described as a "serious offense." Lights out in the nurses' home, a two-story house facing on Junius Street and donated by Mr. and Mrs. F. W.

Johnson of Pecos, was at 10 p.m. sharp, and student nurses were warned that "perfect quiet must be observed after that hour." No "fancy waists or elaborate underwear" were tolerated.

According to the 1910 prospectus, the nurses who endured such rules could expect to earn up to $4 for a twelve-hour day, without rest. Other prices listed by the hospital were also incredibly modest. A bed in a ward cost $10 per week, including board and nursing care; private room rates ranged from $20 to $50 per week. The operating room fee was $15 for major operations and $10 for minor surgical procedures.

Within those first months, patients came from all parts of Texas, as well as from other states, to take advantage of the new facilities. They came as fast as the rooms could be opened up and made ready for them. Superintendent Roberts was convinced that the entire hospital plant would soon be taxed to its utmost capacity—and he was right. But during his two years as superintendent, Roberts displayed excellent organizational abilities, and by the time of his resignation in April 1911, the sanitarium had adopted a comprehensive set of by-laws, setting forth its policies with respect to employes and administration, admissions, patient rules, apothecary, physicians, operating rooms and interns.

Such by-laws and regulations added to the efficiency of the hospital, thereby making it possible to utilize its space and facilities to the greatest advantage. But even with this efficiency, the sanitarium still suffered from financial instability. The board had been forced to borrow money several times during the construction program, and it was forced to resort to similar stop-gap loans in ever increasing amounts through the next several years. As historian Powhatan W. James expressed the situation: "They (hospital officials) discovered that the construction, operation and maintenance of a great general hospital was big business and called for a lot of faith, courage, nerve and *credit*."

But economic factors and the pressures of being underfinanced were to be only one aspect of a tumultuous period of crisis, challenge and change that lay just ahead. Thus far, the hospital had emerged victorious from a series of early skirmishes with fate, but many other battles were still to be fought.

IV

Wounds of War and Peace

Striving for Recognition

As a new decade opened, the world found itself
suddenly ten years deep into the Twentieth Century.
Time and events were somehow moving faster and
faster now with each year that passed, spurred by new
means of communication, the growth of industrial
technology and mounting international political
pressures. The horse-and-buggy era in health care, as
in other aspects of American life, was rapidly fading
into the past. In many respects, the decade that
dawned in 1910 would signal the end of the old, predominantly rural, predominantly slow-paced way of
life in North Texas, and usher in an era of incredible
development and explosive growth—an era that has
continued almost without letup ever since. Before the
decade was over, Dallasites would build their first
skyscrapers, pave their first country roads, adopt the
motorcar as their favorite mode of transportation, see
their own population double, and help fight a war on
faraway battlefields with names that many of them
could not pronounce.

It would be a decade of great demands on the
medical profession and on the educational system
that provided it with doctors, both from the public
and from increasingly powerful watchdog regulatory
agencies. In response, medicine began making impressive strides toward life-giving "miracle cures."
Slowly, the most notorious killer diseases of the Nineteenth Century—typhoid, smallpox, diphtheria,
yellow fever, tuberculosis and pellagra— were being

brought under control. All in all, medicine was poised on the brink of a revolution that would extend the average American's life expectancy at birth from 47 years in 1900 to 71.3 years by the mid-1970s.

But even as medical advancement was bringing the gift of a longer and more comfortable life to millions of people, a segment of the medical community was, itself, dying. Before the reverberations from a highly regarded rating system for medical colleges known as the *Flexner Report of 1910* had run their course, no less than 60 American medical schools would close their doors forever. And by the end of the decade, Baylor University College of Medicine, described as "inferior" in the Flexner study, would be the only surviving school in Dallas, largely because of the support it received from its sister institution, the Texas Baptist Memorial Sanitarium.

Meanwhile, the sanitarium was taking vigorous strides toward becoming one of the outstanding hospitals in Texas. In October 1911, J. B. Franklin of San Antonio became superintendent of the hospital, replacing B. J. Roberts. The following fall, on November 12, 1912, Franklin hired Helen Holliday as superintendent of nurses, who brought with her four other graduate nurses from her prestigious alma mater, Johns Hopkins Hospital in Baltimore, Maryland. Miss Holliday and her young and highly skilled associates—Kathryn Duvall, Helen Rennie, Edith Applegate and Emma Woods—were to be largely responsible for establishing the high standards of nursing for which the hospital became known during those early days.

It was during this period that the sanitarium pledged its full support to the ailing medical college, which had suffered a number of serious setbacks in recent years. Besides the reeling blow hurled by the Flexner Report, the college had also been denied Class A standing—it was ranked Class B—by the

American Medical Association's Council on Medical Education, indicating that the college still had improvements to be made before it could be fully accredited. At the same time, the college was also confronted by two new and powerful state regulatory agencies, the State Board of Medical Examiners, which strengthened medical education requirements for physician licensure, and the State Anatomical Board, which was to oversee "proper procurement" of anatomical materials for medical schools. In addition to the increasing regulatory pressures and their accompanying problems, the college's Commerce Street headquarters had been destroyed by fire in 1902, leaving the students to be shunted from one temporary location to another. Eventually, the school moved to the old Good Samaritan Hospital and, with the approval of the sanitarium board, was allowed to occupy the sanitarium's new Ramseur Science Hall, a three-story structure with basement, when it was completed in September 1909. This generous move on the part of the sanitarium allowed the medical college to turn its attention to more urgent matters—the upgrading of the quality of its instruction and its curriculum.

To help the medical college in this endeavor, the sanitarium made space available for a college library, which was successfully organized during 1910-11.

Then on February 15, 1912, the sanitarium's Board of Directors voted to unite even more closely with the medical college by selecting an executive staff for the sanitarium from the clinical faculty of the college, "each to have special oversight of the classes of diseases which fall naturally under his care as a teacher in the medical school." By 1913, the professional personnel serving the hospital had been reorganized into four staffs—executive, adjunct, dispensary and visiting—and the membership of each was appointed by the directors of the sanitarium upon nomination by the medical college faculty. This was a step toward proper division of responsibility for the care of patients and their use for teaching, as well as toward the departmentalization of the hospital. However, the program was under the direction of two separate boards, one from the medical school and one from the hospital, and there was not always harmony between them.

Meanwhile, the sanitarium was helping Baylor students gain more opportunity for training in the clinical setting. On March 1, 1913, the outpatient clinic, then called the dispensary, was moved from Ramseur Science Hall to the first floor of the sanitarium, except for the genito-urinary clinic and clinical diagnosis laboratory, which stayed behind primarily because the sanitarium refused to see patients with venereal diseases at that time. The dispensary move made more classroom teaching space available at Ramseur Hall and also greatly increased the number of sanitarium patients attended by medical students.

Prior to a visit in 1913 by a joint committee from the Association of American Medical Colleges and the Council on Medical Education, the medical school, in cooperation with the sanitarium, staged an all-out push to attain the all important and long-denied Class A rating. In addition to the improvements already made at the college, Dean Cary urged the heads of the laboratory departments to report immediately everything they needed; clinicians were urged to build up a large clinic at the sanitarium, and a clinical committee was appointed; student records were quickly brought up to date. But despite all these efforts, the medical school was destined to be disappointed again. The joint committee refused to bestow the Class A rating, leaving in its place a list of further suggestions for improvement. The suggestions accentuated the need for still better laboratory and clinical facilities, better student records, additional full-time teaching personnel, correlation of courses, enforce-

Medical students at the Baylor College of Medicine had to attend classes at the Texas Baptist Memorial Sanitarium until the new Ramseur Science Hall, at left, was completed.

Patient No. _____ TEXAS BAPTIST MEMORIAL SANITARIUM

Dallas, Texas _____ 8-22 _____ 1918

Received of _____ Dorothy Russell

$6 _____ in _____ payment of account as listed below:

Private Room			Telegraph and Telephone		
Ward	1		Extra Meals		
Operating Room			Special Nursing		
Dispensary			Board of Sp. Nurse		
Laundry	ok		Surgical Dressings		
Fan					

TEXAS BAPTIST MEMORIAL SANITARIUM

By _____

The Texas Baptist Memorial Sanitarium
Dispensary

EVERY DAY EXCEPT SUNDAYS, TWO TO THREE P. M.

Located on the Grounds of the Baptist Sanitarium
In Science Bldg. on College Ave., between Gaston Ave. & Junius St. Take Main or Swiss Car, Get Off at Junius Street and Walk Two Blocks West

GRADUATE PHYSICIANS AND SURGEONS
:: :: Giving Attention to Various General and Special Conditions in Attendance :: ::

The Worthy Poor desiring Medical or Surgical services, whether of emergency or chronic character are invited to apply for diagnosis and treatment each day Free of Charge

The free dispensary (outpatient clinic) of the Texas Baptist Memorial Sanitarium was located at the Ramseur Science Hall when it first opened. Later, the dispensary was moved to the sanitarium building.

ment of higher standards of scholarship for promotion and graduation, and strict adherence to admission requirements.

It began to seem that no matter how rapidly the college improved its facilities, upgraded its programs and strengthened its requirements, it could scarcely keep pace with the new regulations being imposed by the regulatory agencies, much less gain ground on them. But officials at the medical college and the sanitarium swallowed their disappointment and vowed to try again.

Growing Competition

Meanwhile, the decade beginning in 1910 signaled not only various advancements in treatment techniques and facilities for the ill, but increasing competition among Dallas hospitals as they sought to respond to public demand for more and better hospital care. Facilities for the observation and treatment of tuberculosis patients became available with the opening on July 19, 1913, of Woodlawn Hospital, a 40-bed city-county institution. On February 1, 1914, the new city-county Parkland Hospital opened at Oak Lawn and Maple Avenues in what was then far North Dallas. The $500,000 Parkland project gave birth to the Dallas City-County Hospital System, which also included Woodlawn, Union Hospital for smallpox patients and the hospital at the county poor farm in Hutchins. The city continued to operate its Emergency Hospital separately in the City Hall.

As new hospitals began to appear in other parts of the city, officials of the Texas Baptist Memorial Sanitarium began to contemplate more expansion of their own facilities. In late 1913, Miss Holliday and other hospital leaders proposed the construction of a Nurses' Home and Training School on the sanitarium grounds.

They anticipated that the proposed building

would cost "several hundred thousand dollars," and once again—as he had so often in the past—the ever-faithful Colonel Slaughter pledged his support in the fund-raising campaign ahead. As an incentive for others to give, he offered to contribute $2 for every $3 donated by others, up to the amount of $200,000.

In a spirit of growing cooperation between the sanitarium and the medical school, Dr. Truett moved during a Board of Directors meeting that $100,000 of the money raised in the campaign be applied to a proposed endowment fund for Baylor University College of Medicine. Dr. Truett's proposal would appear to have indicated that he foresaw few difficulties in securing the money for the nurses' building. Unfortunately, however, such was not the case. When international political tensions exploded into World War I in August 1914, the fund-raising drive was still floundering far short of its goal. Construction of the nurses' building began after much delay in 1916—even though the money was still not available to pay for it. It took a final gift of $150,000 from Colonel Slaughter—made at the request of Dr. Truett as he departed for six months' tour of duty in the war trenches overseas—to allow the building's ultimate completion in March 1918.

During this period, the sanitarium also constructed a $15,000 three-story Clinic Building at the rear of its main structure, with the help of a $5,000 contribution from members of the medical college faculty. The building provided space for 100 beds for Mexican and Negro patients, as well as for the outpatient dispensary, which occupied half the ground floor. Complete operating facilities were housed on the third floor.

Just prior to the completion of the Clinic Building, the sanitarium had added a special ward for children. That ward, which cared primarily for children from Buckner Orphans' Home, greatly increased patient services at the sanitarium and made clinical instruction in pediatrics much more accessible to students at the medical college.

In fact, the sanitarium's improvements, coupled with Dr. Cary's determination, had so much impact on the medical college that on June 12, 1916, the Council on Medical Education at long last awarded the college the coveted Class A rating in recognition of its compliance with standards set for curriculum, laboratory and clinical teaching facilities, admissions, advancement and graduation.

But there was scarcely time for lengthy celebrations before another crisis—this one of worldwide proportions—blazed up to confront the sanitarium, the medical school and everyone associated with them.

The War Effort

As late as the first days of January 1917, public opinion concerning the two-and-one-half-year-old war in Europe was fairly equally divided in Texas and the nation.

But on January 16, Germany's Foreign Secretary Arthur Zimmermann sent a fateful secret telegram, by way of the German Embassy in Washington, to the German minister in Mexico, instructing him to propose an incredible "deal" to Mexican President Venustiano Carranza. In exchange for a military alliance with Germany, in the event the United States joined the war on the side of the British and French Allies, Zimmermann offered Carranza the return of Mexico's "lost territory in Texas, Arizona and New Mexico." All Mexico had to do, the telegram said, was to attack across the Rio Grande at the precise moment Germany instructed.

To the chagrin of the plotters in Berlin, however, the telegram was intercepted and decoded by British intelligence, and on February 24 a copy of the clandestine message was handed to President Woodrow

Dr. George W. Truett, left, a world-renowned minister and one of the original trustees of the Texas Baptist Memorial Sanitarium, secured the funds for the much-needed nurses' training home, Holliday Hall, above, before leaving on a six-month tour of duty overseas in World War I. By March 1918, the training home was completed and student nurses, below, were busy attending classes.

Wilson. On March 1, the whole sordid story was headlined in the newspapers.

This development, along with Germany's announcement of unrestricted submarine warfare in the North Atlantic, caused national sentiments to change dramatically within a matter of weeks. In the Southwest, especially, public apathy toward the distant conflict between the great powers of Europe gave way to angry outrage. Texans were particularly inflamed. After all, men like Colonel Slaughter's father had fought one war to secure Texas' independence from Mexico. If another war had to be fought for the same purpose, the talk went on Dallas street corners, let it begin now!

Almost immediately after the United States declared war against Germany on April 6, the conflict placed a heavy double burden on the nation's hospitals and medical schools, siphoning off both students and financial support. Those whose contributions were usually directed at health care institutions were now supporting the war effort, and those who ordinarily would have enrolled in medical school were enlisting in the armed services instead. But both the Texas Baptist Memorial Sanitarium and the Baylor University College of Medicine were now strong enough not only to withstand the drain of wartime, but also to make a vital contribution to the welfare of the hundreds of thousands of American troops who would soon be pouring into France.

Dr. Cary was so smitten with patriotism that he wanted to don a uniform and head for France himself. He had been offered command of a base hospital, but Dr. S. P. Brooks, president of the parent university in Waco, convinced him that he was needed more at home than overseas. Dr. Cary was serving as president of the Texas Medical Association at the time, and, as such, was to play a key role in obtaining the volunteer services of more than 1,000 Texas physicians for the armed forces.

54

Although he was dissuaded from going "over there" himself, Dr. Cary was largely responsible for the organization and training of the Baylor Medical and Surgical Unit, formed in August 1917 and composed of sanitarium staff and medical school faculty. After training at Fort McPherson, Georgia, the unit served with distinction in France under the command of Lt. Col. Mark E. Lott, an orthopedic surgeon at the Texas Baptist Memorial Sanitarium and professor of orthopedics at the medical school. Dr. Cary also secured authority from Washington to develop a Students' Army Training Corps at Baylor, for which the entire student body was organized. The government paid student tuition fees, but Dr. Cary had to borrow and spend more than $100,000 to build barracks and provide food for the students. He was assured, of course, that the government would eventually repay the money.

Amid the glowering war clouds and the flurry of mobilization, medical school enrollment continued to increase, but it was the sanitarium staff and the medical school faculty ranks that were about to be severely depleted by the war effort, as the Baylor Medical Unit prepared to serve its country as the only base hospital unit from Texas to see action during the war.

In addition to Dr. Lott, other officers of the unit included: Dr. W. B. Carrell, captain, and Drs. R. B. McBride, W. W. Shortal, M. L. Brown, George L. Carlisle, M. M. Carr, Dewitt Smith, R. S. Usry, Samuel D. Weaver, C. H. Standifer and Robert E. Kirth, lieutenants. All 12 physicians attached to the original unit were staff members at the Texas Baptist Memorial Sanitarium and members of the faculty of Baylor Medical College. In addition, the unit included 21 nurses and 50 orderlies and attendants. It was designated as the U.S. Army's Hospital Unit V, and before leaving for France, as a full base hospital corps attached to Base Hospital 26, its strength was more than doubled with the addition of a number of other physicians from Dallas and the surrounding area.

As the unit prepared to leave for training in Georgia on February 25, 1918, Dr. Lott expressed his satisfaction with the personnel and their spirit in an interview with *The Dallas Morning News.* "I am more than pleased with our line-up," he said, "and the more I see of it and the more I hear of it through the expressions of others, the more I feel it is one of the best units yet organized. The men and nurses are full of vim and energy and with a little more special training, we will be ready to go."

Dr. Cary's wife presented the unit with a silk American flag just prior to its departure, and wives of other medical school faculty members provided a Red Cross flag for the unit to carry abroad. The Dallas Red Cross supplied enlisted men in the unit with sweaters, helmets, wristlets and mufflers before they sailed for France.

The unit arrived in the war zone in the early summer of 1918. Their arrival coincided with the bloody and climactic final phase of the conflict—a phase in which the more than one million American doughboys then helping to fill the massive line of Allied trenches stretching across Western Europe would prove the decisive factor in turning the German tide.

At 11 a.m. on November 11, 1918, the guns fell silent along a thousand miles of trenches. The Armistice had been signed. The Great War, the "war to end wars," the most tragic outpouring of human life the world had yet witnessed, was over. Almost ten million people, including 115,000 Americans, had been killed. But the Baylor unit, as far as it is known, had suffered no serious casualties.

But with the ultimate victory came a crushing loss for both the Texas Baptist Memorial Sanitarium and the medical school. Colonel Slaughter, whose great wealth and even greater devotion to humanitarian causes had come to the rescue of both

56

the sanitarium and college so many times over the years, died on January 25, 1919, after several years of failing health.

His death dampened some of the enthusiasm of the welcoming ceremonies for the returning Baylor Medical Unit, which came home from France the following month. But before his death, as a last benevolent gesture, Colonel Slaughter had secured the future of the nurses' building at the sanitarium with his $150,000 gift, and, in so doing, laid the groundwork for what would shortly emerge as the Baylor University School of Nursing. His legacy was alive and well.

The war was in the past now. The challenge of peacetime progress lay just over the horizon.

V

A Time of Evolution

Peace and Progress

With the most awesome conflict in human history at an end. Dallasites set out to celebrate the peace with the same exuberance with which they had pursued the war effort. The "modern era" descended on the nation in a flurry, filled with new experiments, new excitement and new challenges. It was an age in which the technological revolution would come into full flower. Before the end of the 1920s, the radio, the phonograph and the "movies" would alter the lifestyle of virtually every citizen in America's cities.

For Dallas, the 1920s were characterized by unparalleled growth. Gone was the rawboned prairie town of the turn of the century. In its place, by 1929, would stand a bustling city of 260,000, a city whose prosperity had already established it as the "market center of the Great Southwest." The 23-story Magnolia (now Mobil) Building, opened in 1922, became Dallas' most famous landmark; the revolving "flying red horse" atop the building was visible for miles across the rolling countryside. The first major paved highway in Dallas County, Belt Line Road, was opened to traffic in 1920, making a Sunday drive in the country in the family Model T a great deal safer and more comfortable. As automobile transportation became less hazardous, exclusive communities began to develop rapidly in such outlying areas as Lakewood and the Park Cities.

The Texas Baptist Memorial Sanitarium and the Baylor College of Medicine burst into a "boom" period of expansion immediately following the war. Bolstered by the desire of the Baylor Board of Trustees at Waco to build a medical center that would equal any in the United States, the sanitarium and medical school acquired more property, erected more buildings, enrolled more students—and borrowed more money to finance the growth. (Some of the new facilities, while serving a much-needed function at the time, were less than luxurious. Dr. H. Frank Carman, a 1922 graduate of the medical school, recalled in a 1960 interview that one building of the period, known as Cary Hall, was actually at first the City Hall of East Dallas and later a converted grammar school. "The building was condemned for the children, but was considered safe enough for medical students," he recalled cryptically.)

This period saw the evolution of the "Baylor-in-Dallas" concept, as the sanitarium, the medical school, the School of Nursing, the School of Pharmacy and the School of Dentistry—a state school purchased in 1918 for the incredibly low price of $3,000—were all placed under the authority of the Board of Trustees of the parent university at Waco. At the time the State Dental College, located at 1420 Hall Street, was sold to Baylor, it had an enrollment of 140 students, all of whom were due to be drafted into the armed services, since their school had no university affiliation. To spare their entire student body from mass induction, therefore, the owners of the school, Drs. T. G. Bradford and C. L. Morey, sold it to Baylor for a small fraction of its appraised value.

In keeping with this new "Baylor-in-Dallas" concept—one that would, before the end of the decade, also give rise to the conviction that Dallas would eventually grow into one of the nation's leading medical centers—the Baptist General Convention of Texas voted in November 1920 at the recommendation of the Baylor Board of Trustees to consolidate Texas Baptist Memorial Sanitarium and the various scientific schools with which it was associated. "Baylor-in-Dallas" was now regarded as an integral part of Baylor University, and the university's 21-member board was divided into two executive committees, one to supervise the affairs of Baylor at Waco, and the other to supervise the scientific units in Dallas, with the entire board in charge of matters affecting both.

The consolidation came about as a result of changing relationships between medical schools and their affiliated teaching hospitals in the years following World War I. Prior to the war, medical schools had devoted much of their attention toward raising admission requirements, improving teaching and laboratory facilities and meeting stricter licensing standards. But after the war, the emphasis shifted toward "clinical" instruction, the direct contact of the students with patients. This required the establishment of a greater abundance of "teaching patients" and reorganization of the clinical faculties to improve methods of instruction with patients. Toward these ends, the Baylor trustees designated Texas Baptist Memorial Sanitarium as the official teaching hospital for the medical school and limited practice in the sanitarium to medical school faculty and members of the sanitarium staff. At the same time, the board pledged to make such additions as "necessary for carrying out in every detail the making of a really great and first-class College of Medicine and Hospital."

In July 1920, a complete reorganization of the internal conduct of affairs of the sanitarium and medical college resulted from the voluntary and unanimous resignation of the school's faculty members and their subsequent reappointments both to the faculty and the hospital staff. The departments of the medical school were more clearly defined with a chairman appointed for each, and an advisory board was established, consisting of the superintendent of the sanitarium, the director of the school of nursing, the dean of the medical college and the department chairmen.

One phase of the reorganization involved the deanship of the medical school. It had been specified that the position of dean should be filled by someone who was not engaged in the active practice of medicine and who could devote full time to the affairs of the medical college. Because Dr. Cary was in private practice, he resigned the post and became dean emeritus and chairman of the advisory board, as well as continuing his faculty responsibilities as professor of ophthalmology and otolaryngology. Dr. W. H. Moursund, a professor of pathology who had recently come back from active military service, was appointed acting dean for the ensuing term. In 1921, Dr. McIver Woody, formerly dean and chief of the surgical division at the University of Tennessee School of Medicine, was named dean and professor of surgery. Dr. Woody resigned the post in 1922 and, again Dr. Moursund was named acting dean—an appointment that became permanent in 1923.

Other Changes

As a part of the changes occurring during this period, the sanitarium was officially renamed Baylor Hospital on January 21, 1921. One thing that even a new name could not change, however, was the ever-present, ever-pressing need for more space and more facilities to absorb an ever-increasing load of patients. As usual, the need for expansion was not easily met and was not without crushing financial problems for the Board of Directors, all of whom served without pay and some of whom taxed their own personal resources and lines of credit to meet various emergencies as they arose. Fortunately, too, banks and other lending institutions adopted liberal policies as a rule when dealing with Baylor Hospital and its allied schools. Otherwise, it is doubtful that they could have survived.

In 1922, the completion of a new five-story building for women and children increased Baylor Hospital's total bed capacity to 400 and greatly expanded its capabilities in pediatrics, obstetrics and gynecology. At the same time, another five-story structure was also completed to connect the old portion of the hospital with the new facility, which was officially named the Children's Building. This connecting structure housed the morgue and autopsy rooms in the basement, rooms for lectures, clinics and conferences on the first floor, clinical laboratories on the second and third floors, the x-ray department on the fourth floor, and all operating rooms on the fifth floor. A new dispensary building had also been planned, intended to house facilities for an outpatient clinic for up to 400 patients per day. Unfortunately, however, there was no money available for this project.

As the physical plant of the Dallas campus expanded, the institutions also began to put more emphasis on the quality of service rendered by the scientific schools. Following the example of the "Class A" medical school, the others also set out to attain top ratings and experienced notable success. Having complied with the requirements of the Dental Education Council of America, the College of Dentistry obtained a "Class A" rating during this time, as did the School of Nursing (one of only two such schools in the Southwest to meet all requirements of the New York Board of Nurse Examiners). Its Nurses' Home and Training School was regarded as the finest facility of its kind in the South.

Despite continuing financial problems, by the end of its second decade of existence, Baylor Hospital had mushroomed into the largest hospital in the Southwest and the second largest in the South. It contained seven fully equipped operating rooms, and the entire hospital was departmentalized. Its clinic had grown so quickly that it now had a staff of 50 physicians treating up to 25,000 patients per year. Most of this treatment was administered free and the service imposed a heavy financial burden on the hospital, causing many appeals for funds, especially to the Baptists of Texas. But the hospital's over-all excellence was unquestioned. It enjoyed the highest ratings of both the American College of Surgeons and the American Hospital Association. It was on its way to fulfilling—indeed, even surpassing—the fondest dreams of the farsighted planners of the early 1900s.

Financial Turmoil

In a sense, though, the hospital and its affiliated schools were being lured by the same impatience for growth and availability of easy credit that were drawing millions of private citizens deeply into debt in those first few prosperous post-war years. But as has happened so often in America since, the boom was followed, suddenly and sharply, by a severe economic downturn in 1923, which left Texas Baptists saddled with huge debts and without the means to pay for the progress they had purchased on credit. In May, 1919, buoyed by peacetime enthusiasm, the Southern Baptist Convention had pledged at its annual convention in Atlanta, Georgia, to raise $75 million to support Baptist institutions. When the recession of 1923 hit the country, only $55 million of that had been raised, however. Texas Baptists' share was to have been $10 million—$1.6 million of which was to have gone to Baylor Hospital and the medical school—but only $5 million had actually been raised. The result was "a drastic and embarrassing shrinkage in the subscriptions" to the Dallas-based institutions.

To complicate matters, the recession was followed by a four-year interlude of "false inflation and artificial prosperity." The seeds of economic disaster that would culminate by the end of the "Roaring 20s" in the greatest national depression in U.S. his-

In 1918, Baylor University at Waco purchased
the State Dental College, located at 1420 Hall
Street in Dallas, above, and spared all of its 140
students from mass induction into the
military.

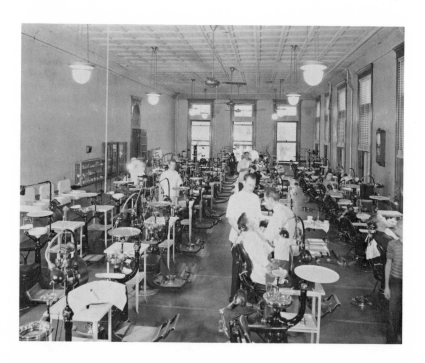

In 1922, the completion of the five-story Children's Building increased Baylor Hospital's total bed capacity to 400 and greatly expanded its capabilities in pediatrics, obstetrics and gynecology.

As medical students at the Baylor College of Medicine busily prepared themselves for careers as physicians, Baylor University at Waco made plans during the 1920s and 1930s to turn the Dallas campus into a leading medical center.

tory were being sown in all directions, but nobody seemed to sense the calamity that lay just around the corner. Wild speculation reached from the towers of Wall Street to the small hamlets of the nation. Millions of people risked their lifetime savings on marginal purchases of watered stocks. Nearly everyone was sailing high on the seas of easy money, bullish markets and Coolidge confidence. It is perhaps symptomatic of the period that the only internal "scandal" ever to touch Baylor Hospital occurred during this time, when a hospital financial officer embezzled several thousand dollars over a period of months, was caught, convicted and sentenced to two years in prison.

By November of 1928, a review of Baylor's finances showed the hospital to be $261,330.52 in debt—a staggering sum for that time. That December, Baylor officials arranged to pay off the debt, but only with the help of a $250,000 loan from the W. C. Bitting Company of St. Louis.

Ironically, the Bitting loan was to be paid off by October 1929, but by that time, the prosperity, optimism and easy credit that had swept America along for almost ten years on a binge of reckless spending had collapsed. On October 24, 1929—Wall Street's infamous "Black Thursday"—the stock market burst like a toy balloon. Frantic speculators, trying to escape the deluge before their narrow profit margins were wiped out, dumped 13 million shares of stock on the reeling New York and American Stock Exchanges. Four days later, on October 29, the market virtually plunged out of sight. Almost overnight, it seemed, the Great Depression had engulfed America. Banks closed by the dozens, businesses by the hundreds. Mortgages were foreclosed, industrial production fell by half, and almost 12 million Americans were out of work. The hungry, homeless and fearful were everywhere.

Realistically, there was no more hope of Baylor paying off its debts than there was for any over-extended American family. Luckily, the Bitting Company showed a great deal of patience. Records show that Bitting and other St. Louis banking firms subsequently financed a million-dollar bond issue for Baylor-in-Dallas, which absorbed the original loan. The indebtedness of that bond issue was reduced to $543,000 by October 1944, when two Dallas banks, First National and Republic National, furnished funds for liquidating the debts owed to the St. Louis firms. From that time on, local banks and Southwestern Life Insurance Company have provided financing for Baylor. In the intervening years, however, debt was to become a way of life for the hospital and affiliated schools—as it was to the rest of the country.

Medical Arts Building

Probably no single development of the 1920s influenced the conflicting ambitions of the Dallas medical community more graphically than the magnificent 19-story Medical Arts Building, erected on Pacific Avenue in downtown Dallas in 1923 by the former dean of the Baylor College of Medicine, Dr. Cary. The Medical Arts Building received national publicity as something of a medical showcase, but locally it also signified a deep internal rift at Baylor, one destined to fester for more than 20 years and finally lead to the removal of the medical college to Houston.

Dr. Cary originally constructed the Medical Arts Building as a centrally located office complex for Dallas County physicians, but by 1928, although still a faculty member at Baylor College of Medicine and still on the staff of Baylor Hospital, he had opened a small hospital of his own on two floors of the building.

Beneath the surface, there were reasons other than mere convenience or a desire for convenient modern office space that prompted such pillars of

Baylor-in-Dallas as Dr. Cary to turn their attentions toward newer facilities for their patients.

While the Baylor units were growing rapidly and improving their facilities at a steady pace during this period, many of those associated with them remained dissatisfied. Two reports submitted within three months of each other demonstrate the concerns of those who felt Baylor was not living up to its full potential. The first was an eight-page typewritten report from the faculty of the medical school, addressed to the Baylor Board of Trustees and signed by Dean Moursund, Dr. Henry M. Winans and Dr. W. W. Looney. Dated December 20, 1928, the report was constructive in some respects, but fiercely critical in others, especially where the School of Nursing and the nursing service at Baylor Hospital were concerned. The second report, submitted on March 26, 1929, to the Executive Board, was addressed to the entire Board of Trustees and the president of Baylor University. It was signed by Drs. Cary, A. I. Folsom and C. C. Hannah, and proposed a new administrative structure for all units of Baylor-in-Dallas, while offering detailed recommendations for improvements in 13 departments. Among other things, the report urged that (1) a proposed new clinic of the City Health Department be aligned with Baylor Hospital's efficiently run venereal disease clinic, and (2) that a proposed Baby Hospital, Cancer and Pellagra Hospital and Psychopathic Hospital, each of which had been authorized by the State Legislature, be located near enough to the Baylor campus to receive the advantages of Baylor's scientific schools.

Although critical of Baylor as it currently stood, the reports showed that physicians associated with the hospital and medical college were beginning to sense that Dallas was on the threshold of becoming a major medical center. They wanted Baylor to have its share in the recognition and to play a larger role in making their vision a reality.

The Baylor trustees, while not insensitive to the physicians' ideas, nevertheless were reluctant to undertake too many large projects, realizing they might put the already debt-ridden hospital and affiliated schools into genuine financial danger. They agreed to make changes, but not as extensive changes as the physicians would have liked. To help resolve the nursing problems, the board again named Mrs. John R. Lehmann (nee Helen Holliday) as head of the Nursing School and the Nursing Service, and under her leadership the nursing situation soon improved. They also designated Dr. J. F. Kimball as a vice president of Baylor University and placed the entire Baylor-in-Dallas complex under his supervision. Bryce Twitty, a man skilled in public relations and finance, was hired as superintendent to overhaul various hospital departments. Simultaneously, the trustees launched strenuous campaigns for increased public financial support, and borrowed still more money against the hospital's equity in the estate of the late W. H. Thomas. (The hospital, along with Buckner Orphans' Home, was to share equally in the estate at the death of Thomas' daughter, Mrs. May Thomas Miller. In 1951, when the estate was settled, Baylor's share came to about $500,000.) In general, all these moves were regarded as steps in the right direction, but were not enough to satisfy the complaining physicians.

That Dr. Cary was genuinely concerned about the future of Baylor's medical school can scarcely be doubted, even though he was also obviously interested in his own Medical Arts Building. Among the nation's medical leaders, Dr. Cary was one of the most respected figures of his day. Not only had he served without pay as dean of the medical school from 1902 until 1920, but his untiring efforts, energy and determination were largely responsible for the school's eventual elevation to "Class A" status.

By 1929, he had already served as president of the Texas Medical Association, the Dallas County

Medical Society and the Southern Medical Association, and was a trustee of the American Medical Association. In 1931, he would become the first Texan ever to be elected president of the AMA.

In years to come, Dr. Cary's expressed ambitions for Dallas to become one of the world's great centers of medical achievement and the development of the life-saving arts would be amply realized. But, as fate would have it, it would be his Medical Arts Building that would fall by the wayside as time went on. Choked by downtown traffic and lack of parking facilities, and outmoded by newer, more modern buildings in more convenient locales, the Medical Arts Building's last physician moved out in late 1977. Even as this book was being written, demolition crews were bringing down the once-proud structure.

The day of the vast medical center complex was coming to Dallas. For the moment, though, it was an idea that would have to wait. After the autumn of 1929, few Americans had either the time or the money to pursue visions. They were too busy struggling for survival amid the social catastrophe of the Great Depression.

VI
Pioneering Again

Birth of Blue Cross

As the Depression swept the country, destroying jobs and capital, closing banks and businesses, and leaving millions of Americans unable to pay for the basic essentials of life, it also struck a devastating blow at the nation's hospitals. Hospital costs had increased dramatically since the days of $5-a-week room and board, and now most patients were simply too broke to pay the higher costs. Baylor's patients were no exception. Overdue bills, ranging from $100 to more than $1,000, quickly piled up at the hospital as the effects of the Depression worsened. Soon, the financial crisis threatened Baylor's very existence. According to one report at the time, "Methodist Hospital was in the hands of the receivers, and Baylor was just 30 days ahead of the sheriff itself."

One afternoon late in 1929, Baylor University Vice President J. F. Kimball, who was in charge of the Dallas units, and Baylor Hospital Superintendent Twitty were discussing the crisis in Kimball's office. Kimball suggested that people be allowed to pay a small amount each month toward future hospital care—an idea he had originated earlier in the 1920s with Dallas teachers while he was serving as school superintendent. The original plan had been put into effect after many teachers had suffered severe hardship from loss of salary due to illness during the "Spanish flu" epidemic of 1918-20. In formulating his original "sick benefit plan" for the teachers, Dr. Kimball proposed that each teacher in the Dallas school district pay $1 per month into the treasury of his or her school. One faculty member in each school would then collect the monthly dues and send the money to the central board for disbursement after due proof of illness and time lost. In cases of long-term ailments, teachers could draw $5 per day for each work day lost, after the first 21 days of illness.

It was the teachers' "sick benefit plan" that Dr. Kimball and Twitty used as a model for what would win nationwide attention as the "Baylor Plan." The first group to be enrolled under the plan was the Dallas teachers, and the plan was aimed at protecting them during the first 21 days of illness that were not covered by the school district plan. Dr. Kimball and Twitty had only the records of previous sicknesses among the teachers upon which to calculate the actuarial risk involved, but they decided that dues of 50¢ per person per month would be sufficient to operate the plan. The first group of 1,356 teachers was enrolled in December 1929.

At first, administering the plan was a relatively simple matter, since only one hospital was involved. There was no detailed list of benefits to which those covered by the plan were entitled. When a subscriber became ill, his doctor merely sent him to the hospital and he stayed until he was discharged; in the interim, he got everything the hospital had to offer. The subscriber's dependents received the same benefits, except that they were charged for one-half the daily room fee.

The first patient to receive hospital benefits under the "Baylor Plan" was Mrs. Alma Dickson, who slipped on an icy pavement in December 1929 and fractured an ankle. Her doctor, a member of the Baylor staff, asked her if she belonged to the new plan. When she said that she did, she was promptly admitted to the hospital and spent Christmas day there.

While Dr. Kimball was signing up the teachers, Twitty called on employes of *The Dallas Morning*

News. He encountered considerable resistance to the new idea, until one of the employe representatives from the *News* was stricken with appendicitis while discussing the plan with Baylor officials. She found her hospital bill paid in full by the plan, and the favorable impression that resulted helped convince the rest of the *News* employes to enroll. They paid a monthly fee of 50¢ for individual or $1.50 for family coverage. A group of employes from a large Dallas bank immediately followed the example of the *News* employes, and from that point on, the plan steadily gained public popularity.

People found it amazing to be able to go the hospital without having to spend a cent of their own money. Ruth Buckner, a *News* employe who was hospitalized for three weeks in October 1932, recalled her own surprise in a 1968 interview: "When I was ready to go home, I was told that I didn't owe anything. I couldn't believe it, but when they assured me it was true. I was very happy."

As the "Baylor plan" grew, Dr. Kimball and Twitty were careful not to enroll more people than the hospital could handle, since Baylor was the only hospital utilizing the plan. That was soon to change, however. With the country gripped by economic chaos and deprivation, the idea of prepaid health insurance was to become the only salvation for the nation's hospitals and their patients. Without it, scores of hospitals would have been forced to close, and the American public—who in the late 1920s had spent as much on chewing gum as they had on health care and who was now in no position to cope with rising hospital costs— would have been left, literally, out in the cold.

All was not smooth sailing, however. The "Baylor Plan" faced stiff opposition from several quarters. First, other Dallas hospitals threatened to obtain an injunction against Baylor for selling group hospital service. But once the hospitals had inspected the plan at close range, at the invitation of the Baylor administration, they decided to follow the old philosophy of "if you can't lick 'em, join 'em," and quickly began to implement plans of their own. Next, some commercial insurance companies charged Baylor with competing with private business in the selling of insurance. The companies contended that Baylor had violated its non-profit status and should, therefore, have to pay taxes. As a result, the state attorney general's office threatened to revoke Baylor's charter if Dr. Kimball and Twitty did not halt promotion of the plan immediately. The bitter dispute finally went all the way to the Texas Legislature, where Baylor won its point.

Contrarily, the Dallas County Medical Society supported the plan from the beginning—and with good reason. Its member doctors were suffering financial hardships, just as Baylor was.

As an outgrowth of its legal victories in Texas, national recognition of the "Baylor Plan" spread rapidly. The first attention given the plan outside Texas came from the Rosenwald Foundation. Rufus Rorem, a representative of the foundation, visited Dallas in 1930 and was so impressed with the plan's results that he helped publicize it across the country. A few months later, a paper was presented on the plan at a National Education Association meeting in Washington, D.C. After the meeting, Frank Van Dyke, executive secretary of the Essex County Hospital in Newark, New Jersey, headed directly to Dallas for a firsthand inspection of the plan. Upon his return to New Jersey, he put the plan in operation with headquarters in Newark, marking the first time the plan had been implemented in another state.

The plan was officially introduced to the American Hospital Association at its annual convention in New Orleans in 1930 by Dr. Kimball. When it was presented for the delegates' approval, some hospital administrators bitterly condemned it, calling the plan "unethical, unreasonable and unworkable," and urged that it be abolished at once. Despite this opposition, Dr. Kimball never faltered in his support of the plan, and, ultimately, it won the endorsement of the association.

Even before the American Hospital Association extended its blessings to the plan, however, the American College of Surgeons became the first important national medical body to give its approval. Over the next few months, more and more hospitals used the "Baylor Plan" as a model for plans of their own, but it would be several years before the powerful American Medical Association officially sanctioned the concept.

The great drawback of group hospital service was the fact that each hospital sold prepaid care in its own facilities only, giving the patient no free choice in the matter. The American Hospital Association wanted to create a central office through which all individual hospital plans would be administered, so that patients could go to any cooperating hospital with the assurance that their bills would be prepaid. At the AHA's 1934 convention in Atlantic City, an advisory group was formed to work toward the coordination of all the plans currently in use in the United States, and Twitty was elected its chairman. (By 1934, more than 10,000 persons were covered under the "Baylor Plan," making it one of the largest such plans in the country.)

Several months later, the AHA's Commission for Hospital Care was formed and a national office set up in Chicago. Rorem, the former Rosenwald Foundation official who had first helped spread the word about the "Baylor Plan," was picked to head the office. The name selected for the national organization was one that would become a household term in America over the next few decades—Blue Cross.

During 1934 and thereafter, various commercial insurance companies added hospitalization to their lines of coverage. But the Blue Cross plans across the nation remained non-profit service organizations, operated by unpaid boards of trustees. In 1938, the Texas Legislature passed a bill creating Blue Cross of Texas. By the following year, the "Baylor Plan" had grown into a nationwide Blue Cross system, and, by 1940, its membership would exceed five million persons. In 1946, the Blue Cross Plan was supplemented by the Blue Shield Plan, which provides insurance for the payment of doctor bills. And now, nearly five decades after Dr. Kimball and Twitty originated the idea, more than 90 million Americans are covered by Blue Cross. The tiny "acorn" planted at Baylor Hospital in December 1929 has grown into an institution of massive proportions. In the lobby of today's Truett Hospital of Baylor University Medical Center is a bronze plaque inscribed as follows: "To Baylor University Hospital, Dallas, Texas—the birthplace of the Blue Cross program of prepaid hospital service. The Board of Trustees and the Blue Cross Commission of the American Hospital Association jointly present this plaque in appreciation of the origin of this movement which has contributed greatly to progress in health care and which has made hospital service available to millions."

The plaque is a small, inauspicious reminder of one of the major health care developments of the Twentieth Century—one born of sheer desperation on a bleak long-ago afternoon in Dallas.

Breakthroughs in Blood

While the "Baylor Plan" was creating a national sensation during the 1930s, a number of important events which were to cast worldwide attention on Baylor were occurring back home in Dallas—especially in the field of hematology, the study of the human blood.

Perhaps some of Baylor's greatest contributions to

medical research came during this period as a result of the work of Dr. Joseph M. Hill, a native of Buffalo, New York, who was appointed director of the Baylor laboratories in 1934, and a staff of physicians, scientists and technicians. Under Dr. Hill's leadership, Baylor established one of the first and most progressive blood banks in the world and initiated extensive investigation in 1935 into the problems of blood diseases, blood cell structure and techniques of preparation, preservation and handling of blood.

In 1938, Dr. Hill began the development of a machine called ADTEVAC (Adsorption Temperature Control Vacuum) that could dry blood plasma. In the process, blood plasma was reduced to a powdered form that did not require refrigeration to prevent bacterial growth and spoilage. The powder was mixed with a dissolving liquid immediately prior to its use in transfusions to form "instant blood plasma."

As Dr. Hill recalled in a 1978 interview: "We really started the development of a machine for another purpose. We were trying to culture human cells, and one of the requirements for that was fetal calf serum, which we obtained from slaughterhouses. We felt at that time that the culturing of human cells would be a useful tool in the study of blood diseases and cancer. To preserve the fetal calf serum, we decided to attempt to build a device that would freeze-dry it. Somehow, though, we decided to try freeze-drying blood, and the fetal calf serum idea just got lost in the shuffle."

Because of the difficulty of obtaining research funds during those days, Dr. Hill and his associates searched everywhere for any material that might be used in the construction of the machine and finally "scrounged together enough odds and ends" to successfully complete the project. A discarded autoclave formed a vacuum for the machine, for example, and motors from illegal slot machines destroyed by the Dallas County sheriff also proved quite useful. To

In 1929, Dr. Justin F. Kimball, above left, and Bryce Twitty conceived and implemented an insurance program that would later become the Blue Cross program of prepaid hospital service. As Dr. Kimball's plan was creating a sensation nationwide, Dr. Joseph M. Hill, head of Baylor's laboratories, brought further attention to the hospital with the creation of an ADTEVAC machine, below, that could dry blood plasma.

78

Blood serums were dried in the ADTEVAC's vacuum chamber, left, and the dried serum was then placed in ampoules and sealed, above, for shipment to other hospitals. Because of the success of this project and others in the field of blood research, James K. Wadley, center, below, a Texarkana millionaire, and his wife, Susie L., seated, donated the funds to Dr. Joseph M. Hill, left, for the construction of a new blood center on the Baylor campus.

perfect the machine, Dr. Hill hired D. C. Pfeiffer, an engineer with Dallas Power and Light Co., as a consultant, and Pfeiffer became so enthralled with the project that he resigned his DP&L job to devote full-time to the machine. Their first effort, built on a $7,500 grant from the late Fred Luhnow, a Dallas businessman, would produce only one-half liter of dried plasma at a time, while a perfected version could produce as much as 100 liters a week. Like all the group's discoveries, the process was released as a free gift to the scientific community and was rapidly adopted by other blood plasma services, and with certain modifications was used to supply the United States armed services with blood plasma during World War II. With the development, Baylor became the first hospital in the world to have a routine dried plasma service.

Due to the widespread interest generated by the new machine, Baylor received a $13,000 grant in December 1939 from Dr. and Mrs. Stanley Seeger, a Milwaukee couple who had recently moved to Dallas, to start a blood center in memory of the late William Buchanan, Mrs. Seeger's father and a millionaire Texarkana lumber dealer and oilman. The center, officially known as the William Buchanan Blood, Plasma and Serum Center, was located on the hospital's fourth floor and provided the additional space and laboratory facilities necessary for further blood research.

Among the projects initiated after the establishment of the center was the revolutionary development of a method to mass-produce serum that could be used to determine the Rh factor of a person's blood before that person received a transfusion. Without such blood typing, there was a chance the person might receive an incompatible blood transfusion that could result in death. At the time the center began its research, the serum necessary for such blood typing—a routine procedure in today's hospitals — was available only in minute quantities at extremely high prices for medical research. But using the ADTEVAC machine, the Baylor scientists found a way to dry the serum and produce it in large-scale quantities. In 1945, in a report of the *Journal of the American Medical Association*, the staff announced its discovery—a breakthrough that made Baylor the first hospital in the world to have a routine Rh blood-typing service. Immediately, Baylor made the serum available to other hospitals throughout the United States and in many foreign countries. Proceeds from the sale of the serum were used to finance further research at Baylor. By the early 1950s, the center had produced and sold 155,867 ampoules of serum, and its caseload of patients with Rh-related problems, especially women who had lost babies because of Rh incompatibility, was continuing to increase.

As the demand for services grew, the need for more space and newer equipment and facilities became paramount. Those needs were met in 1951 when J. K. Wadley, a Texarkana millionaire and protege of William Buchanan, and his wife, Susie L. Wadley, donated $700,000 for the establishment of a new blood institute to be located on land leased to it by Baylor at Gaston and Adair Streets. The Wadleys had become interested in blood research, and had decided to donate a large portion of their wealth to such efforts, after the death of their six-year-old grandson, Keener Bob Mosely, from leukemia in 1943. With the approval of Dr. and Mrs. Seeger, the name of the William Buchanan Center was officially changed in 1951 to the J. K. and Susie L. Wadley Institute and Blood Bank and was put under the administration of a joint Baylor-Wadley Institute board. That facility would one day form the nucleus for another independent health care institution in Dallas, the Wadley Institutes of Medicine, a blood and cancer treatment-research facility located at 9000 Harry Hines Boulevard.

More Changes

All in all, the patterns of patient care in America probably shifted more rapidly in the 1930s than in any similar period in American history. While the country's population increased by 30 per cent between 1910 and 1935, the number of hospital beds increased by 150 per cent (or 1,076,350 beds) during that same 25-year period. When the decade of the 1930s opened, the vast majority of American babies were still born at home. Indeed, as late as 1935, only 37 per cent of the nation's births took place in hospitals. But by the beginning of the 1940s, well over half the births were in hospitals, and by 1945, seven out of every ten U.S. infants entered the world in hospital surroundings.

To accommodate the growing demand for maternity and obstetrical services, Baylor opened the Florence Nightingale Maternity Hospital on its Dallas campus in 1937. Construction of the facility was made possible by a gift from Mr. and Mrs. E. R. Brown of Dallas, but, as had often happened in the past, the project ended up costing a great deal more than originally anticipated. Baylor officials first believed the new unit of Baylor could be built for $75,000, but the final cost totaled $148,695.55—or almost twice the first estimates. Fortunately, the Browns generously increased the size of their donation to cover the cost overrun. A modest man and a devout Presbyterian, Brown also insisted that his name not be attached in any way to the name of the hospital. When Dr. Kimball suggested that it be named Florence Nightingale Maternity Hospital, to honor a noted pioneer in the field of nursing education, the Browns gave their prompt approval.

The new hospital at the corner of Gaston Avenue and Adair Street was considered the ultimate, the "last word" in facilities for newborn babies and their mothers, and Dallas area mothers-to-be lost no time in taking advantage of them. During the 12 months immediately preceding the opening of Florence Nightingale on May 12, 1937, 1,055 babies were born at Baylor; at the new hospital's peak, in the early 1950s, some 6,800 births per year were recorded.

With the opening of Florence Nightingale came another important development in the process that would, over the years, transform Baylor Hospital into the sprawling complex now known as Baylor University Medical Center. Florence Nightingale was the first hospital facility on the Baylor campus to function under a separate name, in a separate building (although it was connected with Baylor by an underground tunnel), and with a separate staff. In the brochure distributed at the formal opening of Florence Nightingale, officials of Baylor-in-Dallas used the term "Baylor University *Hospitals*" for what may have been the first time.

As early as 1932, official papers had added the word "university" to references to Baylor Hospital, but as far as can be determined, the name was not formally changed to Baylor University Hospital until July 16, 1936, when a new 50-year charter was issued to Baylor University and the hospital name change became a legal fact.

Other changes were also taking place during the 1930s—many of them unhappy changes. The Baylor University School of Pharmacy, which had operated in Dallas since 1904 as one of the oldest components of Baylor-in-Dallas, became a lost cause in 1931, the victim of inadequate financing and more stringent laws regarding the education of pharmacists. Along with its fellow scientific schools in Dallas, the School of Pharmacy had suffered during most of its 27-year existence from a shortage of funds. (The parent university in Waco had made it abundantly clear to its Dallas branches from the very beginning that they would have to generate their own operating funds, and that no financial assistance would be possible from Baylor-at-Waco.) By 1931, there was simply no money left to run the School of Pharmacy, much less to upgrade the curriculum and expand the facilities as newly enacted state legislation would have required.

During that same year, Dr. S. P. Brooks, who had served as president of Baylor University since 1902 and who had been one of the early advocates of the university's sponsorship of a hospital and medical school in Dallas, died. If President Brooks had lived, there is some slight chance that the School of Pharmacy might also have survived, at least for a while. Two years before his death, he had warned Baylor's trustees that Baylor's "problem in Pharmacy (is) very acute," but had firmly recommended expanding the school's course of study from two years to three in order to comply with "certain laws passed by the State."

Dr. Brooks' successor, former Governor Pat M. Neff, was believed by some Baylor-in-Dallas officials to have had difficulty understanding the needs of the scientific schools in Dallas and in realizing their importance in relationship with the parent university. But by the time Neff took office on June 1, 1932, the School of Pharmacy was already dead and buried.

Death and disaster—as well as Depression— seemed to be among the tragic trademarks of the 1930s. Desperadoes like John Dillinger and Clyde Barrow and Bonnie Parker spread homicide and high-speed terror across the continent. An assassin's bullet felled Chicago Mayor Anton Cermak and narrowly missed President Franklin Roosevelt in Miami. The giant German airship *Hindenburg* exploded into a ball of flaming death at Lakehurst, New Jersey. The kidnap-murder of Charles A. Lindbergh's infant son made headlines around the world.

But to Texas befell what must rank as the most awesome disaster of the decade, the most tragic loss of human life medical professionals from Baylor Hospital would witness between the two World Wars.

On March 18, 1937, a school building at New London, Texas, filled with hundreds of unsuspecting children blew up without warning a few minutes before classes were to be dismissed for the day. The blast, later blamed on a huge accumulation of leaking gas in a sub-basement beneath the four-year-old school, killed 294 persons instantly—280 of them children—and left almost 100 others injured, many critically. It was the most horrible disaster involving children in all of American history.

Within minutes, news of the catastrophe reached Dallas, slightly more than 100 miles away. Many of the victims—both the dead and the living—were buried beneath tons of crumbled brick and twisted steel, and it was first feared that as many as 500 of the approximately 600 persons who had been in the building at the time of the blast might have lost their lives. In the days to follow, the task of treating the survivors and of recovering, identifying and burying the dead would be monumental.

Soon, doctors, nurses and other medical personnel from Baylor were hurrying to the scene, and the hospital was designated as the central clearinghouse for all supplies going to the town. In all, 30 physicians and 100 nurses from Dallas went to the aid of the stricken townspeople of New London. Many were from Baylor, although the exact number is not recorded. Some would stay for days in the town that had lost virtually an entire generation of its young, and the vivid memories of what they saw there would remain for a lifetime.

Even though they were frequently characterized by calamity, the Thirties also brought dramatic advancements in the healing arts and in the saving of human lives. The term "wonder drug" entered the American lexicon before the end of the decade, with the discovery and development of the first powerful infection fighters—the sulfa drugs.

Dr. John S. Bagwell, now an internist on the

At the time the Florence Nightingale Hospital
opened on May 12, 1937, on the Baylor campus,
its facilities were considered among the finest for
newborns and their mothers.

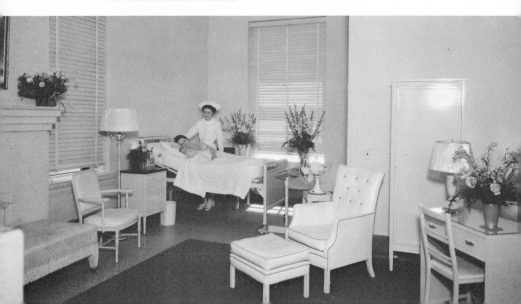

The ambulance corps for Baylor Hospital poses beside the newly completed Florence Nightingale Hospital.

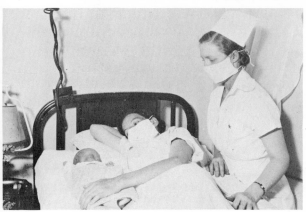

At its peak period in the 1950s, almost 7,000 births per year were recorded at the Florence Nightingale Hospital, and it was not long before the facility could no longer accommodate all the maternity patients who came to its doors. The only solution was to place the patients in the hallways.

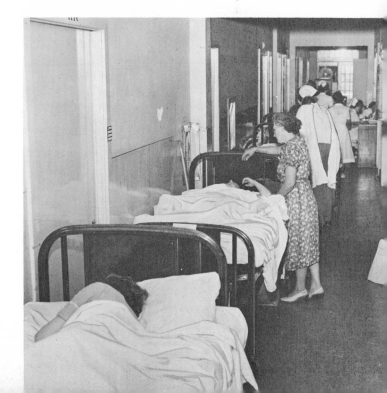

Baylor staff, was an awed young intern at the hospital at the time a sulfa drug was first used there to combat a deadly infection in a seemingly doomed patient. That was more than 40 years ago, in 1937, but Dr. Bagwell's voice is still charged with excitement as he recalls the drama he observed so long ago: "The drug was a bright red solution in a quart fruit jar. We gave it to a young woman who had a severe infection. She was running a fever of 106 degrees and was on the brink of death. None of us had any experience with the drug, but it was our only hope. Within 24 hours after she received it, the woman's fever had subsided, and a few days later she walked out of the hospital fully recovered. It was a crude drug compared to the antibiotics of today, but its results were truly miraculous."

How Firm a Foundation

Except in its very earliest days, enrollment had never really been a problem for Baylor University College of Medicine. Even in the midst of the Depression, the number of students rose steadily year by year, until, in 1938, the number of students entering the freshman class had to be limited for the first time. That year, there were 83 freshmen and a total of 338 students enrolled.

But the tuitions paid by the larger numbers of students could not resolve the basic problem that had always plagued the school—lack of money. It had no endowment, no support from a major financial foundation or granting agency, and no monetary assistance from its own parent university. But there were even greater problems than financial insolvency. Most of the faculty members were engaged in private medical practice, and their primary concern was, necessarily, the treatment of patients, not the teaching of medical students. There was little research at the school and instruction was basically limited to lectures. These drawbacks, coupled with a still-inadequate physical plant, were jeopardizing Baylor's position as a Class A institution.

Thus, even as the hospital was making its way successfully through a time of great economic hardship and finding innovative ways to solve its dilemma, the medical college was floundering. Its part-time faculty was composed of dedicated men who had given countless hours of their time without pay to give Dallas a medical school, but they could not continue forever to do it alone.

It was in this troubled climate that Dr. Cary, who had become one of the wealthier members of Dallas society and an integral part of the city's Establishment, decided to form the Southwestern Medical Foundation. On January 21, 1939, with the support of other leading figures in the community, Dr. Cary obtained a charter for the foundation, which declared it to be a non-profit corporation with no capital stock. In addition to Dr. Cary, the incorporators were E. R. Brown (the Florence Nightingale benefactor), show business entrepreneur and Interstate Theater owner Karl Hoblitzelle and Dr. Hall Shannon. Shortly after its incorporation, the foundation added Herbert Marcus and Rhodes Baker, both of Dallas; Jesse H. Jones and R. C. Fulbright, both of Houston; and T. O. Walton, president of Texas A&M College at Bryan, to its Board of Trustees.

The charter of the foundation permitted collection and disbursement of funds for medical education and research. It also gave the foundation the right to own and operate a medical school. And it set forth as the broad purpose of the foundation "the establishment of facilities and clinics in the study of causes, the prevention and cure of diseases of the minds and bodies of needy persons residing in the southwestern section of the United States and elsewhere, and for the development and training of laboratory workers, physicians and nurses in the treatment of diseased persons, in the study of individual and community hygiene and in promoting public health and in medical research."

Historian Dr. John Chapman, a chest specialist formerly at Baylor Hospital and now on the faculty at the University of Texas Health Science Center, offers the following observation on Dr. Cary's goals and motives in establishing the foundation: "The wording of the charter suggests that Cary had reached a decision to bring medical education in Dallas to the level he regarded as appropriate. Through his associations in the American Medical Association, he would have been aware of Baylor's uneasy status in comparison with other medical schools. And, obviously, he was completely aware of the local situation . . . . One can only infer that its (the foundation's) purpose was to change Baylor, or—failing that—to set up a competitive, more 'modern' school."

Although Dr. Cary was himself a faithful Baptist, he had gone on record as early as 1929 as wishing to "dispel the impression among many that Baylor is wholly denominational and sectarian." He and other leaders of both the medical and civic communities in Dallas were deeply disturbed by the fact that Baylor's scientific schools were firmly controlled by a Baptist institution, and one that was not even providing the schools with adequate financial support.

At a formal dinner sponsored by the Southwestern Medical Foundation on January 23, 1939, at the Adolphus Hotel in downtown Dallas, those responsible for the foundation emphasized that, although it was located in Dallas, it would belong to the entire Southwest and would be strictly nonsectarian in its pursuit of its goals. It was expected that endowments would come from private sources; unofficial estimates of the amounts needed ranged from $5 million to $25 million.

That same month, in one of its earliest formal actions, the foundation appointed a committee consisting of Dr. Cary, Dr. Kimball (who earlier that month had resigned as vice president of Baylor University to devote his full time to the newly organized Group Hospital Service, Inc., which later became Blue Cross-Blue Shield of Texas), Hoblitzelle, Marcus and M. J. Norrell, who represented E. R. Brown on the group. The committee's purpose was to raise a $5 million endowment for the promotion and support of medical research at Baylor College of Medicine. Enthusiasm and hopes ran high for a while, but, as it had a habit of doing where the medical school was concerned, the money proved difficult to obtain. Within a few months, the nation's eyes were once again focused on a dangerous and spreading war in Europe, and perhaps this is the reason the endowment failed to materialize. Whatever the cause, the failure meant that more difficult times were still ahead.

But even as the uneasy rumblings of discord and dissatisfaction grew louder around Baylor—and as the thunder of armed conflict grew more ominous overseas—there were those who could find a large measure of comfort and fulfillment in the amount of distance Baylor-in-Dallas had covered since those embryonic beginnings in the first years of a new century.

As the curtain came down on the 1930s, sage old Dr. Rosser, whose wit and humor had carried him and the medical school he had fathered through the toughest of times, summed up those feelings with this comment:

"Yesterday, the spacious parking place of the Baylor University Hospital and College of Medicine was so crowded with cars of staff and other visiting doctors that for a time I could find no place to park my own. The first reaction was one of annoyance, but remembrance traveling backward more than 30 years to the time when, day by day, my buggy rig and George Loudermilk's horse-drawn, rubber-tired ambulance were the only two such vehicles to frequent the premises, I was content. Sadly enough, too often do pioneers who conceive, plan and promote great enterprises pass on before the fulfillment of their dreams."

Fate had dealt kindly with Dr. Rosser in that respect. But now there were other dreams occupying other minds. And looming on the horizon was the horrendous nightmare of World War II.

VII

Courage and Conflict

A World at War

In August 1940, at about the same time a triumphant Adolph Hitler was viewing the capital of a conquered France from atop the Eiffel Tower, the Board of Trustees of Baylor University Hospital and Baylor University College of Medicine received a telegram from U.S. Surgeon General James C. Magee, asking that an executive committee be formed at the college to organize a medical unit for the Army. The unit was to be designated as the 56th Evacuation Hospital, and it would, in the beginning, be composed almost entirely of hospital staff and medical school faculty and alumni, just as its predecessor had been 22 years earlier in World War I.

Technically, of course, America was still at peace that hot, fateful summer of 1940. In Europe, the situation was desperate. Hitler and his pompous partner in Rome, Benito Mussolini, held dominion over all of the western European continent. Across the English Channel, debilitated by the disastrous retreat from Dunkirk and fearing imminent invasion by the German Army, Britain stood alone. Night after night, the Luftwaffe dumped hundreds of tons of bombs on a reeling London while Nazi stormtroopers goose-stepped through the streets of Paris. Poland, Czechoslovakia, Norway, Denmark, the Netherlands, Belgium and France—one by one, they had all fallen before the Axis onslaught.

But on relaxed family outings at White Rock Lake, on the roller coaster at Fair Park, in the bleachers at a

Dallas Rebel baseball game, or at a backyard watermelon party, Dallasites could still pretend for a while longer that all was well. Europe was still a long way off, although not nearly so far away as it had been in 1917. And this time, there was another threatening presence on the other side of the world, where the Japanese warlords had sent their armies knifing deep into China and were now casting greedy eyes on the French, British and Dutch colonies in Southeast Asia.

That autumn, at President Franklin D. Roosevelt's urging, Congress approved the first peacetime draft in American history, even though equipment was so scarce that those first draftees were forced to train with wooden rifles and broomsticks. Through the Lend-Lease program, the United States was already sending ships, arms and other war materiel to the embattled British; soon it would be sending men as well.

The physicians and surgeons who had volunteered as members of the 56th Evacuation Hospital were given their commissions in the U.S. Army in February 1941. Dr. Henry M. Winans, a specialist in internal medicine at Baylor University Hospital and professor of medicine at the medical college, was commissioned a lieutenant colonel and given the responsibility of organizing the hospital unit, in collaboration with Dr. G. M. Hilliard, administrator of Baylor University Hospital. During the summer and fall of 1941, the largest peacetime maneuvers ever seen on the North American continent were conducted by the Army, as Roosevelt and British Prime Minister Winston Churchill moved closer and closer toward a binding military alliance. Still, the American people were sharply divided in their attitudes toward American participation in the war. But while American attentions were focused largely upon the war in Europe, something was about to happen in the Pacific that would dramatically alter public sentiment within the space of a few hours.

Shortly before 8 o'clock on the pleasant Sunday morning of December 7, 1941, hundreds of Japanese planes attacked the giant U.S. naval base at Pearl Harbor in the Hawaiian Islands without warning. Fighters and dive bombers emblazoned with the emblem of the Rising Sun struck U.S. airfields, while Japanese high-level bombers and torpedo planes mounted a furious attack on the assembled warships of the U.S. Pacific Fleet. The devastating sneak attack left 2,330 Americans dead and another 1,145 wounded, and sent a wave of shocked outrage across the country. The next day, the American people gathered around their radios to hear President Roosevelt call for a declaration of war against Japan—a request that was approved in Congress by an overwhelming vote of 470 to 1. Three days later, Japan's Axis partners, Germany and Italy, declared war on the United States. Congress reciprocated, and the American people became full participants in the most monstrous conflict in human history.

As a result, the organization of the 56th Evacuation Hospital was suddenly and drastically accelerated. As originally constituted, twenty-nine of the unit's officers were staff members at Baylor University Hospital, faculty members of the Baylor College of Medicine or medical college alumni and two were from the College of Dentistry. Charter members of the unit included Lt. Col. Winans, Lt. Col. Christopher B. Carter, Majors Andrew B. Small, Raymond S. Willis, Edwin L. Rippy, Charles D. Bussey, James Hudson Dunlap and Festus J. Sebastian; Captains George M. Hilliard, Robert J. Rowe, Weldon E. Bell, William P. Devereux, Sidney Galt, Hugh E. McClung, John B. Peyton, Rowan E. Fisher, Samuel A. Allesandra and Gustavus W. Thommason; and First Lieutenants Ben A. Merrick, Lawrence D. Collins, C. J. Hicks, Charles N. LaDue, Richard E. Martinak, George J. Merriman, Robert H. Johnson, Byrd E. White Jr., Jabez Galt, Hugh Arnold, Elmer K. Jones, William W. Brown and Mack

F. Boyer. Margaret Rea was named commanding officer of the hospital unit's original 31-member nursing complement, which included Laura Alsup, Sara B. Alvey, Vernie Brazelton, Elizabeth Brooks, Helen Agnes McCullough, Madge Teague, Jean Richey, Elsie Moore, Frances Raymond, Helen Pfeiffer, Martha Tate, Marjorie LaVerne Kester, Johnny Christina Hatchett, Mary Ann Corey, Dorothy Thralls, Elizabeth Herndon, Sybil Mosely, Ruth Hungerford, Louise Hughes, Myrtle Elkins, Ruse Curry Craig, Thelma Dennis, Mary Louise Roberts, Iris Ruth Ritchie, Charlotte Sellman, Frances Lee Springer, Pansy Jo Thompson, Victoria Skrow, Ruby Gadberry, Marjorie Gray and Elizabeth Wright.

It was not long, however, before the unit began to grow rapidly, as additional nurses and physicians, caught up in the wave of patriotism that was sweeping the country, began volunteering for duty with "the fighting 56th." On March 17, 1942, all commissioned officers and nurses under Lt. Col. Winans' command were ordered to report for duty at Fort Sam Houston in San Antonio, and on March 29, the unit was officially activated. Bets were being made among eager members of the 56th that the unit would be overseas within six to eight weeks, but the bets were wrong. It would require almost a year of training, outfitting with equipment and expansion to full strength before the unit would reach the combat zone. But when combat finally came, there would be more than enough of it to satisfy even the most eager and patriotic members of the 56th.

In the meantime, though, amid the sound and fury of global conflict, there were also signs that another kind of conflict was brewing at home.

Collision Course

Just as the attack on Pearl Harbor had alerted the federal government to the urgent need for many more physicians, the huge and demanding task of training more doctors for the war effort became the priority for the nation's medical colleges. Doctors had become important "war materiel," and both the Navy and the Army had decided that medical students must be made militarily ready—even while they were still in school.

Since Baylor had experienced continuous difficulty, even in meeting peacetime demands, and since the Southwestern Medical Foundation had by this time acquired enough money (mostly from Hoblitzelle) to give it considerable power, Dr. Cary decided the time was right to make changes in both the financing and control of the ailing Baylor College of Medicine. Regardless of how generous the motives for such a move may have been, this decision was to place Baylor-at-Waco on an irreversible collision course with the foundation—a course that would only end with the move of the medical college, in July 1943, to Houston.

Early in 1942, as the 56th was going into training, the Southwestern Medical Foundation, with the support of a number of Baylor Hospital staff and Baylor Medical College faculty members, began actively pursuing the "joint operation" of a medical school with Baylor University. It seemed that their long-awaited objective was about to become reality when *The Dallas Morning News* carried this announcement on March 12, 1942:

"Plans for a great medical center on a 35-acre tract on Hines Boulevard, including the Parkland Hospital grounds, were announced Wednesday, March 8, 1942, by the Southwestern Medical Foundation through its president, Dr. E. H. Cary of Dallas. It is stated that buildings planned for the center and necessary equipment will cost $1 million for the start and run up to $25 million when completed. Baylor University College of Medicine has been offered the opportunity of sponsoring the medical school which would be an integral part of the center. The plan would not involve Baylor Hospital. The Southwestern Medical Foundation is nonsectarian. The medical school at the projected center as well as all other activities would be nonsectarian. The Baylor Dental College also is included in the proposal. Under the proposed group plan, Baylor would direct the educational or academic aspects while the foundation would control the fiscal affairs."

The announcement marked the beginning of a year of confusion for both Baylor and the foundation.

After the formal announcement of plans for a "great medical center," a push began to get Baylor to agree to have its medical college become a part of the complex. Committees from the clinical faculty and the foundation's Board of Trustees met with the trustees of both Baylor-at-Waco and Baylor-in-Dallas. The proposal for joint operation of the college was endorsed by the Dallas County Medical Society, the Southern Clinical Society of Dallas, the staffs of various hospitals and the Dallas Baylor Alumni Association.

Terms of the proposed agreement called for the foundation to provide 20 acres of land and a minimum of $1 million, of which at least $750,000 would be used for new quarters for the medical and dental colleges. This construction was to be completed within two years after the lifting of wartime building priorities. Title to all buildings constructed by the foundation was to remain at all times with the foundation. The college of medicine was to be governed by an administrative committee consisting of three members appointed by the foundation and two members appointed by the trustees of Baylor. Meanwhile, effective with the oncoming term, 1942-43, the foundation was to furnish a minimum of $20,000 per year in additional financial support to the medical college.

By May 12, a called meeting of the Dallas trustees of Baylor unanimously approved "in principle" a proposed contract worked out by lawyers for the two

98

parties, Robert G. Storey, representing the foundation, and J. M. Penland, representing Baylor. As a result of that action, the board of Baylor-at-Waco approved the agreement on June 23 at a meeting in Dallas, and on July 7, the agreement was also approved by the executive board of the Baptist General Convention of Texas, after Penland had given his assurance that "control of the schools will never pass from the hands of the Baptists." Finally, in November 1942, the entire Baptist Convention approved the agreement. For a while, as the war raged elsewhere, all was quiet on the Dallas front. But it was not to remain so for long.

As the academic year went on, misunderstandings between Baylor and the foundation over which entity had control of the college began to grow. Baylor felt that the foundation was attempting to take complete charge of the school, and Baylor trustees had no intention of allowing that to happen. Amid increasing dissension, Baylor trustees began having second thoughts about the agreement with the foundation, and their doubts rapidly festered into deep misgivings. As early as January 1943, it was reported that the Baylor trustees had spent an entire day pondering the problems of the medical school, but had taken no action. It is known, too, that Dean Moursund was opposed to Baylor's alliance with the foundation because he feared it would cause control of the medical school to shift from Baylor and its dean to Dr. Cary and Dallas' "downtown establishment." There also was speculation that many others at Baylor opposed the agreement because it would change the medical school's hospital affiliation from Baylor to Parkland, since the new medical school facilities would be located adjacent to Parkland.

In the final analysis, the agreement was destined to come apart because of four main points of disagreement—points the foundation viewed as essential, but which Baylor simply could not accept. They were: (1) the physical removal of the medical school from the

This collection of photographs offers a glimpse of the 56th Evacuation Hospital unit during overseas duty during World War II. The photographs were furnished by Dr. Ben A. Merrick.

Dr. Henry M. Winans, a Baylor internist and professor of medicine, organized the 56th Evacuation Hospital unit.

In the spring of 1942, these officers and nurses, below, departed for military maneuvers in Louisiana. Almost all of them were graduates of Baylor University College of Medicine, and many were on the staff of Baylor Hospital.

Baylor-in-Dallas campus, (2) its designation as a non-sectarian institution, (3) the foundation's majority on the administrative committee, and (4) a separate accounting system for the medical school. Whether it was Dean Moursund's objections, general concerns among the Baylor Board of Trustees or bolder pressures from the foundation representatives that caused the final splintering of the agreement seems unimportant. Whichever the case may have been, according to historian Dr. Chapman, responsible parties at Baylor and within the Baptist denomination apparently concluded as early as March 1943 that the agreement was unacceptable.

During the same month, the 56th Evacuation Hospital got its orders to ship out for its long-anticipated overseas assignment. As the physicians and nurses of the unit made out their wills, told their families and loved ones goodbye and packed their belongings for the long ordeal ahead, none of them knew what the fate of the medical college or Baylor University Hospital would be.

The Breaking Point

An ominous and uneasy silence followed the March meeting of the Baylor-in-Dallas trustees. While little was said publicly about their agreement, it was now obvious that both the Southwestern Medical Foundation and Baylor were looking for alternatives.

Setbacks and rumors notwithstanding, Dr. Cary was still determined to have a medical school and to see it operated on his own terms. Informed of the apparent reluctance of the Baylor trustees, he tartly told the press that the foundation would proceed with its plans for a medical school, with or without Baylor. Before the end of March, the foundation began negotiations with the City of Dallas and Dallas County (the joint operators of Parkland Hospital) for use of Parkland as a teaching facility for a medical school.

102

As the *Dallas News* noted at the time: "The foundation agrees, under the terms of the contract, to assume the administration and responsibility and exercise financial control over the operation of a nonsectarian medical college . . . ."

In his *Oral Memoirs*, a history compiled in 1974 by Baylor University, Dr. Milford O. Rouse recalled that, not long after the March meeting of the Baylor trustees, Baylor University President Neff came to Dallas to confer with the local trustees. He brought with him the news that members of the parent university's board from Waco, San Antonio and Houston were unanimously in favor of revoking the contract with Southwestern Medical Foundation, but there were no reports of this sentiment—or even of Neff's visit—published in the Dallas newspapers. Officially, the trustees of Baylor-in-Dallas were still in favor of continuing the agreement with the foundation. In his book, Dr. Rouse describes an emotional meeting with the Dallas trustees:

> Now, I might mention, about that time our Dallas Baylor trustees were kind (enough) to invite three of us Baylor graduates—all of us were Baptist deacons, Dr. H. F. Carman, Dr. Gordon Maddox, and myself—to come and just talk about the problem. And so, as best we could, we outlined the tremendous financial needs of Baylor College of Medicine. We needed new buildings, we needed new facilities, we needed more full time teachers if Baylor was to continue to be recognized as a Class A medical school. . . . So, we tried our best to point out to these friends there that night that we were interested in our medical school—their medical school, going ahead and joining hands with this group of business and professional men to assure getting what we needed. To my sincere regret, one fine friend there shook his finger in Dr. Rouse's face and said, "Dr. Rouse, you're a traitor to Baylor." Well, as kindly as I could, I said, "No, my friend. I'm just as loyal and interested in Baylor as you or anyone else. I'm a Baptist, but I feel very strongly that we Baptists ought to provide this money. But we've never done it, and still, you don't hear of any effort for us Baptists to increase our financial support of Baylor (Medical College). Therefore, I don't think it's fair for us to con-

tinue to get the credit for a Baptist institution if we're going to let it, literally, starve. I'd much rather we Baptists would do it. But if not, I think in all fairness we owe it to the medical school to release it if we're not going to support it as we should. But please remember, I'm trying to help my Baylor.

At the next meeting of the entire Baylor University board on April 27, a majority of the trustees voted "to annul" the original agreement. In a statement to the press following the meeting, Neff blamed a "misunderstanding as to the objectives to be realized by the agreement" for the breakdown in the contract, and said that it had existed "from the beginning" of negotiations between Baylor and the foundation. He also announced that Baylor had received an offer to move the medical school to Houston, and three days later he called a special session of the board to weigh the Houston offer. Attorneys for the foundation, meanwhile, informed the public that Baylor's action had effectively canceled the entire contract. Neff publicly accused the foundation of being the first to break the accord, as a consequence of its agreement with the City of Dallas and Dallas County concerning the use of Parkland. The foundation countered with its own accusations. Obviously, neither side was in a conciliatory frame of mind, and any chance for compromise had passed.

(Although no specifics of the Houston proposal were made public immediately, the offer had come from the M. D. Anderson Foundation, specifying that the foundation would provide 20 acres of land for the Baylor medical and dental colleges, and would set aside $1 million for permanent buildings and another $1 million for research—all without taking part in school management or attempting to control school operations or policies. Although Baylor later decided to leave the dental school in Dallas, the basic terms of the offer remained the same.)

Four days after the announcement that the Baylor College of Medicine was leaving Dallas, the newspapers carried an announcement of the arrival of the new dean of the newly created Southwestern Medical College. The die was cast. As Dr. Chapman put it: "The divorce was complete and irrevocable."

But now, the student body and the faculty at the existing Baylor University College of Medicine fast became the "spoils of war." On one occasion, according to Dr. Chapman, Neff reportedly visited the Dallas school in a personal effort to convince the students they should go with Baylor to Houston. One account says that when the Dallas students balked at Neff's invitation, the former governor became "curt." When the question was raised as to the use of the medical school buildings, Neff was quoted as saying, "Those buildings are owned by Baylor University . . . and will be used by it." Asked if Southwestern Medical College would be allowed to use the buildings on a temporary basis, he reportedly replied, "Under no circumstances."

By this time, according to Dr. Chapman, "workmen in the Baylor buildings were . . . dismantling and preparing to ship to Houston everything salvageable, including the plumbing. This gutting was a little less retaliatory than it sounds; under the conditions of war, materials for construction were almost unobtainable, even if one could obtain a high priority for their purchase." Even the new library, which had been completed in 1941 with the support of the student body, the faculty and the Baylor Alumni Association, was moved from its quarters—further irritating those who wanted to keep the medical school in Dallas.

Dean Moursund, who moved with his school and continued to serve as its dean in its new location, contended that "many things were done to embarrass Baylor Medical College. Pressure was brought to bear on the salaried faculty to join the foundation school. Even the applicants who had been accepted for admission to the freshman class for the next year were besieged by telephone, telegraph and other means to try to persuade them to accept admission to the new school. Attempts to embarrass the college were directed towards creating unfriendliness and non-cooperation among the members of the Houston medical profession."

Through it all, though, students and faculty somehow continued to go about their daily routines. Amid the turmoil, and despite the flaring tempers and flying charges and counter-charges, commencement exercises for 77 graduates—the last in the 43-year history of the medical college in Dallas—were held on May 31, 1943, at the First Baptist Church. During its four decades as a Dallas institution, Baylor University College of Medicine had graduated a total of 1,670 medical doctors, not counting the 37 M.D. degrees awarded by the University of Dallas Medical Department during three years of operation. Its financial and other limitations were obvious but the quality of its educational programs was such that many of them are outstanding physicians and leaders in their specialties.

By July 1943, the school was gone. In its wake, it left a struggling Southwestern Medical College (the original unit of today's University of Texas Health Science Center), a shaken Baylor University Hospital, more than half of its students and faculty, and a residue of bitterness and regret that would linger for years.

But overshadowing all the events of this localized conflict was the larger conflagration of World War II.

To Hell and Back

On April 16, 1943, the men and women of the 56th Evacuation Hospital, by now under the command of Col. Henry S. Blesse of the U.S. Army Medical Corps, boarded the S. S. Mariposa, a converted luxury liner of the Matson Line, and sailed from

New York Harbor. Their destination, although no one in the unit knew it until they were well out to sea, was the legendary *Arabian Nights* port city of Casablanca, where the Mariposa docked eight days later after a perilous, unescorted voyage across the Atlantic, so that the unit could undergo further intensified training.

From Casablanca, the 56th crossed 1,300 miles of mountains and desert in a convoy of 112 trucks (many of which were driven by physicians pressed into service as truck drivers) to the big American base at Bizerte, near Tunis, where the unit came under fire for the first time on July 6 during a massive air raid by some 200 German planes. That was only the beginning. Allied forces were massing for the invasion of Sicily and the Italian mainland. On August 8, Sicily fell to combined British and American forces, in a campaign marked by fierce German resistance and spiritless defense by the Italians. Mussolini was ousted in a coup d'etat and Italy tried to make a separate peace with the Allies, but the Germans kept fighting. In September, the Allied carried out a triple landing on the embattled "boot" of Italy, at Reggio di Calabria, Taranto and Salerno. On September 26, the 56th landed at Paestum, 30 miles below Salerno, and from there began the slow, bloody march toward Rome. Once, counterattacking Germans almost pushed the Allies into the sea at Salerno, but they held on, and the march continued.

On January 22, 1944, Allied troops stormed ashore behind enemy lines at Anzio, 30 miles south of Rome, to launch one of the most brutally fought engagements of the war. Two days later, on January 24 and 25, the officers, enlisted men and nurses of the 56th boarded six small British landing ships and left Pozzuoli harbor in turbulent seas and under the constant threat of enemy air attack. Destination: the bloody beachhead at Anzio.

The first ship, carrying one officer and 24 enlisted men with some supplies and equipment, reached Anzio on January 25 as an advance detail sent to prepare a hospital building. German fighters strafed the docks as they were unloading and the building in which they were staying suffered direct hits from German bombs twice during the next two days. A second ship broke in half in the heavy seas; another experienced engine trouble and was forced to return to Pozzuoli. The last ship in the small armada, with several officers and all the unit's nurses aboard, was also forced back to Pozzuoli by foul weather. But in the meantime, 26 seasick nurses were transferred to a larger ship, only to find themselves trapped in Anzio harbor and unable to land because of incessant German air raids. Sixteen times in a little more than 36 hours, the ship was bombed and strafed by the Luftwaffe. Only after Major Edwin L. Rippy went ashore and demanded that the nurses be allowed to disembark did the ship dock. Even then, the nurses were forced back below decks twice more by attacking German planes before they finally managed to reach shore. En route to the hospital, they were forced from their trucks by yet another air raid. The date was January 27, 1944—D-Day plus five at Anzio.

During the weeks that followed, the 56th learned to recognize the terrifying sound of the "Anzio Express" as the Germans in the hills above the town rained death down on the invading Allied forces from their long-range 170 millimeter guns. Repeated bombings, meanwhile, drove the unit from its original hospital site, a former tuberculosis sanitarium that had been chosen on the basis of aerial photographs, but which was now deemed too dangerous for use. So the men and women of the 56th moved out to a "tent city" three miles east of the town of Nettuno.

By late January, they were swamped with wounded. All the space in the receiving and pre-operative wards was filled to overflowing; all surgical wards were overtaxed, and even the dental tent and

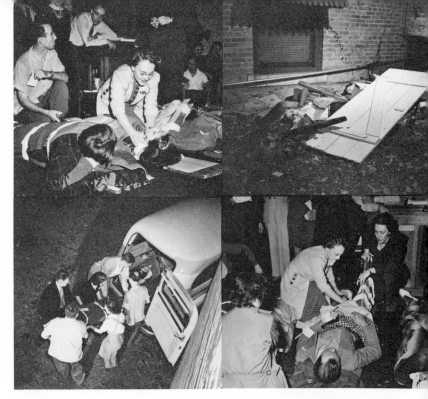

As physicians and nurses from Baylor Hospital saw duty overseas during World War II, another Baylor physician, orthopedic surgeon Ruth Jackson, top photo, left, helped to prepare Dallasites in case of an air raid at home. Dr. Jackson simulated realistic disaster drills, as these photographs show.

Dr. Edward H. Cary was instrumental in gaining Class A status for the Baylor College of Medicine, but during the war years, his efforts in forming the Southwestern Medical Foundation caused the loss of the medical college to Houston.

Baylor Hospital served as a site for collection of blood for use overseas during the years of World War II.

supply tents were used for pre-operative patients. Ambulances brought more loads of wounded men day and night. In one 36-hour period, the 56th treated 1,129 battle casualties.

Air raids and artillery attacks became just another fact of everyday life—and death. On the evening of February 10, the 56th was hit by shellfire from the infamous German 88s. Three shells struck the 56th's area and three others hit the nearby 33rd Evacuation Hospital, where two nurses and one enlisted man were killed. On February 12, the heaviest German air raid of the battle hit Anzio. It lasted for an hour and a half. One anti-personnel bomb landed in the 56th's officers' area, fatally wounding Lt. Ellen Ainsworth, and slightly injuring several other personnel.

On March 22, a massive artillery attack began at 4 a.m., devastating the nearby 15th Evacuation Hospital and moving ominously toward the 56th, with shells from more than forty 88s bursting at two-second intervals. At the 15th, seven patients were killed and many wounded when a ward received a direct hit, but only a few shells landed in the 56th's area before the barrage moved away. On March 29, the 56th was again hit by German bombs, one of which seriously wounded Private Nick Gergulas, who died of his wounds three days later. On April 3, Private Harvin C. Estes of the 56th was killed in another artillery attack. A fourth member of the unit, Private First Class Hulon V. Lofton, was killed on October 4, 1944, during a strafing attack by German planes at Scarperia.

After 76 days and nights in hell, "the fighting 56th" was relieved at Anzio. But the full story of the heroic unit from Baylor, which was told after the war in a book edited by Dr. Ben Merrick, did not end there. Subsequent chapters were to be written throughout the Italian campaign, over 25 months of continuous operation on foreign soil, during which the unit admitted and cared for 73,052 patients, a record its personnel believe was unsurpassed by any

Army evacuation hospital in either the Mediterranian or European Theaters of Operation. Many of its members were decorated for valor. One of them, Lieutenant Mary Roberts, one of the original 31 Baylor University Hospital nurses to join the 56th, became the first woman in the history of the U.S. Army to receive the Silver Star for bravery. The unit as a whole was awarded the Meritorious Service Unit Plaque in July 1945 "for superior performance of duty in the accomplishment of exceptionally difficult tasks." The award citation read in part: "The technical skill and resourceful initiative of this organization during the final victorious Po Valley offensive resulted in the saving of countless lives and the alleviation of much suffering. Its accomplishments reflect great credit to the Medical Department of the Army of the United States."

On August 4, 1945, the 56th admitted its last patient at Udine in northern Italy, and turned over its operations to another hospital unit in preparation for redeployment to another area. Two days later, the first atomic bomb fell on Hiroshima and on August 14, Japan unconditionally surrendered.

The war overseas was at an end. But at home, an uncertain future awaited—a future Baylor would have to face without the aid of two of its founding fathers whose courage and dedication had helped to see the hospital through four decades of almost unceasing struggle. Dr. George W. Truett, the farsighted minister for whom Baylor had become the embodiment of a fond dream, had died on July 7, 1944, after a lingering illness. And Dr. Charles M. Rosser, the father of Baylor Medical College and the founder of the Good Samaritan Hospital from which Baylor had evolved, had followed Dr. Truett in death on January 27, 1945.

The death of Dr. Truett, in particular, was the occasion for a period of citywide mourning, but the 77-year-old minister was also mourned by people of all creeds in every corner of the globe. During a worldwide ministry that had spanned more than half a century, he had touched the lives of countless millions at home and abroad.

Three days after he died at his home on Live Oak Street, just a few blocks from the hospital he had helped bring to life, nearly 6,000 persons attended funeral services for the North Carolina-born pastor at the First Baptist Church in Dallas, whose congregation he had served for almost 47 years. Tens of thousands more had paid their last respects as his body lay in state at the church prior to the funeral.

The man they called "the world's first Baptist" had become a school teacher when he was only 17 years old and had planned a career in law. But a few years later, after moving to Whitewright, Texas, he was literally "drafted" into the Baptist ministry by a group of deacons and preachers who were convinced he was destined to be one of the greatest clergymen of all time. And in 1891, not long after his ordination, he became financial secretary of Baylor University at Waco, where his first job was to raise enough money to pay off a staggering debt, a task he accomplished in less than two years. In the meantime, he had also enrolled as a student at Baylor, and in the summer of 1897, just a few weeks after his graduation, he was invited to speak at the First Baptist Church in Dallas. That September, he delivered his first sermon as the church's new pastor.

He spoke an estimated 17,000 times after that, to some of the largest religious gatherings of the Twentieth Century. In Stockholm, Sweden, in 1923, where he was chosen to deliver the keynote address to the Baptist World Alliance, his speech was translated into the language of delegates from 33 countries. An audience of 16,000 heard him on one occasion in Kansas City. Another time, he spoke from the steps of the Capitol Building in Washington to a crowd of nearly 15,000. During World War I, he was one of only 20 American ministers selected by President Woodrow

Wilson to go to the war zone to work with U.S. troops, and he was one of three ministers called to Paris to confer with Wilson, British Prime Minister David Lloyd George and French Premier Georges Clemenceau while the Treaty of Versailles was being drafted. Perhaps the largest audience ever to hear him "live" was in Atlanta in 1939, when more than 40,000 persons packed a football stadium for an address by Dr. Truett, then president of the Baptist World Alliance. Hundreds of thousands who never saw him heard his sermons on radio.

Through all of this, he remained the dedicated friend and benefactor, promoter and servant of Baylor Hospital. At the time of his death, he was the longest standing member of the Baylor Board of Trustees. His dream of a "great humanitarian hospital" in Dallas had already been amply fulfilled, and no matter what the future might bring, Baylor would not forget George W. Truett.

Before the echoes of the last eulogies had faded, Texas Baptists were already planning a fitting memorial to the boy from the Blue Ridge Mountains who grew up to become the silver-haired, silver-tongued "Prince of Preachers."

VIII

A Time of Transition

The Turning Point

The first post-war decade was to bring the greatest transition up to that time for Baylor University Hospital. There had been many pivotal periods between the founding of the Texas Baptist Memorial Sanitarium and the end of World War II in 1945, but the next ten years would bring some of the most momentous changes of all. By 1955, the hospital had successfully turned the corner from its status as primarily a local hospital (albeit one of the largest such institutions in the South) to take on new stature as a regional medical referral center. The period in between was also a time during which Baylor's leaders made the far-reaching philosophical decision to stay on the hospital's original inner city site in old East Dallas and to stand their ground against whatever urban problems might come their way. That same decade saw the hospital's first major construction program since the erection of the original sanitarium in 1909. And it also saw the emergence of a dynamic new leader in the person of Boone Powell, who became chief executive officer of Baylor University Hospital in 1948 and who gave it the impetus it needed to become "the Johns Hopkins of the Southwest" in the years ahead.

None of Baylor's accomplishments in the years between 1945 and 1955 came easily. When the war ended, the hospital found itself facing many formidable obstacles. The fact that it had lost the medical school to Houston touched off widespread public speculation that the hospital itself might also be moved—or, worse yet, simply be closed down. The combined effects of the Depression and the war had left the physical plant of the hospital deteriorated and in danger of becoming outdated. For more than 15 years, there had been a shortage of funds for maintenance and an almost total absence of funds for expansion. To complicate matters further, the leaders of the hospital's medical staff had been called away to serve in the armed forces, depleting the number left at home to train young doctors for the staff. The result of all this was a desperate shortage of practically everything a hospital must have to function efficiently— physicians, nurses, beds, materials, scientific equipment, and even food.

But while these obstacles might have signaled the demise of other, less determined institutions, they merely served as a catalyst for new growth and renewed vitality at Baylor. That indomitable pioneer spirit that had given birth to the hospital in the first place was making its presence felt again. The Board of Trustees and the administration, then headed by Lawrence Payne, realized that, for Baylor to survive, it would have to change its role completely. It would have to be moved from caring primarily for charity patients, as the association with the medical school had dictated, to serve private patients. This, in turn, would necessitate the building of vast new facilities.

In 1944, shortly after the death of Dr. Truett, Baylor had begun raising funds for the construction of just such a new medical complex—to be known as the George W. Truett Memorial Hospital. But because of the war and other factors, it took almost three years to accumulate enough money to get the project under way, and its eventual completion did not come until 1950. Nevertheless, this modern new hospital, incorporating the latest and finest facilities for health care at that time, plus the strength and dedication of Baylor's medical staff, were the two indispensable factors that made possible the beginning of the transition to the giant Baylor University Medical Center we recognize today.

When the Baylor University College of Medicine pulled up stakes and departed for Houston, it left behind its primary asset—namely, the bulk of its clinical faculty, including some of the most respected physicians in the state. These men stayed on to serve Baylor University Hospital and to provide the impetus for the complete reorganization of the hospital staff in 1946—a move that, in the words of Board Chairman Charles R. Moore, led to "our greatest improvement in patient care" up to that time. To implement the reorganization, Baylor physicians circulated a petition throughout the medical staff, obtaining enough signatures to submit an official request that the trustees appoint a chief of service for each department within the hospital. The chiefs, in turn, would serve as Baylor's Medical Board and would be personally responsible for establishing professional standards for all physicians serving under them. Approval of the request by the Board of Trustees had the effect of unifying the medical staff more closely than ever before. Up until that time, there had been chiefs in only three departments—radiology, pathology and anesthesiology. But with the reorganization, Baylor placed its top men in their fields in positions of responsibility and influence, thus insuring decisive leadership for the medical staff and the close cooperation of the medical staff with the administration and the Board of Trustees. The original chiefs and members of the first Medical Board included: Dr. Henry M. Winans, internal medicine and board chairman; Dr. A. I. Folsom, urology and vice chairman (who was fatally injured in a tragic auto accident on October 3, 1946, shortly after his appointment); Dr. J. M. Hill, pathology and secretary; Dr. Earl F. Weir, anesthesiology; Dr. Albert D'Errico, neurological surgery; Dr. W. K. Strother Jr., obstetrics and gynecology;

116

In the wake of the Texas City disaster, which left 500 persons dead and another 3,000 injured, the William Buchanan Blood, Plasma and Serum Center at Baylor Hospital collected blood from hundreds of Dallasites to aid the victims.

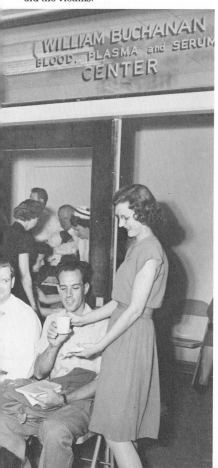

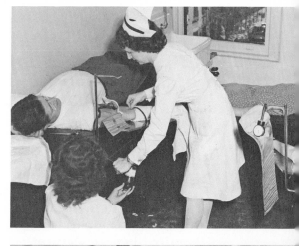

Dr. Lester H. Quinn, ophthalmology; Dr. Felix L. Butte, orthopedic surgery; Dr. Lyle M. Sellers, otolaryngology; Dr. Robert L. Moore, pediatrics; Dr. Curtice Rosser, proctology; Dr. Guy F. Witt, psychiatry and neurology; Dr. Frank M. Windrow, radiology; Dr. H. Walton Cochran, surgery; Dr. C. B. Carter, attending staff representative; Dr. Joseph G. Riley, associate attending staff representative, and Dr. Robert S. Sparkman, junior attending staff representative.

At the same time, the medical staff took a further step, organizing what is believed to be the first hospital surgical tissue committee in the United States. It was the purpose of the Tissue Committee, with the approval of the Board of Trustees, to avoid unnecessary surgery at the hospital by requiring that samples of tissue from each operation be thoroughly examined by the hospital's Pathology Department. If the tissues were found to be normal, then the physician performing the surgery would be called before the committee for an explanation. If he were judged guilty of performing surgery without proper reason, he was severely reprimanded or expelled from the hospital staff. All reports were identified by number, rather than physician and patient names, so that physicians on the committee could be totally objective during the review process. Later, the success of the Baylor committee caused the accrediting agency for hospitals at the time, the American College of Surgeons, to require that tissue committees be a part of each hospital in the country. That requirement is still in effect today for hospitals which want to be accredited by the current accrediting agency, the Joint Commission on Accreditation of Hospitals.

Basically, the structural organization of the staff has remained the same ever since, with the exception of one change in 1955 which provided for staff members to express their preferences among physicians being considered for appointments as chiefs of service. This is done by confidential written ballot, with the results of the tabulation of those ballots being presented to the board for consideration in making their selections. Also in 1955, patient admissions to the hospital were limited to physicians who were members of the active, consultant or courtesy staffs of Baylor, rather than to any member of the Dallas County Medical Society.

In the 1950s, the Board of Trustees found it necessary to declare a moratorium on admissions of additional physicians to the Baylor staff—a development which spilled over into the 1960s. Because of extremely crowded conditions, patients were waiting two to four weeks to be admitted to the hospital. Had Baylor allowed its medical staff to continue to expand, then the problem of overcrowding would have increased simultaneously. Therefore, the Medical Board, with the approval of the Board of Trustees, instituted the moratorium on new staff members, with the exception of associates of present staff members, for five years. Prior to that time, most of the specialists who came to Dallas had wanted to be on the Baylor staff. With the moratorium, these specialists went to other hospitals throughout the city. Thus, Baylor's loss was a great boon to Dallas as a whole.

In another medical development of the early 1950s, anesthesiology was emerging as a medical specialty and was attempting to gain recognition in private practice. This was difficult because most anesthetics were administered by nurse anesthetists, in some instances supervised by an anesthesiologist under a salary arrangement with the hospital. Baylor had an outstanding school of nurse anesthesia and hospitals throughout the Southwest were dependent upon its graduates. Anesthesiology-society actions such as discouraging anesthesiologists from supervising and teaching nurse anesthesia students and nurse anesthetists became an increasing hardship for Baylor's school, but Baylor felt an obligation to continue operating the school. This, along with the severe shortage of anesthesiologists and Baylor's special needs for anesthesia service for its very large obstetric service and emergency surgery and for its surgical teaching programs created tensions in relationships in anesthesiology which persisted into the 1970s.

Even though facilities, equipment and personnel were in short supply during the immediate post-war years, Baylor continued to serve the people of Dallas faithfully and well. Each day, it coped with crises large and small. Designed with a capacity to handle just 352 patients per day, Baylor's average patient load was running between 450 and 500. Beds from jam-packed rooms and wards overflowed into the hallways, and still the list of patients waiting to be admitted stood at around 300 most of the time. "With such overtaxing of our capacity, and with heavy depletions among our personnel, it has been impossible to render to all patients the 'plus' service we desire," administrator Payne remarked. "But by giving basic care to a maximum number, we have met the challenge at a time when physical expansion had to be delayed." Payne and his staff found themselves battling the first of the post-war inflationary spirals that were to become so familiar to Americans in the 1950s, 60s and 70s. During this time, the hospital's total operating budget was soaring by as much as 80 per cent per year. Meanwhile, the Truett expansion project was being held up until Baylor could substantially reduce its indebtedness for construction that had taken place years before—a debt that stood at $333,809 in 1946.

While coping with the exploding demands of its own city, Baylor also continued to serve outlying areas in time of tragedy and disaster. On April 16, 1947, for example, one of the greatest peacetime catastrophes of modern times took place in the bustling Gulf Coast port of Texas City. A merchant vessel loaded with chemicals caught fire in the intercoastal

120

waterway, triggering a series of huge blasts among the oil tankers anchored there, and leaving more than 500 persons dead and another 3,000 injured. The dead and dying filled every available square foot of space at nearby John Sealy Hospital in Galveston, where officials issued an urgent appeal at 5 p.m. that fateful afternoon for massive quantities of blood from Baylor's Buchanan Blood Bank. Within a half-hour after the appeal was broadcast, Dallasites were lining up at Baylor to donate blood, and the Dallas County Society of Laboratory Technicians had volunteered its services to Dr. J. M. Hill, the blood bank director, and his staff. Except for a few pints reserved for local emergencies, Baylor's entire blood supply was being loaded aboard Navy planes bound for Galveston within the hour. Three days later, on April 19, a second appeal for blood was made to Baylor, and broadcast over Dallas radio stations. Within 45 minutes, the Buchanan Blood Bank was filled again. This same procedure continued around the clock for four days and four nights in one of the greatest outpourings of public concern ever witnessed locally.

The following month, Baylor officials were instrumental in establishing the American Association of Blood Banks at an organizational meeting held November 17-19, 1947, in Dallas, with representatives of 57 blood banks attending. Marjorie Saunders, administrative assistant at the Buchanan Blood Center, formulated the idea for the association in 1945 when she became interested in learning about administrative procedures used in other blood banks. She began to make inquiries throughout the country, compiled a list of 1,200 blood banks and later sent a questionnaire to the banks to see if they would be interested in forming an association. Seventy-five per cent answered affirmatively. Shortly, the blood bankers began to press Miss Saunders to organize a meeting for the purpose of forming such an association, and with the permission of Baylor administrators, she did just that. Since that time, the association has grown to include member blood banks from all over the United States and in several foreign countries. Their cooperative efforts now make blood supplies more readily available in emergencies than was the case 31 years ago at Texas City.

The Truett Hospital

One week after Dr. Truett's death, the Board of Trustees of Baylor University Hospital officially approved plans for the construction of a "Truett Memorial Tower" to honor the visionary minister who had been so instrumental in the founding of the hospital four decades earlier. The plans called for the tower to be approximately 15 stories tall and to be located adjacent to the existing Baylor Hospital structure. At the time, the hospital was already involved in an eight-month-old community drive to raise $750,000, but the trustees decided to increase that goal to $1.2 million in order to finance the Truett Memorial Tower. By November 1944, they found it necessary to add another $400,000 to the goal, and eventually the goal reached $2.4 million, $1.2 million of which was to be raised in the Dallas area, with the rest coming from Baptist churches in the state. The funds were to pay not only for a new Truett Memorial Hospital (now envisioned as a 450-bed facility, rather than a tower), but also for enlargements and improvements at the Baylor School of Nursing and Baylor College of Dentistry.

In one of the most extensive publicity campaigns in the history of the Dallas medical community, the fund drive drew editorial endorsements from all local newspapers, one of which termed the proposed hospital not only a "fitting monument to a great preacher, but . . . an institution of immense value to the citizenry in this area." The campaign also enjoyed the full support of the Dallas business community.

Building Truett

In **1946**, the campus we know today as Baylor University Medical Center was barely recognizable. It consisted of a conglomeration of old houses and outdated hospital buildings, but then a massive fund-raising drive began for a new hospital, to be named in honor of the late Dr. George W. Truett. People watched . . .

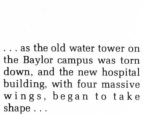

. . . as the old water tower on the Baylor campus was torn down, and the new hospital building, with four massive wings, began to take shape . . .

. . . As construction continued, sculptor José Martín, below, was commissioned to design a bust of George W. Truett to be placed in the lobby of the hospital. When the new facility finally opened on November 30, 1950, it was hailed as "the hospital of tomorrow." The first phase of construction that was to shape the Baylor campus of today was over.

125

Dallas banker Fred Florence called the fund appeal "a once-in-a-generation campaign for the community's permanent investment in essential health facilities." Paul Carrington, a local attorney and general chairman of the appeal, also tried some innovative approaches to raising money. He announced that plaques would be placed on various units within Truett Memorial, bearing the names of loved ones specified by the donors. Such dedication opportunities included endowments of private patient rooms for donations of from $1,200 to $3,600 each; $9,000 for an operating suite; $4,200 for a fracture room; $12,000 for an x-ray laboratory; $18,000 for a library or chapel; $6,000 for a solarium and $48,900 for the blood bank and plasma department. Gifts of this type were to be made in six quarterly payments.

Baylor received such all-out community support in the campaign because the public had become well aware of the pressing need for more health care facilities. Dallas was 800 hospital beds short of the needs of its booming population, and every hospital in the city was severely overcrowded. Hopes that funds for the Truett Memorial would be quickly raised ran so high that administrator Payne and architect Arthur E. Thomas made an inspection tour of major U.S. hospitals in October 1944 to insure that the new building incorporated the most modern features available. En route, Payne stopped off in St. Louis to liquidate a 19-year-old debt of $496,239 covering bond obligations on the old medical school which had been assumed by Baylor in 1921 as well as construction costs of the hospital's east wing, added in 1922. This did not mean that the hospital was debt-free, but merely that a new mortgage loan had been executed with two Dallas banks at a lower rate of interest, to allow its retirement with funds raised through the Baptist denomination and from other sources. News reports said that money obtained in the current fund drive would not be used for any old debts, but only for the erection of new buildings.

By November 1944, however, only 65 per cent of the money for the Truett Memorial—or $726,433—had been raised. Despite continual appeals, the total had reached only $851,945 a week later, when the campaign was officially scheduled to end. Carrington urged his workers to take heart and extend the drive another week, but even then the drive was still $272,177 from its goal. Desperation appeals continued for a time, but the remainder of the money simply was not to be forthcoming in 1944—or for quite some time hence. The main reason for the drive's failure was probably that Dallasites had been asked to give more than they could afford at this particular time, just as the war was drawing to a close. They had just finished donating $1.7 million to a War Chest campaign as the Baylor drive began. Simultaneously, St. Paul Hospital had launched a $300,000 fund drive for a new 100-bed addition; Southern Methodist University was trying to raise money for a blood center, and the Southwestern Medical Foundation was continuing its quest for $200,000. It was simply too much for Dallasites to absorb all at once.

It would have been simple to apply for federal funds at this point, but Baylor refused to take this route, even though it was eligible. "Texas Baptists not only believe in separation of church and state, but also in standing on their own financial feet, instead of seeking help from the government," said Boone Powell, then the hospital's young business manager.

Finally, in October 1947, another massive fund-raising effort began, with Dallas insuranceman W. C. McCord serving as its general chairman. By this time, though, inflation had driven the projected cost of Truett Memorial to $4 million, leaving Baylor further from its goal than it had been three years earlier. But this time, with the return of peacetime prosperity, the campaign was successful. Dallas citizens contributed $1 million, which was matched dollar for dollar by

127

funds from the Baptist General Convention of Texas. This was added to the $1 million left in trust from the previous campaign, and the remaining $1 million was to be borrowed and amortized over a 20-year period.

Meanwhile, the same inflationary pressures that had sent building costs skyward were still having a profound effect on Baylor's day-to-day operations. To expedite and simplify organizational functions and trim costs, Baylor retained a firm of professional and technical experts to study the hospital's operation and suggest improvements. This resulted in the hospital's Board of Trustees making a major change in the management structure of the institution in October 1948. In keeping with similar organizational setups in other large hospitals, administrator Payne was named to the newly created position of director of the hospital, and Powell was designated as his successor in the position of administrator. Payne's attentions were to be focused on overall planning for the hospital, while Powell devoted his full efforts to overseeing daily operations.

Powell, a native of Tennessee who had joined Baylor Hospital as business manager just over three years earlier, and who had later been promoted to the post of assistant administrator, had served in various administrative capacities with the federal government for nine years. With him, he brought to the Baylor administrator's office a farsightedness, a down-to-earth businesslike approach and a keen organizational ability that was destined to serve Baylor well during the next three decades of growth and challenge.

The Hospital of Tomorrow

When it opened at last, on November 30, 1950, the eight-story, 436-bed George W. Truett Memorial Hospital had exceeded its cost projections of three years earlier by another $1.5 million. Its final price tag was $5.5 million, but Baylor and the rest of Dallas were convinced that it was worth every penny it had taken to build it and every day of effort that had gone into financing it. Its formal opening ceremonies represented, in the words of Rabbi David Lefkowitz, "the dedication of a magnificent building to a magnificent personality."

Even as 175 dignitaries crowded into the main lobby (financed by *The Dallas Times Herald* in memory of its late publisher, Edwin J. Kiest) to attend a 60-minute dedicatory ceremony, the upper floors of the Truett Hospital were already humming with the business of caring for the sick and injured. Parts of the new building had been put into use, wing by wing, floor by floor, as they were completed in the weeks prior to the dedication.

A bronze bust of Dr. Truett by noted sculptor José Martín stood in the lobby as Dallas officialdom crowded around. On it was inscribed a quotation from Dr. Truett: "Never let it be said that Baylor Hospital has become just another boarding house for the sick. The science and knowledge of man must combine efforts with the Great Physician to render the ultimate in service to God and mankind."

In the dedicatory prayer, Dr. J. Howard Williams, executive secretary of the Baptist General Convention of Texas, said: "We dedicate this building to Thee, Oh Lord. Let Thy spirit pervade its rooms, give deftness to the surgeon's hands, wisdom to the attending physicians, gentleness and understanding to the nurses."

Speaking for the civic leadership of Dallas, George L. MacGregor commented: "Too long have we waited to enlarge the hospital facilities of our city. Baylor is the first to expand. Others must go ahead. Fast-growing Dallas is like *Alice in Wonderland*—we must run like everything to stay in one place."

When the Truett Hospital opened, the reinforced concrete and brick structure was described as "The Hospital of Tomorrow" because it contained all pieces of equipment and departments of service considered necessary for the ideal hospital. Its innovations included the use of soft pastel colors instead of "hospital white" for walls, telephones in every room, a patients' library, its own chapel, piped-in oxygen, pillow radio "soft speakers" for patients, and special elevator arrangements so that patients could be moved from floor to floor without being in contact with the general public. With the exception of one or two areas on the ground floor, the Truett building was completely air conditioned—a rare amenity that was almost eliminated because of a shortage of funds. It contained 17 operating rooms with adjacent preparation areas, the 50-seat John A. and Sally Truett Penland Memorial Chapel, and the Austin Moore Memorial Orthopedic Center, named in honor of the late son of Baylor Board Chairman Moore.

But over and above its distinctive and unique features, the Truett Hospital's greatest overall impact on the future status of Baylor can be summed up in one short sentence. Before the opening of Truett Memorial, Baylor had ranked 95th in size among general hospitals in the United States; with the opening of Truett, it became overnight, the fifth largest hospital in the entire country, based on number of beds.

Truett Hospital was completed at a time when Dallas was adding about 30,000 people to its population each year. Since Truett was the newest hospital in the city, and since its addition made Baylor far and away the largest medical complex in Dallas, it gave Baylor the boost it needed at a highly opportune moment in local history. With its medical staff and administration strengthened, its physical plant vastly expanded and improved, Baylor had achieved a position of prominence unlike any it had ever known before. But new administrator Powell felt that this was no time for the hospital to sit back and rest on its laurels. The treatment of disease was making huge strides in all directions, and to keep pace with these developments, Powell knew that Baylor must plan boldly, continue seeking top-flight personnel in many areas, and still use its available money very carefully. To these ends, he strengthened the hospital's management team and greatly broadened the range of services offered at Baylor. Under Powell's aggressive leadership, some key developments took place in the early 1950s, including the following:

—In March 1950, headquarters of the Baylor School of Nursing were moved to Waco, and it was decided that students would attend one year of school at the Waco campus, followed by two years of clinical service at Baylor Hospital. By 1952, the program had been expanded from a three-year course to a four-year baccalaureate program.

—In December 1950, the Office of Chaplaincy Services was established, and B. F. Bennett was named to fill the post—a job he still holds today. Marjorie Saunders, who had served as an assistant at the Buchanan Blood Center, was appointed as Baylor's first full-time director of public relations. She had been editor of *Baylor Progress*, the employe magazine, since it was founded in September 1948.(Nancy Cooper, a seamstress in the housekeeping sewing room, submitted the winning entry in a name-the-magazine contest; if her *Baylor Progress* had not been chosen, the publication might have been called either *Baylor News and Views* or *Scars and Gripes*, the second and third place entries.)

—In January 1951, the Department of Oral Surgery and Dental Service was established, and the following July, Dr. D. Lamar Byrd, the first residency-prepared oral surgeon in the City of Dallas, was appointed chief of the service.

—In June 1952, David H. Hitt, who had been administrator of the University of Alabama Hospital at

Tuscaloosa and then a research fellow with the University of Minnesota graduate program in hospital administration and on the staff of the Minneapolis hospital consulting firm of James A. Hamilton and Associates, became administrative assistant at Baylor. Within a year, he was named assistant administrator. He now serves as executive director of the Medical Center.

—In May 1953, a new centralized campus library was opened to serve the dental college, nursing school and hospital, and that same year a contract was awarded for further construction at the dental college, an expansion program that had begun in 1948.

—In April 1954, the Baylor Volunteer Program was initiated. By that December, its volunteer members had completed more than 3,000 hours of service to patients. Also in 1954, the hospital established a unique approach to providing a new service for patients—"the mobile recovery service." At the time the hospital had been built, the value of having a recovery room for post-operative patients had not been fully realized, and by the time the decision was made to incorporate such a unit in the hospital, there was no conveniently located space for the service. Therefore, Baylor instituted its "mobile recovery service," consisting of carts of the type used in a grocery store and equipped with a suction machine, drugs, oxygen units, IV solutions and other emergency supplies that a nurse might need as a patient recovered from anesthesia after surgery. The specially-trained nurse and her mobile unit would accompany the patient from surgery to his hospital room and remain there until he had awakened from the anesthetic. The service proved very reassuring to patients and their families and was in use at Baylor until 1962 when space became available for a central anesthesia recovery department.

132

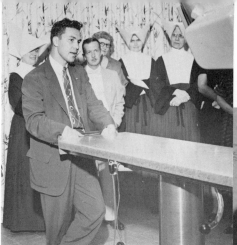

In 1955, Dr. John T. Mallams, left, Baylor's first full-time radiotherapist, gave a preview of Baylor's new cobalt unit for the treatment of cancer patients to members of the Dallas Hospital Council.

In January 1957, a group of individuals at Baylor, right photo, from left, E. H. Barry, Boone Powell, Dr. Jerry E. Miller, Dr. John Mallams and Charles A. Sammons announced the purchase of another machine for cancer treatment—the supervoltage x-ray unit. By June 1957, the unit, below, was installed in the New Charles A. Sammons Department of Radiation Therapy and Nuclear Medicine.

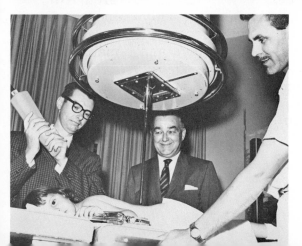

Dr. Richard Collier, left, and technician Bob Torson, right, demonstrate new equipment in the Department of Nuclear Medicine in June 1961 to Charles A. Sammons, who donated the funds to make the facility possible.

Physical Medicine Expands

While all this was happening, important developments were also taking place in other distinct areas of treatment and diagnosis of disease as Baylor made major advances in the fields of physical medicine, cancer treatment and cardiovascular disorders.

Among a number of highly regarded specialists who had been attracted to the Baylor staff during this period was Dr. Edward M. Krusen, who came to Baylor from the Mayo Clinic in 1950, while the Truett Hospital was still under construction, to become the first specialist in physical medicine in the North Texas area. It was Dr. Krusen who was to guide the future development of the Grady H. Vaughn Department of Physical Medicine, which was established in the new Truett Hospital late in 1950, and who continues today in that role at Baylor.

The original physical therapy department had been started at Baylor in 1934, operating in an un-air-conditioned basement "cubby hole" that did not even have a door. The department was sparsely equipped and staffed, containing four treatment tables and a lone Hubbard tank with which one physical therapy technician and an orderly were capable of treating six patients per day—at the maximum.

But in 1947, a Baylor patient decided to change the shape of physical therapy at the hospital for many years to come. His name was Grady H. Vaughn, a self-made millionaire who had been partially paralyzed by a severe stroke. Every day for two and one-half long years, Vaughn received physical therapy in the old basement facility, staring up at the utility pipes overhead and at the grayish patch of sunlight that filtered in through a grille on a small window. As grim as the surroundings were, Vaughn made a remarkable recovery because of the therapy he received there. And when Baylor doctors wanted to set up a full-scale Department of Physical Medicine in the new Truett

Hospital, Vaughn volunteered to donate the money—and told planners to spare no expense.

With Vaughn's generous donation and Dr. Krusen's expertise, Baylor thus acquired one of the most modern such departments in the world. Built at a cost of $133,000, the department contained four rooms with heat lamps, treatment tables, devices for muscle testing and electrical stimulators to help patients with hundreds of different ailments. It also boasted two hydrotherapy rooms containing whirlpool baths, contrast baths, paraffin baths and Hubbard tanks in which the whole body can be immersed, plus a large gymnasium with a wide variety of rehabilitative exercise equipment.

Within a few years, partly as a result of the polio epidemics of the 1950s, demands for the department's facilities had grown to such an extent that it was necessary to expand it into five separate areas in the Truett Hospital and the old sanitarium building. In the meantime, Baylor had also established the Grady H. Vaughn School of Physical Therapy, requiring still more room for the department. In 1955, a residency program for physicians in physical medicine was also begun, with four or five residents in training each year. (Today, the department is headquartered on the first floor of the Jonsson Hospital with additional units in other areas of the Baylor complex. The move from the Truett Hospital into the expanded quarters in the Jonsson Hospital was financed by a $120,000 gift in memory of the late Mr. and Mrs. Grady Vaughn Sr. by their sons and daughters-in-law, Mr. and Mrs. Jack C. Vaughn and Mr. and Mrs. Grady Vaughn Jr. The department now serves a phenomenal 600 patients per day and provides in excess of 216,000 treatments each year.)

Other Advancements

When the Truett Hospital opened, Baylor owned

just three small radiation therapy machines for the treatment of cancer, and these units were used by only eight or ten patients in an average day. The entire radiation department consisted of three treatment rooms, an examining room and a secretary's office. There was only one staff radiologist, who divided his time between treating patients and diagnostic radiology.

But by early 1953, the patient load had approximately doubled, to as many as twenty patients per day. It was at about this time that a Baylor patient with lung cancer had to be sent all the way to California to receive treatment on a super-voltage cobalt therapy machine. Concern over this situation led to the purchase, in 1954, of Baylor's first cobalt machine, with a $75,000 gift from the Reserve Life Insurance Company of Dallas. This, in turn, led to the construction of a new facility and the establishment of a separate cancer treatment center, to be named in honor of Dallas philanthropist Charles A. Sammons, chief executive of Reserve Life. The Charles A. Sammons Radiation Therapy Center was established in 1956, and Dr. John T. Mallams became Baylor's first full-time staff radiotherapist, to be assisted by a physicist and a nurse. For the first time, an operating room was made available for radium applications.

The installation of the new radiation therapy machine also gave rise to another innovation at Baylor. The cobalt machine was massive, and there was concern that the overwhelming size of the machine would add to the anxiety of the patient, who had to be alone in the treatment room. To minimize the machine's size and to add to the patient's comfort during treatment, Powell designed a room, decorated in pastel colors with one entire wall covered with a mural of Mirror Lake, to house the cobalt unit. The room was widely known as "The Baylor Room" and was copied in hospitals throughout the United States and as far away as Africa, and, as a result of the innovation, the idea of designing special environmental effects into facilities for treating patients with serious illnesses has become common practice.

After the opening of the new center and the Department of Radiation Therapy, the number of cancer patients increased so much that the purchase of a second super-voltage unit became necessary. This two-million-volt machine was purchased with another donation from Sammons and Reserve Life. Shortly afterward, the Department of Radiation Therapy was combined with the Department of Nuclear Medicine, which had been founded in 1955, to form the Charles A. Sammons Department of Radiation Therapy and Nuclear Medicine. Dr. Mallams became director of radiotherapy, and Dr. Richard Collier was named director of nuclear medicine. (The latest development in radiation therapy came in 1977 with the opening of the new Sammons Cancer Center in its own modern building, containing the most advanced equipment for detecting and combating cancer in North Texas.)

Meanwhile, in June 1953, a cardiovascular service was inaugurated at Baylor, with Dr. John Osborne as its first director. It was Osborne, a cardiologist, who established the hospital's first laboratories for cardiac catheterization, a surgical procedure in which a long, flexible catheter is passed through a vein or artery into a chamber of the heart to determine the extent and severity of a patient's heart disease. The catheterization laboratories, the latest development in heart disease diagnosis, were the first such facilities established in the North Texas area.

In addition to the catheterization laboratories, the cardiovascular service also housed other diagnostic equipment, electrocardiography and electroencephalography. The hospital's first electroencephalograph (EEG) was purchased in December 1952.

The first location of the service had been in a converted storage area, but it was soon moved to larger quarters on the third floor of the sanitarium building. (This was the beginning of an emphasis on specialized treatment and diagnosis of cardiac disorders that would be culminated in 1977 with the opening of the H. L. and Ruth Ray Hunt Heart Center, one of the outstanding facilities of its type in the country.)

A Golden Anniversary

As Baylor University Hospital celebrated its 50th birthday in October 1953, it stood at the proud pinnacle of five decades of service, achievement and expansion. Its sleek Truett Hospital towered above the site where the tiny, ill-equipped Good Samaritan Hospital had struggled for survival against overwhelming odds so many years before. From that humble beginning, through the vision and determination of many men and women, Baylor had grown to 850 beds, an accomplishment that still amazed the old-timers who had watched medical history being made in East Dallas over the past half-century. One of these was Dr. Cary, the man who had played such a prominent role in Baylor's fortunes during those first 50 years. Dr. Cary lived to witness the hospital's golden anniversary, but he died two months later, on December 11, 1953, at the age of 81.

It must have seemed to many that Baylor had reached its peak. Indeed, after the myriad accomplishments of recent years, what could the hospital hope to do for an encore? It was already internationally recognized, not only as a hospital but as a teaching center. As *Dallas Morning News* reporter Helen Bullock phrased it: "Its medical staff includes so many noted specialists, and its physical plant so much up-to-the-minute equipment, that it attracts 'problem cases' from throughout the Southwest for diagnosis, special treatment and surgery." On top of all this, the thrust of Dallas now seemed to be outward, away from the cramped inner city, toward the suburbs and the "good life" that post-war America supposed awaited it there. Ahead lay the problems of urban decline, and a greater period of transition than the founders of the Texas Baptist Memorial Sanitarium could have comprehended in 1903.

But if those who observed that golden anniversary during a six-day celebration October 11-16, 1953, could have looked into the minds of Baylor administrator Powell and his staff, they would have been amazed at the unfulfilled visions there—especially those who felt Baylor might have "peaked out" or be about to.

In many respects, the first 50 years had, indeed, been golden—if not in a monetary sense, then at least in a sense of accomplishment. Baylor had enjoyed some fine and soul-satisfying moments in the past. But the finest hours of all still lay in the future.

IX
Demolition and Construction

Building Hoblitzelle

On the day the Truett Hospital was dedicated, Boone Powell was already contemplating the erection of a second ultra-modern addition to the mushrooming Baylor complex. Immediately after the Truett dedication, Dr. Warren E. Massey, a longtime member of the Baylor staff in obstetrics-gynecology, handed Powell a $2,500 contribution—the first donation toward the construction of another new hospital. "Now, Mr. Powell, we need a new women's and children's building," Dr. Massey told the administrator. "I won't be around to see it finished, but I want to be a part of it." (As it turned out, Dr. Massey's prediction was, unfortunately, correct. He died in 1957, some two years before the opening of the new facility he had helped make possible.)

Slightly more than a year after that meeting, on November 21, 1951, Powell presented an architect's schematic drawing of the proposed Women and Children's Hospital—a name that would be officially changed in 1968 to the Karl and Esther Hoblitzelle Hospital—to the Board of Trustees. Although the overall planning process was destined to take several years, the board gave Powell its permission to proceed with the preliminary steps that would lead to the eventual construction.

By now, it had become obvious that Baylor was locked into an unprecedented pattern of growth, one that would make it appropriate in 1959, the same year Women and Children's opened, to change its name

140

from Baylor University Hospital to Baylor University Medical Center. In the words of board chairman Ben H. Wooten, a new name was required to adequately describe the various hospitals, departments and schools that now comprised Baylor-in-Dallas.

At the time the new hospital was authorized, almost 7,000 babies were being born at Baylor each year, placing it sixth among 6,600 hospitals in the United States and Canada in the number of births. Emergency beds had to be placed in the hallways at Florence Nightingale, the existing maternity facility, to accommodate new mothers and mothers-to-be. As Powell recalls, "When Florence Nightingale was built, it was described as the most modern maternity hospital in America and the only air-conditioned building of its kind. But when compared with today's hospital standards, it was poorly designed. The hallways were only six feet wide, instead of eight, and we had so many beds in the corridors because of overcrowding that we had to stagger them to allow hospital personnel to walk down the halls. I don't remember a day when we didn't have beds in the hallways on the first and second floors. The hospital was also designed with six-bed wards, and to save money, the nurse-call buttons had been draped from a single spot in the middle of the room. It looked like a maypole, and doctors swore they were going to be hanged some night by the things. Also, the doors of the building weren't wide enough to get the stretchers through."

To alleviate some of the overcrowding, Baylor added a maternity nursing unit in another building. Later it constructed a labor-delivery area and three maternity nursing units in the original sanitarium building, and the maternity patients and babies were moved to the top two floors of the Veal Hospital. It was Dr. W. K. Strother Jr., chief of the Department of Obstetrics-Gynecology at the time, who was in charge of making the transition. "Those months in the 'penthouse' suite of Veal were really something else," recalled Dr. Strother. "Even there, we had to keep some patients in the halls." In 1954, 17 years after it had opened its doors amid great fanfare, Florence Nightingale was boarded up. And, in 1956, it was torn down to make way for the new hospital.

On June 15, 1957, Baylor launched a $4 million fund-raising campaign to finance construction of the new Women and Children's Hospital, under the leadership of Baylor trustee G. H. Penland, who also served as general chairman, and Fred O. Detweiler, campaign chairman. The citizens of Dallas were asked to provide $2.5 million, with the rest to be secured through a long-term loan. At this point, the city's population was growing so rapidly that it was still short of hospital beds. A survey showed Dallas with only three beds per 1,000 population or 50 per cent fewer than the recommended minimum safety requirement of 4.5 beds per 1,000. Fund-raising literature called attention to the disastrous tornado that had struck the city just a few weeks earlier, on April 2, 1957, and noted that only limited hospital facilities had been available to meet the emergency, since all Dallas hospitals had been operating at or above 100 per cent of capacity. "The disaster of April 2 is a grim warning to Dallas to take steps now to provide the hospital facilities it needs and must have," the campaign brochure read.

When the campaign started, Baylor ranked first in number of admissions among the 1,101 church-affiliated hospitals in the country and third among the 3,097 voluntary hospitals. Out of the 6,600 hospitals in the United States and Canada, Baylor stood ninth in admissions, but only 69th in bed capacity. Again, the campaign drew strong support from the civic and business leadership of Dallas, including written endorsements from Mayor R. L. Thornton Sr., and Chamber of Commerce president Erik Jonsson. The Baylor medical staff, following the example of Dr.

Massey, contributed heavily to the campaign.

This campaign proceeded much more smoothly than some of its predecessors, and on September 18, 1958, just 15 months after the drive began, construction got under way. Mrs. Louise Ramsey, nurse supervisor of the Baylor maternity unit, laid the first brick.

Before the new building was opened, on October 28, 1959, its cost had risen to $4.5 million. It contained 128 maternity beds, 150 bassinets, 60 beds for gynecology patients, 44 for children and 21 for teenage patients.

The new building contained a total of 196,000 square feet in two seven-story wings, plus a full basement and a two-story machinery penthouse. Again, the interior was in soft pastels and muted tones, rather than the stark white usually found in hospitals at the time, with furniture and other color coordination planned by administrators C. L. Stocks and John L. Towers. Bedside units developed by Boone Powell provided patients with fingertip control of services, including television, five radio stations, piped-in music and chapel services, telephone (not black, but beige-colored) and luminous-dial electric clock. All rooms were equipped with all-electric beds which lowered to normal home height, except when patients were being examined or treated. All rooms had private or adjoining bathrooms with colored plumbing fixtures.

The installation of television in hospital rooms was still considered somewhat revolutionary at the time. Taking note of this, Baylor's trustees said their decision to provide TV in the new hospital was based on the belief that the medium had passed from the "luxury" classification to one of "necessity for most people."

The new hospital also contained a labor and delivery suite with 16 private labor rooms, five delivery rooms, two combination labor-delivery rooms and a

143

recovery room. The recovery room, a new feature at Baylor, was equipped with six beds and special equipment to serve the needs of patients during the period of post-anesthesia recovery.

Among other noteworthy features were the newborn nurseries, located on each of the three maternity floors, each composed of two rooms separated by an examining area. Two isolation nurseries were also provided for infants with infections, along with a premature nursery offering maximum safeguards for premature infants. Hospital procedures called for each newborn to be placed in an incubator for the first two hours of life to provide added warmth until the body temperature had stabilized. It was innovations such as these that laid the groundwork for the reputation Baylor would gain in the 1970s as one of the best newborn care centers in Texas, especially in the care of premature and low birthweight babies.

Not overlooking the problems of expectant fathers, the hospital also incorporated a "Dad's Den" on the first floor, adjacent to the labor-delivery suite, where expectant fathers could smoke, pace the floor and talk to others awaiting the same big event. The room was, according to press releases, "strictly off-limits to members of the opposite sex."

With the opening of the Women and Children's Hospital, Baylor became the first hospital in the Southwest to establish a separate division for teenage patients. The unit demonstrated the awareness of Baylor officials that teenagers had special problems which deserved more attention than they customarily received, and that they were apt to feel out of place if hospitalized with small children or adults.

A major attraction of the large entrance court now formed by the matching front facades of the new Women and Children's Hospital and the Truett Memorial Hospital was a large 18-foot circular pool with a fountain. The pool and fountain, with their ever-changing water effects and colorful lighting, are a major Baylor landmark today. A seven-foot wall of ceramic mosaic tile rises behind the fountain and serves as a background for the 12-inch cast aluminum letters spelling out "Baylor University Medical Center."

Most important, from the standpoint of the increasingly particular consumer of hospital services, the new hospital eliminated the necessity for keeping patients in corridors. The actual number of beds in the entire Baylor complex now stood at 825, and virtually all of these were in private or semi-private rooms.

At the time the hospital opened, Baylor ranked first in Texas in the number of births, first in births among American church-related hospitals, and second in births among all voluntary general hospitals in the country, so it is easy to see why such facilities were so important. And Dallas area mothers-to-be lost no time in utilizing the new hospital. Within the first 24-hour period after the hospital opened, a total of 19 babies were born there.

Prior to the opening of the new hospital, Baylor had been serving some 37,000 patients per year. With the additional space and facilities, that number was increased to 39,000 patients per year. In addition to all the extra room and equipment it incorporated into the Baylor complex, the Women and Children's Hospital also served as a catalyst for a new administrative approach at the Medical Center. The complex was growing at such a rate that it was in danger of losing the individualization of patient care. To make sure that the needs of the individual patient would continue to be a major concern in all sections of Baylor, the pattern of the entire administration began to change. A separate director of nursing was named in 1959 for the new hospital—a move that led in the 1970s to the designation of four hospitals, each with its own nursing director and administrator.

In 1956, the old Florence Nightingale Hospital, above, was torn down to make way for another new health care facility on the Baylor campus—the Women and Children's Hospital. The new hospital was later named in honor of Karl and Esther Hoblitzelle, right.

With the completion of the Women and Children's Hospital in 1959, the Baylor campus took on a new look and gained a new landmark, the lighted fountain, below, located in the entrance court fronting on Gaston Avenue.

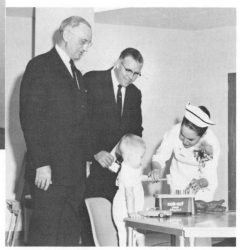

Dallas Mayor R. L. Thornton, right, above, congratulates Fred O. Detweiler, chairman of the fund-raising for the Women and Children's Hospital, on his successful campaign. In photo at right, Dr. J. W. Duckett, left, Dr. M. B. Carroll, center, a Baylor trustee, and Louise Ramsey, the nurse who laid the first brick for the new hospital, visit the pediatrics unit during dedication ceremonies on October 23, 1959.

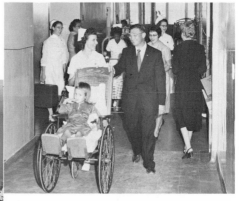

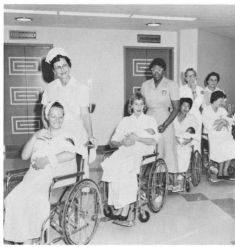

On October 28, 1959, new mothers, their babies and pediatric patients were moved from temporary quarters in the Veal Hospital to the new Women and Children's Hospital. Among those making the cross-campus trek was the little fellow, right, who just happened to be the last baby born in the Veal building.

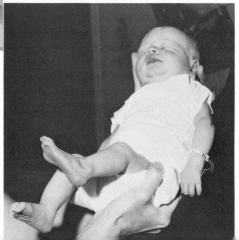

The Planning Process

It was no accident that the Women and Children's Hospital included many of the amenities of a home-style atmosphere, plus the most modern and sophisticated medical equipment and concepts of the day. Innovations in the new facility—many of which had never been used in a hospital building before—were the result of careful research and planning by doctors, nurses, administrators, architects, and even former patients. At the time, it was considered unusual to design an entire hospital from plans formulated by committees of both professional and lay people, as was the case with Women and Children's. The major part of this unique planning project was carried out by six committees in all, each made up of doctors, nurses, hospital administration representatives and a staff representative from the architectural firm of Thomas, Jameson and Merrill (which was retained to develop a master plan for the Baylor-in-Dallas campus in conjunction with plans for the new hospital). Each of the six main committees was given a patient service area to study, and plans for improved services or new innovations were made at daily meetings, even before funds were assured for construction. As definite conclusions were reached by the committees, reports were drafted and presented to a central planning committee for final review. The central committee was composed of the chairmen of the six other committees, plus the chief of the Department of Pediatrics, Dr. Robert L. Moore, and the chief of Obstetrics-Gynecology, Dr. Strother.

Some of the suggestions made by the various groups could not be carried out with equipment then available on the market. This necessitated considerable in-house research, out of which came some innovations for hospitals—such as the bedside unit, which combined all its controls on a single panel for patient convenience.

148

Besides the input of the professional members of the committees, numerous sound and practical ideas came from three committees of lay persons. One of these, consisting of six Dallas mothers, all of whom were recent patients at Florence Nightingale, quickly pointed out aspects of the old hospital which could be improved in the new one. A committee of fathers recommended "plenty of phones and plenty of dimes" for the "Dad's Den." And the eight-member teenage committee's first recommendation was to drop the word "Teenagers," since they felt it was synonymous with "delinquents" in the minds of some, and substitute the name "12-to-20 Club" for the adolescent division. (The teenage committee also soberly recommended the hiring of "middle-aged nurses" for the youth division, but when pressed on the members' exact definition of "middle-aged," the committee's tongue-in-cheek response was, "Oh, about 18 years old.")

This innovative and many-faceted planning process was the brainchild of administrator Powell, and was the forefunner of a more comprehensive long-range planning program initiated in 1962. "My basic belief," Powell says today, "is that if you're going to accomplish something significant, you've got to have a lot of people with you. The only way to get people to understand an institution is to get people involved."

New Names, New Roles

Baylor's Board of Trustees voted in April 1959, several months before the Women and Children's Hospital received its first patients, to change the institution's name for the fourth time in its 56-year history. It was also agreed that the name of the Medical Center's original building, still bearing the inscription of Texas Baptist Memorial Sanitarium, be changed to the Minnie S. Veal Teaching and Research Hospital,

149

in honor of Colonel Slaughter's eldest daughter, who had continued her father's tradition of generosity toward the hospital long after his death. The trustees also decided that the Veal Hospital should house three inpatient units, the outpatient clinic, cardiac laboratories and the Rose and Henry A. Weinberger Research Laboratory, as well as other special teaching and research activities. To fill these new roles, the board agreed, a complete renovation of the old building would be necessary.

So, six months after Women and Children's opened, remodeling began at the Veal Hospital. All maternity services, which had occupied the third and fourth floors of Veal for several years during the transition from Florence Nightingale to the new hospital, were removed. The Weinberger Laboratory, established in 1958 and named in honor of the founder of Ward Drug Company and his wife, found a new home on the fourth floor, and the third floor was used to house patients of the charity teaching service. After the remodeling, the medical education department and the outpatient clinics were housed on the first floor, and the second floor was converted into living quarters for the intern-resident staff. In addition, new lecture rooms and demonstration areas were located throughout the building.

In commenting on the significance of the name change and the new roles the Veal Hospital would play in the future, Dr. W. R. White, president of Baylor University at Waco, had this to say: "Mrs. Veal's personal interest was in the clinic and charity program of the hospital. Her substantial gifts were directed toward the development and expansion of this aspect of the hospital's program . . . . Members of the board, therefore, feel that it is particularly appropriate that the teaching and research hospital of Baylor University Medical Center be named in her honor."

The name change to Baylor University Medical

Center was announced during opening ceremonies for the Women and Children's Hospital. As board chairman Wooten pointed out: "The present name no longer described the several hospitals, departments and schools represented here on the Dallas campus. Baylor University Hospital now has practically all the aspects of a full-fledged medical center.

"The addition of the Women and Children's Hospital, the expansion of our teaching and research hospital and the establishment of the Sammons Department of Radiation Therapy and Nuclear Medicine, the Weinberger Laboratory and other specialized departments and laboratories that have come into being within the past few years required the new designation. As time goes along, we will be adding to our physical plant in order to take advantage of new developments."

There would, indeed, be many new developments for Baylor and its ever-expanding complex in the climactic decade of the 1960s that was about to begin. Unfortunately, though, not all those developments would be favorable and positive.

Out beyond the Medical Center's handsome new hospitals, along the quiet, tree-shaded streets of old East Dallas, other changes were taking place. Many of the old middle-class families were moving away, and a younger, more transient element was seeping into the neighborhood. Homes that had remained neat and well-kept for two generations were beginning to fall into disrepair. Police sirens were heard more often at night. "For sale" signs were popping up here and there, and some said property values were on the decline.

Gradually, almost unnoticed amid the flurry of growth and activity at Baylor, a perilous new crisis was developing around it. It was a crisis that would overwhelm East Dallas before the end of the next decade, one that would test Baylor's will to survive in ways it had never been tested in all the years before. It was to be a crisis of deterioration and inner city blight and even more—a crisis of community.

X

Change and Continuity

Landmark of Stability

As the decade dawned with the election of a young and vigorous new President, there was a mood of buoyant anticipation across the country—and even in conservative Dallas, which did not necessarily embrace the policies of John Fitzgerald Kennedy. In the beginning, hopeful Americans were referring to the ten-year period just ahead as the "Soaring Sixties." And soar they did for a time, only to crash back to the hard, unyielding surface of reality. Slightly more than three years after his election, the young President would be shot down by an assassin on a Dallas street, and before the end of the 1960s, the Texan who succeeded him in the White House would be forced to step aside and let someone else try to lead a nation bitterly divided over a far-away war.

In a sense, it was a decade when hopes and dreams faded, and when a bright national enthusiasm soared into cynicism and divisiveness.

Over the last years of the 1950s, the character of East Dallas had begun to change rapidly. The children who had grown up there moved to the suburbs when it was time to have children of their own, and the parents they left behind frequently followed. Old homeplaces gave way to new apartment houses, and once-elegant mansions were converted into rooming houses. The population of the area increased tremendously, but it was now largely a transient population of renters, which lacked the on-going stability and the sense of community that had been an integral part of

153

the home-owning East Dallas of prior years. All along Gaston Avenue, the street on which Baylor University Medical Center faces, semi-fashionable apartment complexes sprouted overnight, attracting predominantly single young career men and women. But along the area's back streets, amid less desirable surroundings, the poor, the uneducated, the unemployed and the disenfranchised began to gather. Even the fine homes along Swiss Avenue, once the showplace of the entire city, began to fall into disrepair.

Amid this deterioration, Baylor stood as an oasis of order, stability and new growth in a dangerously declining community. The Medical Center's leadership quickly grasped the significance of what was happening under Baylor's very nose and realized that the situation called for drastic and unprecedented action. To safeguard its perimeters against encroaching blight, Baylor began to buy up chunks of surrounding property, as administrator Powell and his staff demonstrated their determination to stand their ground. One of the properties acquired by Baylor during this period was the old Gaston Hotel across the street from the Medical Center, which was demolished to make room for expanded parking facilities. In all, from the early Fifties through the 1970s, more than 100 deteriorated buildings were acquired and torn down by the Medical Center.

Baylor also continued to build, even as it seemed everything else around it was going in the opposite direction. The new Wilma Bass Memorial Residency Hall was opened for the Baylor School of Nursing. The W. W. Caruth Surgical Research Laboratory was also built, and plans were made for the construction of two more major hospitals in the early 1970s. Such positive moves left little doubt that Baylor intended to ride out the storm.

Medicine was going through another period of rapid change and advancement during the 1960s. Procedures such as kidney dialysis and cardiac catheterization were making medical news and were being performed at Baylor. In 1963, Dr. Ignatios Papanicolis, an internationally known heart specialist from Athens, Greece, visited Baylor to study innovations in cardiovascular surgery. During his visit, he predicted that the next two major steps in the fight against heart disease would be the development of an artificial heart and heart transplantation. Before the decade was over, heart specialists would be experimenting with both.

During the 1960s, the cancer treatment program was again expanded at Baylor. One of the newest pieces of equipment, a cesium radiation therapy unit, was donated to the Medical Center in January 1961 by friends of Mary Andrade of Dallas. The million-volt unit reduced the radiation protection requirements to about half of what was needed by patients undergoing traditional cobalt treatments. And in 1962, Charles A. Sammons and the Reserve Life Insurance Company made another $100,000 gift to finance research at the hospital. It was Sammons' fifth major contribution to Baylor.

Besides advances in diagnostic and treatment capabilities, there were also advances in research. In March 1964, Baylor became part of an 18-month program of research at the request of the National Institutes of Health, Division of Biologic Standards, at Bethesda, Maryland, in a research project to accumulate data on blood typing serum. The results were used to make needed changes in regulations and minimum standards for producing the serum in the United States. In August 1966, the study was extended for another year at Baylor. Dr. Donald Paulson, one of the nation's foremost thoracic surgeons, was invited in the fall of 1965 to present a scientific paper at the sixth annual meeting of the Japanese Association for Lung Cancer Research. In February 1966, Dr. William D. Gaither, a Baylor resident in oral surgery, presented a paper based on research performed at the

Medical Center to a meeting of the American Academy of Oral Surgeons in Denver. For his work, Dr. Gaither won the Oral Surgery Research Award.

It was also a decade in which many prominent national newsmakers came to Baylor. When House Speaker Sam Rayburn was admitted for cancer treatment in November 1961, he was visited by many of America's top political leaders, including President Kennedy, Vice President Lyndon Johnson and his wife, Lady Bird, former President Harry S Truman and John Connally, then secretary of the Navy. It was Kennedy's last visit to Dallas before the assassination. In March 1963, famed evangelist Billy Graham also was a patient at Baylor.

Little six-year-old April Freeman of suburban Mesquite was another sort of newsmaker at Baylor. At 1:30 p.m. on June 17, 1964—to April's great surprise—she was honored as the Medical Center's millionth patient.

And a young man named Jerry Ward also made newspaper headlines as what one report called "a living symbol of a superhuman effort" by Baylor doctors and nurses. Ward received a total of 521 transfusions of whole blood and blood products—a record at the time—during a successful 86-day fight to save his life. A hemophiliac, Ward underwent three operations to correct a bleeding ulcer that threatened his life. When he went home to Borger, Texas, on November 19, 1963, he had received charity care amounting to $35,523.55—even with 267 replacement pints of blood given by donors.

There were impressive strides in other areas, too. Dr. Ralph Tompsett, who had become chief of internal medicine, director of medical education and director of infectious diseases at Baylor in 1957, steadily increased the strength of the medical staff through renewed emphasis on the training of young doctors. Dr. Paul J. Thomas had served as part-time chief of internal medicine for four years prior to Dr. Tompsett's arrival and played a primary role in getting the associate professor of clinical medicine at Cornell University Medical College to come to Baylor as the first full-time chief of the department. That move greatly improved the Medical Center's medical education programs, which had declined in quality and numbers after the war and the medical school's move to Houston.

Under Dr. George Race, who became chief of pathology and director of laboratories in 1959, Baylor's labs were remodeled and their space almost doubled, greatly increasing the Medical Center's capabilities in diagnostic medicine. In May 1963, the Medical Center and public relations director Marjorie Saunders received the Silver Anvil Award, the highest award of the Public Relations Society of America, Inc., in recognition of Baylor's program to recruit, orient and train volunteers for supplemental service to patients, interpret the institution to the community, and familiarize it with the advantages of careers in medicine.

More and more, Baylor was becoming a model to be copied by medical experts from around the world. In 1963, a hospital management delegation from the Soviet Union, including four physicians, an architect and a psychiatrist, visited Baylor under the provisions of a State Department agreement. In 1965, N. I. Latinsky, a South African architect, came to Baylor to study the design of the Women and Children's Hospital in preparation for designing a 140-bed hospital in Johannesburg. "This is the best unit I've seen in the States so far," he commented.

Baylor personnel also brought recognition to the institution. Boone Powell became president of the American College of Hospital Administrators in August 1965. In March 1966, Dr. Jerry E. Miller, chief of the Radiology Department, was installed as chairman of the Board of Chancellors of the American College of Radiology. In June 1966, David Hitt became president of the Texas Hospital Association, and in 1969 was named chairman of the Council on Financing of the American Hospital Association. And in June 1967, Dr. Milford O. Rouse, a Baylor specialist in gastroenterology, was installed as the 122nd president of the American Medical Association.

In addition to recording its millionth patient, Baylor was also setting records in other areas. Dr. William (Fred) Lucas, a resident in obstetrics-gynecology, became the first Air Force flight surgeon to win the U.S. Air Medal for gallantry after flying 35 missions over Vietnam in 1965. In July 1967, six children of Mr. and Mrs. Ronald Hartman had their tonsils out on the same day at the Medical Center. During one 24-hour period in August 1968, three sets of twins were born at Baylor, helping to set a record for multiple births. In May 1969, the first class of patient aides was graduated at the hospital, and in August of that year, the Volunteer Service Corps passed the 500,000-hour mark in its service to patients.

Baylor celebrated its 60th birthday in October 1963, and its Woman's Auxiliary turned 50 years old that same year. The organization had begun at the suggestion of Dr. J. H. Snow, pastor of the Haskell Avenue Baptist Church, and his wife, as a means of supporting the Texas Baptist Memorial Sanitarium. Mrs. Kenneth Foree, who had been elected the first president of the auxiliary at its organizational meeting on June 10, 1913, lived to help celebrate that 50th anniversary. (She died at the age of 100 on December 23, 1968.) Other charter members of the auxiliary included Mrs. Snow, Mrs. W. W. Lathimore, Mrs. M. B. Hunt, Mrs. W. J. Smith, Mrs. M. Williams, Mrs. O. F. Travis, Mrs. M. V. Turner, Mrs. A. U. Puckett, Mrs. J. H. Gambrell, Mrs. W. A. Hewitt, Mrs. W. J. Warriner, Mrs. W. R. Covington and Mrs. J. M. Moncrief. Dr. Snow was elected to honorary membership.

Initially, the auxiliary established a fund for

charity patients (which, in the recollection of Mrs. Moncrief, "grew and grew like Mrs. Finney's turnip vine until it went all around the farm"), and purchased gifts for the sanitarium, such as a sun dial that stood in front of the building on Junius Street. In its modern form, the auxiliary's goals included the promotion and advancement of the Medical Center, the initiation of projects to aid it, the interpretation of its purpose to the community, and the maintenance of a scholarship and small loan fund for nursing students.

In August 1969, Baylor University Medical Center was honored as a fifty-year member of the American Hospital Association at the organization's 71st annual convention in Chicago.

During the 1960s, a number of deaths depleted the ranks of leading figures at Baylor in previous decades. Dr. Lyle M. Sellers, chief emeritus of the Otolaryngology Department, died in 1963, and a special library was constructed in his honor. Dedicated in May 1966 as the Ruth and Lyle Sellers Medical Collection, the library fulfilled Dr. Sellers' expressed desire that his books be kept intact so that young physicians could see one doctor's broad scope of interest. Dr. Sellers had become the hospital's first chief of otolaryngology in 1946 and was the first physician west of the Mississippi to perform an inner ear operation known as "fenestration." At one time, his waiting list of patients for the operation was booked two-and-one-half years in advance. Dr. Henry M. Winans Sr., one of the most respected Medical Board chairmen in Baylor history, died in 1965, and Dr. Sol Haberman, who had gained widespread recognition as the Medical Center's director of microbiology, succumbed in 1968. John B. Franklin, who had served as sanitarium administrator from 1911 until 1925, died in 1963 in Georgia.

Meanwhile, numerous leadership changes were also taking place. Dr. Geddes McLaughlin became act-

In 1968, Baylor lost two of its pioneers, who had distinguished themselves in different fields of endeavor—Dr. Sol Haberman, left, the first director of microbiology, and Mrs. Kenneth Foree, below, the first president of the Baylor Auxiliary.

In this Associated Press photo, taken on October 9, 1961, Boone Powell, right, escorts President John F. Kennedy on a visit to Baylor. President Kennedy came to the Medical Center to visit U.S. House Speaker Sam Rayburn, who was critically ill with cancer.

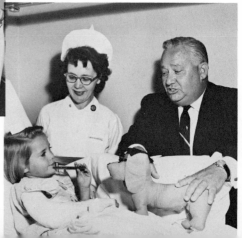

Jerry Ward, in wheelchair above, is escorted by Baylor nurses Wanda McDonald and G. Ayers, as he leaves Baylor on November 19, 1962, after receiving a record 521 blood transfusions. At right, Boone Powell and nurse Nellie LupPlace visit Baylor's millionth patient, April Jean Freeman.

David H. Hitt, left, then associate administrator at Baylor, escorts N. I. Latinsky, an architect from Johannesburg, South Africa, on a tour of the Women and Children's Hospital on January 19, 1965. "This is the best unit I've seen in the States so far," Latinsky commented after the tour.

The Wilma Bass Memorial Residency Hall, above, was built on the Baylor campus with funds donated by the late Mrs. Bass' husband, Harry W. Bass Sr., center, below, and her sons, Harry W. Bass Jr., left, and Richard D. Bass.

161

ing dean of the Baylor School of Nursing in February 1965, replacing Anne Taylor, who resigned. On September 1, 1965, Dr. McLaughlin was named dean of the school. It was under the direction of Dean Taylor, who served as head of the nursing school from July 15, 1961, until February 1, 1965, that the Baylor School of Nursing received in 1964 the national accreditation for which it had been striving several years. Due to a financial deficit and an inadequate curriculum, the accreditation had been denied in 1959, and there was discussion in Waco about closing the school. But with the urging of Boone Powell, the Board of Trustees decided to let the school remain open if the Medical Center would underwrite its deficit. It was Powell who launched the search committee that found Dean Taylor, who was then serving as dean of the University of South Dakota School of Nursing. Dr. Kenneth V. Randolph assumed duties as dean of the Baylor College of Dentistry in August 1968, after 29 years as a dental educator and previous service as dean of the West Virginia University School of Dentistry. Dr. Randolph replaced Dean Harry B. McCarthy, who had led the school through a difficult financial period and problems with accreditation. Dean McCarthy had put the institution on solid financial ground and gained national recognition for its academic standards. Boone Powell became executive director of the Medical Center and vice president of Baylor University in 1965, in charge of all the Baylor units in Dallas. At the same time, David Hitt was named associate director. W. Dewey Presley, who became board chairman in 1965, was appointed to the Board of Trustees in 1964, filling the seat held by Ben Wooten, who was retiring after serving as a Baylor trustee for 18 years.

Baylor, which in 1958 was the site of the pioneering national feasibility study of the potential benefit of computers in hospitals, obtained its first major computer system in 1966. The 1960s were also the decade in which the Medical Center loosened its ties with the Wadley Blood Bank by eliminating the institutions' interlocking board, and the blood bank began a new campus on Harry Hines Boulevard, the Wadley Institute of Medicine.

Long-Range Planning

The changes and challenges that loomed on the horizon as the Sixties unfolded caused Baylor trustees to approve a formal approach to the long-range planning process that would be vital in meeting them. In April 1962, the trustees endorsed the concept of "tomorrow-mindedness" to maintain Baylor's reputation for progress, as well as its leadership in the community. The board also approved the hiring of outside consultants to assist in the pre-planning state of the long-range program. Overall planning was to be undertaken for ten-year periods, subject to updating annually.

These innovative moves brought Baylor widespread national recognition in the health care field. In the first phase of the planning process, a series of task forces, representing all major medical specialties in the Medical Center were charged with (1) examining potential developments in all clinical areas; (2) evaluating requirements and capabilities for reaching that potential; and (3) making recommendations for developing the medical staff and operating departments, as well as the physical facilities necessary to fulfill those requirements. The process utilized more than 200 Baylor physicians, all its board members and management, and a variety of other personnel in a carefully structured procedure.

The task forces were told that Baylor's long-range plans should meet a number of important criteria. They should be logical, moving from objectives to the means of accomplishing them; comprehensive, covering all aspects of the work of the Medical Center, in-

163

cluding its relationship to the community and the Baptist denomination; flexible and action-oriented, providing guidance and stimulating action, yet adjustable to changing circumstances and needs; extended into the future, covering the decade ahead and, in some aspects, even beyond; continuous, reviewed annually and updated with extension for another year; formal, so that major determinations would be definitely recorded and available to all concerned. Task force recommendations were to be evaluated by five review committees—the Committee on Patient Care Programs, the Committee on Education Programs, the Committee on Christian Emphasis, the Committee on Research and the Committee on Community Service. These groups, in turn, would present their recommendations to the Coordinating Council, which would then develop the final comprehensive plan for presentation to the Board of Trustees.

By 1964, the Medical Center had its objectives for the next decade fully outlined. Once a recommendation had been adopted, it was assigned to an administrative staff member for continuous monitoring until it was carried out. By 1974, all the objectives set forth ten years earlier had been accomplished, and another long-range program was instituted. (In 1974, two additional review bodies were added to the original five, including a Committee on Composition and Organization of the Medical Staff and a Committee on External Relationships.)

More Developments

During the late 1950s, Powell had conceived the creation of a Credit Union for Baylor employes and had received permission from the board to establish the new program, which came into full flower during the decade of the Sixties. L. G. "Chick" Evans, who had come to Baylor 23 years earlier as a $75-a-month groundskeeper and risen to the position of superintendent of buildings and grounds, was one of the first employes to act on the proposal. He and nine other employes raised $570 to get the Credit Union started, and when that was still not enough, Evans contributed his entire savings toward the cause. "After that, you'd better believe I got interested," he recalls.

Remembering his own financial difficulties during the Depression of the 1930s, when he had lost both his home and his job within a six-month period, Evans believed the added security employes would gain from a Credit Union was well worth his own personal risk in funding it. Evans became the president and manager of the Baylor Credit Union with its inception in 1957, and for the first five years of its operation, he also continued to supervise the buildings and grounds, often spending weekends and holidays on Credit Union business. In 1962, after 28 years at Baylor, Evans reached retirement age, but his "retirement" did not last long. After just eight hours, Evans decided he had "had enough," and he came back to Baylor as the full-time president and manager of the Credit Union—a job he still holds, as of this writing, at age 83. "I wouldn't have lasted three years if I'd gone home and jumped into a rocking chair," he says. When his assistant, Hurene Walker, retired after 21 years of service, she also came back to the Credit Union. Together, she and Evans have watched that initial $570 swell to more than $2 million in assets and the Credit Union membership grow from 10 to 1,870. Evans recently noted that he had not taken a vacation in about ten years and still often works on weekends. But he believes his time has been well spent. "We have the life savings of many people here," he says, "and I feel responsible." (The Credit Union operates independently of the Medical Center, answering to its own Board of Directors and the Texas Credit Union Bureau; it has no mandatory retirement age.)

Another innovation during the 1960s was a pilot

project testing a new "unit manager" system of patient care—the system that is in operation at Baylor today. The project, initiated in February 1969, was the outgrowth of a nationwide shortage of nurses, and its goal was the reassignment of certain patient care supervisory tasks to other personnel to allow nurses to spend more time at the bedside of the patients. Some of the former responsibilities of the nurses, many of them non-medical in nature, had been taken over by a new group of personnel, including secretaries, assistants, technicians and patient aides, and these personnel were placed under the supervision of a unit manager. The system was ultimately put into effect throughout the Medical Center, with the unit managers accountable to the administrators of the hospitals for providing assistance to nurses and physicians and a wide variety of activities for patients and their families.

More Construction

Mrs. Wilma O. Bass was a well-known Dallas clubwoman and the wife of wealthy Dallas oilman Harry W. Bass. Her basic interests were medicine and human welfare, and for many years she contributed generously to provide equipment for childhood victims of cerebral palsy in her home state of Oklahoma. A few months after Mrs. Bass' death on June 4, 1963, of leukemia, her husband of twenty-seven years and her sons, Harry W. Bass Jr. and Richard D. Bass, decided that the most appropriate way to honor her memory was through the erection of a permanent facility that would help countless people in the years ahead. With this in mind, the Bass family donated $500,000 to Baylor to help finance a new women's residence hall for nursing students. The entire cost of the building was estimated at $1.3 million, the balance of which was to be financed by a self-liquidating loan.

166

In presenting the gift to Baylor, Harry W. Bass Sr. recalled his wife's lifelong interest in human welfare and expressed the family's hope that, by providing facilities to be used over the years by thousands of students in the health care field, they would be contributing to the improvement of human welfare for generations to come. In accepting the Bass gift, Baylor Board Chairman Ben Wooten said: "In view of the fact that one of the most critical problems facing Baylor and all hospitals today is the acute shortage of professional and technical personnel, we are deeply grateful for this gift, which will make possible the erection of a modern, well-equipped building in which to house women students in the various educational programs of Baylor-in-Dallas. Baylor has always been known as a great teaching hospital, but due to inadequate housing facilities . . . recruitment has been a problem, particularly in the School of Nursing. This new dormitory . . . will enable Baylor to retain its place of leadership among hospitals in the Southwest as a teaching center, and to move forward with expanding services."

By the time the architect began drawing up plans for the new residency hall, Clare H. Zachry, chairman of the board of Southern Union Gas Company, had become chairman of the Baylor trustees. When the architect presented the plans to Zachry, the board chairman questioned how many oak trees would have to be cut down to build the dormitory in the manner the architect had outlined. The architect responded that he had planned on leaving two trees, but that was not good enough for Zachry. He told the architect to redesign the building, and he did, leaving all but one or two of the oaks on the site where the dormitory was to be built.

Construction of the new hall at Worth and Adair Streets began in January 1964, and the 51,528-square-foot, six-story (plus basement) building was dedicated a year later. It provided living quarters for 246 stu-

Bernice Miller, a nurse technician, works in the old laboratory at Baylor in the 1930s. The lab, considered modern at the time, does not compare to today's Medical Center laboratories, which consist of 38 units and perform a combined total of more than two million tests per year.

Dr. George Race, at left in right photo, director of laboratories and chief of pathology at Baylor; Dr. Dighton F. Rowan, center, director of virology; and Dr. Floyd Norman, chief of pediatrics, discuss testing procedures for rubella in this 1968 photo.

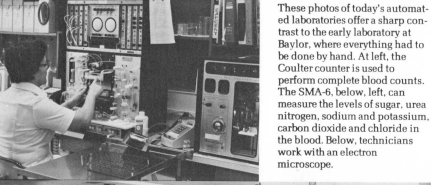

These photos of today's automated laboratories offer a sharp contrast to the early laboratory at Baylor, where everything had to be done by hand. At left, the Coulter counter is used to perform complete blood counts. The SMA-6, below, left, can measure the levels of sugar, urea nitrogen, sodium and potassium, carbon dioxide and chloride in the blood. Below, technicians work with an electron microscope.

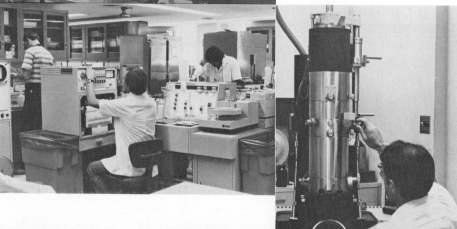

By the 1940s, the laboratories at Baylor had improved somewhat, and there was more equipment available for the procedures performed there.

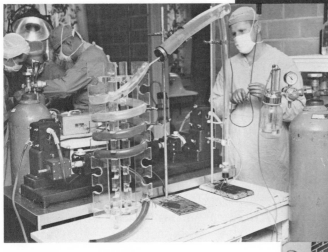

Dr. Paul Ellis, right, experiments with a pump oxygenator, which was used in early open heart surgery cases, in the old experimental animal research laboratory at Baylor.

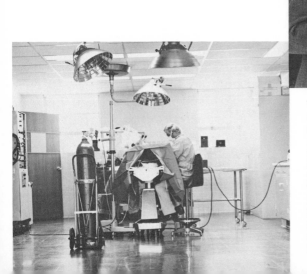

W. W. Caruth Jr., left, above, donated the funds for the construction of a new animal research facility at Baylor, which was opened on March 17, 1964. Caruth's gift was made through the Dallas Community Chest Trust, for which Dr. Frederick M. Lange, right, serves as president. Facilities at the animal research facility, below, are equivalent to those provided for humans in the Medical Center.

dents and replaced facilities at the old Holliday Hall, which had been in use for fifty years (before being torn down to make way for construction of the new Jonsson Hospital a few years hence). It also contained a recreation room, parlor and meditation room, housemother's quarters and other facilities, as well as a swimming pool and recreational areas for badminton, shuffleboard and horseshoes. At the dedication, Mrs. Bass, a native of Chickasha, Oklahoma, was lauded as a woman of "quiet grandeur." The Reverend Ira Gallaway, pastor of the Walnut Hill United Methodist Church, speaking at the dedication, said: "The true meaning of the Wilma Bass Memorial Hall will come to life through the tender hands, loving hearts and willing minds of the nurses who live here. The life of one we honor here, who died in suffering, goes on to relieve the suffering of others." Among those present at the dedication were Helen Holliday Lehmann, first dean of the Baylor School of Nursing, and Mrs. Ola Chumley, a member of the school's first graduating class.

On February 18, 1970, Harry W. Bass Sr., who had been described as possessing the ability of "turning everything he touched to gold," also died. Shortly afterward, his sons made another significant contribution to Baylor, resulting in the completion in 1977 of the Harry W. Bass Memorial Education Center, adjoining the Wilma Bass Memorial Residency Hall. The four-story education center provides classrooms for nursing education and other programs, a lecture hall and offices for the School of Nursing faculty.

Bass, a native of Enid, Oklahoma, who had served as an artillery battery commander in the U.S. Army during World War I, had entered the oil business in 1919 and had come to Dallas in 1932, where he became, at one time, the largest independent processor of liquid hydrocarbons in the oil industry, a pioneer in the recycling of natural gas, and the developer of the universally used portable drilling mast.

The Bass Foundation, a trust established by Bass in 1945, had aided many charitable, scientific, religious and educational causes.

Laboratories Expanded

In 1961, Charles A. Sammons and the Reserve Life Insurance Company provided funds for the construction of the Sammons Department of Virology, the first such clinically oriented laboratory of its kind in the United States. With the funding secured for this new department, Baylor immediately began a vast expansion and remodeling program involving all of its laboratories to incorporate the latest developments in diagnostic medicine, including the purchase of an electron microscope and ancillary equipment with a $75,000 grant from the Moody Foundation of Galveston. By October 1962, the $575,000 expansion project was complete, and the Medical Center's laboratory space had virtually doubled, from 12,000 to 23,000 square feet.

As the new Virology Department was dedicated in Sammons' honor, Dr. John S. Bagwell, then president of the Baylor medical staff, commented that "Baylor will not be the only recipient of Mr. Sammons' contribution. Through their doctors, the whole community of patients . . . will benefit."

The main speaker for the dedication ceremonies was Dr. Clayton G. Loosli, dean of the University of Southern California Medical School and one of America's foremost virologists. "When you have laboratories devoted to diagnostic problems in virology," he said, "it makes a tremendous contribution to the total care of the patient. Spotting these diseases in the community also makes a tremendous contribution."

The first laboratory at Baylor was started in about 1912 by Dr. James Harvey Black, a general practitioner and 1907 graduate of the Southern Methodist

University College of Medicine. Dr. Black, the first physician in Dallas to perform a blood transfusion, later became interested in pathology and went to Philadelphia in 1912 to learn to do autopsies and serologic tests of syphilis. His wife, who accompanied him on the trip, was taught to do cultures for bacteria. When the Blacks returned to Dallas later in 1912, Dr. Black taught pathology and bacteriology at both the SMU and Baylor medical colleges and performed autopsies for the Texas Baptist Memorial Sanitarium, while his wife confined her work to doing cultures for bacteria. At that stage in the development of the laboratory, there were no other tests that could be done.

In 1922, Dr. George T. Caldwell succeeded Dr. Black (who by this time had become interested in the treatment of allergies) as a teacher of pathology at Baylor College of Medicine. Dr. Caldwell also did lab tests and autopsies for Baylor Hospital in a small basement room in the old sanitarium building. He was assisted in his work by his wife, Janet.

In those early years, scientists spent long, lonely hours peering into their laboratory microscopes in search of the elusive origins of disease, and their work was primarily pathological tissue studies. Gradually, however, as technology advanced, the laboratory evolved into a complex and comprehensive unit, where basic science could be applied to the treatment of all types of illnesses.

It was under Dr. Joseph M. Hill, who became director of the Baylor laboratory in 1934, that development of specialized clinical units within the laboratory began. Sol Haberman, a serologist and bacteriologist, was named director of microbiology in 1941, and Gwendolyn Crass, who later received an MD degree, became chief technologist of the hematology laboratory in 1935. Dr. Robert Speer, who had worked on the atomic bomb project during World War II, joined the Baylor staff as director of the chemistry laboratory in 1951, and introduced the use of radioisotopes to the Dallas medical community. Just prior to Dr. Speer's arrival, the laboratories had been relocated from the third floor of the sanitarium building, their location since the 1940s, to new and expanded quarters on the fifth floor of the new Truett Hospital.

In September 1959, Dr. George J. Race was named director of the Baylor laboratories and chief of pathology, succeeding Dr. Hill, who resigned the positions to devote full-time to his job as director of the Wadley Institutes of Medicine. Before joining the Baylor staff, Dr. Race had served as an associate professor of pathology at the University of Texas Southwestern Medical School. In 1958, he had gained international recognition by performing a unique autopsy on a 48,000-pound whale. Parts of the giant cadaver had been returned to Dallas by Dr. Race after preliminary work in Peru.

A native of Everman, Texas, Dr. Race received his M.D. degree from Southwestern Medical School, his Ph.D. from Baylor University and his Master of Science Degree in Public Health from the University of North Carolina at Chapel Hill. He served an internship in surgery at Boston City Hospital, a residency in pathology at Duke University and served as a flight surgeon during the Korean War. In 1973, a major four-volume series of books entitled *Laboratory Medicine*, with Dr. Race serving as their editor-in-chief, was published by Harper and Row. The volumes originated in the Baylor laboratories and are now in their sixth edition. They are only one example of the worldwide recognition Dr. Race has brought to Baylor, while establishing himself as a medical statesman of international repute.

At the time he assumed directorship of the laboratories at Baylor, technology was changing them from a place where every test had to be performed by hand into a whirling world of automation. Such new equipment as the early autoanalyzer, which evolved into the SMA-12 and SMAC systems, can do chemical analysis on 40 or more blood samples at a time, and the Coulter counter, which can click off a count of millions of blood cells in seconds, were taking their place in the Baylor labs by the early 1960s. And by the time the 1970s came along, the automated revolution was in full flower, rapidly increasing the number of lab tests performed at Baylor to more than two million per year. By contrast, Dr. Speer recalls that only about 15 chemistry tests were even available when he first came to Dallas, and that only about 450 chemical laboratory procedures were performed at Baylor in an average month. Today, no less than 265 chemistry tests are available, and the number of procedures averages 114,000 per month.

As part of the massive 1961 expansion program, the labs under Dr. Race's direction were moved from the Truett Hospital to the third, fourth and fifth floors of the Laboratory Building, formerly the Children's Building. Today, there are 38 laboratory units under the auspices of the Pathology Department, including Central Collecting, Chemistry, Special Hematology, Histopathology, Electron Microscopy (there are three electron microscopes at Baylor), Endocrinology, Immunology, Microbiology and Cytogenetics, Mycology, Nephrology, Urinalysis and Parasitology, and Virology and Clinical Microbiology. Among the millions of laboratory procedures performed at Baylor in 1977 were 296 autopsies, 24,664 surgical pathology specimens, 4,289 cytology specimens and 810 bone marrow aspirations. The labs perform not only for Baylor but for 40 other hospitals throughout the Southwest.

Since 1959, the Pathology Department has also conducted a strong educational program, including residency training that has produced more than 100 pathologists. Baylor residents have gone on to such important posts as medical examiner for the State of

Oklahoma, professor and head of the Liver Section of the Armed Forces Institute of Pathology and heads of numerous pathology departments in large hospitals across the country. In addition, Baylor's School of Medical Technology has graduated more than 1,000 technologists in the years since its founding in 1934. The school, made possible when the American Society of Clinical Pathologists organized a Board of Regents for schools of medical technology in 1928, replaced an on-the-job training program that had been available previously at the hospital. Dr. Hill served as the first director of the school and was followed by Dr. Race, Dr. Crass and Dr. G. Weldon Tillery, who serves in the position today. Marjorie Saunders became registrar of the school in 1943, serving in that capacity until 1952, when she became director of public relations and was succeeded by John L. Sills. The current registrar is Dora M. Parker, who was named registrar upon Sills' retirement from the post in 1973.

Caruth Research Lab

On March 17, 1964, Baylor opened an entirely different type of laboratory facility—the Caruth Surgical Research Laboratory. This new animal research facility was made possible by a $55,000 gift from the W. W. Caruth Jr. Fund of the Dallas Community Chest Trust and was named in honor of Caruth, a nationally recognized land planner and developer.

The first floor of the two-story reinforced concrete building at Junius and Walton Streets was devoted to operating rooms, laboratories, x-ray and darkroom facilities, receiving and storage rooms and offices. One of the main considerations in planning the research laboratory was to provide comfortable, healthy and sanitary facilities for the research animals on the second floor. Several veterinarians were consulted

175

and a number of animal hospitals visited before the accommodations were designed. The operating rooms for the animals were judged equivalent to those found in any modern operating room for humans. X-ray facilities including fluoroscopy were made available in a special room to make extensive cardiovascular studies possible.

The new laboratory replaced the Medical Center's old animal research facilities, which were located in "shacks" behind the Wadley Blood Institute at Gaston and Adair Streets. The original laboratory had been started in 1950 by Dr. LeRoy J. Kleinsasser, who had come to Baylor as director of surgical education after serving four years as chief of surgery at the Dallas Veterans Administration Hospital. Although the old laboratory was started under less than desirable conditions, it provided facilities for testing the validity of such vital procedures as open heart surgery and heart-lung pumps before they were used at Baylor.

Onward and Upward

By 1965, Powell was already laying careful plans for yet another major hospital requiring another fund-raising effort—this time with a goal of $4 million—to finance still another major hospital. Before the decade was over, the goal had been exceeded by more than $1 million, with a total of $5,441,651 obtained in a campaign directed by Dallas banker James W. Aston and Baylor board chairman Presley. The final $1 million, presented in the form of 7,500 shares of stock in the electronics manufacturing firm of Texas Instruments on the very day of the victory luncheon for the campaign, came from one of the company's founders, Dallas Mayor Erik Jonsson (who quipped at the luncheon, "That's the last time I'll sign an attendance card!") and his wife, Margaret.

Appropriately, the new hospital would bear the name of Erik and Margaret Jonsson. During the same period, Dallas developer-manufacturer-insurance magnate Carr P. Collins Sr. also donated $1 million for the construction of yet another hospital at Baylor.

By the beginning of the 1970s, as the "Soaring Sixties" were fading into history, construction projects valued at approximately $18.5 million were under way at the Medical Center. With each new building erected and each new expansion of staff and facilities, Baylor's day-to-day operations became increasingly complex and intricate, and more and more pressures were felt from governmental regulatory agencies, especially at the federal level.

In the meantime, though, Baylor had successfully bucked the current of decay and defeat that had swept through East Dallas in the 1960s. Through it all, Baylor had stood like Gibraltar, continuing to build and to provide not only a spirit of continuity and courage, but a symbol of prosperous, enlightened accomplishment.

East Dallas, indeed, was destined to slide even further before its fortunes would "bottom out" and start again to progress. But there was no longer any doubt about where Baylor stood, where it would stay, or what it would be doing in the future. Regardless of what might happen around it, Baylor was moving in only one direction—upward.

XI

Growing Toward Greatness

A New Era

America went soaring into the Seventies, propelled by phenomenal breakthroughs in science and technology. Machines had long since taken over most of the physical labor of mankind, and now machines were also doing much of the thinking for the human race. Space-age technologists, who succeeded in placing the first man on the moon in June 1970, also brought new thrusts to medicine—thrusts that were, simultaneously, both reassuring and disquieting. Nuclear technology, monitoring and instrumentation for medical use all were direct byproducts of space and military programs. Surgeons had succeeded in transplanting human hearts, kidneys and other organs. Other medical pioneers were far along toward the development of mechanical replacement parts for natural organs. A simple-looking electronic device no bigger than a pocket watch—known as a pacemaker—was keeping hundreds of hearts beating that might otherwise have stopped long ago.

In the midst of all this, a sizable percentage of the American public had developed a lackadaisical attitude toward prevention of disease and the maintenance of health. "So what if I wear out this set of organs?" popular sentiment seemed to say. "The doctors can always fix me up with a new set." But not even the fantastic achievements of science and technology could keep Americans from dying in record numbers from cancer, heart attacks, strokes and other degenerative disorders that might easily have been avoided or lessened through proper attention to diet, habits and lifestyle.

Americans were demanding—and getting—the highest level of health care in the history of civilization. And patients were flocking to hospitals as never before in often-belated attempts to take advantage of the newest discoveries in medicine. From a purely technical standpoint, it would soon become possible to extend human life—or a semblance thereof—almost to the borders of infinity. And new and nagging questions were arising, regarding the very concept of life and death. It was the dawn of a new era in which time-honored definitions and once-basic laws would be severely tested.

As the 1970s began, Baylor also stood on the threshold of a new era. A quarter-century of dramatic, dynamic growth had carried the Medical Center far beyond the questions of sheer survival or mere stability. The challenge now was to maintain the drive and energy that would firmly establish Baylor as a health care institution not only of national, but international reputation.

In a period of 25 phenomenal years, the Medical Center had increased its bed capacity from 200 to 800, the number of employes from 500 to 2,300, its medical staff from 200 to 600. It had also purchased 40 pieces of property and demolished 74 buildings to provide space for new construction and adequate parking facilities for physicians, employes and patrons. Meanwhile, the impact of medical research had led to a significant expansion in Baylor's professional and scientific programs, and its emphasis on medical education had increased to the point that it operated almost on the same level as a medical school. When the new decade opened, a record-breaking $18.5 million construction program had been under way for several months. It included the Erik and Margaret Jonsson Medical and Surgical Hospital, the Carr P. Collins Hospital, a 550-car underground parking garage, an expanded Vaughn Department of Physical Medicine, a new Department of Emergency Services, enlargement of the Radiology Department to double its previous size, and a further expansion of Baylor's clinical laboratories by 2,500 square feet. A coronary care unit of 12 beds had already been put into use, and three intensive care units totalling 48 beds had also been completed.

With completion of the new construction in progress, Baylor's total number of beds would jump from 800 to 1,300; its number of employes would increase from 2,300 to 3,600, and its overall scope and capabilities would be substantially enlarged to accommodate the accompanying increase in the number of patients and medical advancements.

Simultaneously, many changes were taking place in the health care industry in general. Costs of all types of goods and services used in hospitals were spiralling. Along with the rapid-fire advances in medicine and medical technology had come changes in the public's pattern of health care utilization. Health care in America was becoming increasingly institutionalized, triggering a growing demand for huge urban complexes to provide not only traditional inpatient services, but outpatient services, facilities for routine care and programs for disease prevention and control, as well. Hospital emergency units were now frequently being used as an extension of the private physician's office, necessitating expansion of those facilities. Other factors contributing to the growing complications of providing up-to-date patient care included the unprecedented diversity and specialization of the practice of medicine, greater emphasis on medical research, increased complexity in medical staff relationships as a result of more specialization and diversification and the need for hospital management to maintain close contact with many influential groups outside the health care system.

More and more, the growth and direction of the

health care industry were being affected by the activities of state and federal regulatory bodies. In 1970, for example, it was estimated that more than 200 governmental agencies, regulatory authorities and professional groups were involved in establishing various licensing, accrediting and approval standards for hospitals. To complicate matters still further, the regulations within each of these agencies were constantly changing. The issue of health care financing—especially with the inception of Medicare in 1966—was also rife with confusion and complexities, in the form of complicated third-party reimbursement formulas and regulations.

Baylor's own growth, plus these unprecedented external changes in the delivery of health care services, made it apparent that a new plan of management organization would be necessary to prepare the Medical Center for its increased responsibilities in the decade ahead. On July 1, 1970, that new management structure was implemented by the Board of Trustees. In effect, the new structure was a broadening and strengthening of an organizational plan that had served Baylor well during its past years of mushrooming growth.

Under the revised plan, Powell continued to serve as executive director and chief executive officer, and long-range planning and development remained his area of major emphasis, along with educational and medical staff relationships. David Hitt assumed broadened responsibilities as associate executive director and chief operating officer, with authority over the day-to-day internal management of the various hospitals and supporting services. Serving in the positions of associate directors, each with a group of operating units and services under his charge, were Paul M. Calmes, Howard M. Chase, Glen R. Clark, Herman A. Walker and William W. Wissman. George J. Tsamis was appointed administrative analyst.

Within the organizational structure, Baylor in-

The generosity of former Dallas
Mayor Erik Jonsson and his wife,
Margaret, made possible the con-
struction of a new hospital on the
Baylor University Medical Center
campus in 1970.

In May 1969, the Erik and Margaret
Jonsson Medical and Surgical
Hospital was still in the construction phase, but, by September 1970,
the new hospital was completely
finished and ready for patients.

Early-day x-ray machines looked complex, but their technology was fairly simple when compared with modern radiological equipment, available at Baylor today in the Department of Radiology, the Department of Nuclear Medicine and the Department of Radiation Therapy in the Charles A. Sammons Cancer Center.

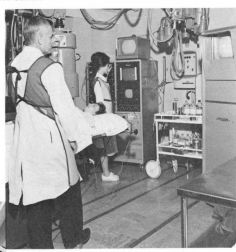

Dr. A. D. Sears, chief of radiology at Baylor, performs a cardiac radiological procedure in a special room that became available at the Medical Center in the 1960s for such purposes. In 1976, Baylor purchased the first computerized axial tomographic (CAT) scanner in the North Texas area. Two views of the machine, at left, show Don Cundy, supervisor of the Department of Nuclear Medicine, as he looks through the partially-assembled scanner and the scanner in use. Several new diagnostic rooms in radiology, below, were made possible in the 1970s when the department was remodeled with a gift from Baylor trustee Herman Lay.

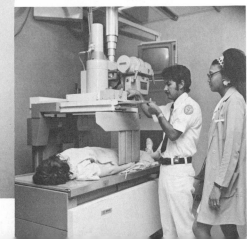

cluded an innovative safeguard against the de-
personalization of patient care as the Medical Center
became ever larger. This was accomplished by creating three new administrative positions for hospital
units. Philip C. Loofburrow, a graduate of the
University of Minnesota graduate program in hospital
administration who had retired as an Air Force colonel before joining the Baylor staff in 1969, was
named administrator for the Truett and Veal
Hospitals. William W. Young Jr., who had joined
Baylor as an administrative resident in 1969, took the
administrator's position for the Women and
Children's Hospital and yet-to-be-completed Jonsson
Hospital. And L. Gerald Bryant, a member of the
Baylor staff since 1967, was chosen to head the
Collins Hospital, then under construction.

In evaluating the challenges posed by Baylor's
vast expansion, the trustees, management and professional staff focused on the importance of top
management people maintaining personal contact, not
only with the nurses and hospital employes who provide direct service to patients, but with the patients
and their families as well. Equally important, the
Baylor leadership felt, was the contact between physicians and management regarding patient services. The
new organizational plan mirrored this concern by
facilitating such contact and communication. The
plan also provided each of the four hospitals with its
own nursing service department headed by a director
of nursing service, and its own food service department directed by a chief dietitian. It was decided that
the director of nursing service and the chief dietitian
in each hospital would report directly to that
hospital's administrator, as would the unit managers
in each hospital.

As impressive as Baylor's development had been
during the 25 years just past, Dr. H. Lawrence Wilsey,
a management consultant with the firm of Booz-Allen
and Hamilton, concluded in the 1970 reorganizational

study that there was every reason to believe even greater changes would occur in the decade of the 1970s. These would bring with them, the study emphasized, an intensification of past pressure on Baylor's leadership.

But challenges also imply opportunities, the report continued, and Baylor's responsiveness was foreseen as leading to many major advancements, particularly in such important areas as outpatient treatment, acute care and rehabilitative services. And even before the report was finished, those advancements had already begun.

The Jonsson Hospital

Private dedication ceremonies for the $6 million Erik and Margaret Jonsson Medical and Surgical Hospital were held September 2, 1970, in the lobby of the new building. Facing Junius Street and consisting of seven stories and a basement, the 200-bed hospital was financed through a 1967 fund drive that had raised $5.4 million and was described as "the most successful in Dallas history."

Perhaps more important than the singular success of this particular fund-raising effort was the fact that it marked the turning point in Baylor's ability to finance its construction programs through community support. A final contribution of $1 million by Mayor Jonsson and his wife had sent the campaign total soaring far beyond its $4 million goal, and prompted banner headlines in the *Dallas Times Herald* editions of May 2, 1967, the day the gift was announced. Announcement of the gift was made by Dallas banker James W. Aston, who had chaired the campaign, James F. Chambers, publisher of the *Times Herald*, and wealthy Dallas industrialist John Stemmons, vice chairman of the campaign, at a final victory luncheon. The fund-raising drive was also significant because it represented a classic interdenominational effort in behalf of a Baptist institution that would, in years to come, benefit citizens of every religious persuasion. The Jonssons, for example, are Methodists. And Aston, a member of the Christian Church, stepped across both denominational and business lines to help another banker—namely, Baylor board chairman Dewey Presley, a life-long Baptist—to reach the campaign goal.

It was Presley, chairman of the Medical Center's Board of Trustees since 1965, who successfully engineered the game plan for the fund-raising campaign and who has been a vital part of each advancement at the Medical Center since then. As president of First National Bank at the time of the campaign, his close ties with the city's wealthy business community enabled him to place some of the most powerful men in the city in the campaign's leadership positions. Born at Wills Point, Texas, on May 26, 1918, and reared at Gilmer, Presley received his early business training as an employe in his stepfather's cotton ginning and sweet potato business. He entered Baylor University during the Depression because he liked the campus and was able to get a job there as a waiter in the boys' dining room. In 1939, he received his Bachelor's Degree in Business Administration and became the first member of his family to be graduated from Baylor University. Presley's brother, Longview oilman Jim Fred Presley; his wife, Virginia; his three daughters and his three sons-in-law are also Baylor graduates.) After college, Presley became an accountant with Magnolia Petroleum Company in Dallas, but his career was interrupted by World War II and his appointment as a special agent for the FBI, during which time he concentrated on war-related security investigations. He joined the First National Bank in 1952 and became its president in 1965. Today Presley serves as chairman of the executive committee of First International Bancshares. He is also in his second term as chairman of the

Medical Center's Board of Trustees.

At the dedication ceremonies for the new hospital, Aston and Presley both paid tribute to the Jonssons. "Erik Jonsson, the distinguished Mayor of Dallas and honorary chairman of the board of Texas Instruments, is one of the most respected men in this country," Aston said. "He is recognized not only as an outstanding mayor but as an astute businessman and extraordinary citizen . . . . As a citizen, his broad community interests and efforts have been shared by industry, science, technology, education, medicine, health and humanitarian organizations, as well as the cultural life of our city. He has long recognized and has publicly stated that among the most important factors in the sound and steady growth of a city is the health of its citizens."

Presley, speaking in behalf of the trustees, praised Mrs. Jonsson. "Dallas' gracious first lady shares her husband's zeal for its welfare," he said. "She is widely known and greatly esteemed for her own contributions to the educational, civic and cultural activities of the city."

"Underlying all these activities," Aston told the Jonssons, in conclusion, "is the changeless attitude that you care."

In response, Jonsson said, "These facilities are everything. They are beautiful beyond compare, and I'm sure they're as functional as they are attractive. For Margaret and me, I'd like to say thank you to all the other people who made it possible. One gift doesn't do it."

Jonsson's informal and unassuming remarks were typical of the man who served as mayor of Dallas from February 3, 1964, to May 3, 1971, and who breathed new life into his adopted city after the assassination of a President had shaken it to its very core. Jonsson had come to Dallas three decades before he became its highest elected official as a young man from New York, who was only 34 at the time, but who had been struggling for 20 years to make his way in the world. His philosophy for community service, born of a working man's heritage, was simple. He put it this way: "The worth of a man to his society can be measured by the contributions he makes to it—less the cost of sustaining himself and his mistakes in it."

Although he attained wealth and community stature, Jonsson remained a humble man who never forgot his early background as the son of impoverished Swedish immigrants, a boy who went to work at 14 to make something of himself. "My parents came here (to America) to work hard, to strive to escape poverty, to be good citizens," he said. "They taught me freedom is never easily or cheaply won, and the necessary effort to maintain it is inextricably linked to it. You can grow up poor and see nothing but grief, or you can learn to play games—to win, to lose, to get along with other people. Learning to scramble for whatever you get is good, because later in life there's going to be lots of competition. Through the struggle, people learn an important thing—man alone among the animals can change his environment and make it less hostile."

Accordingly, even in the matter of his gifts, donations and contributions, Jonsson did not distribute his wealth indiscriminately, but in a down-to-earth and businesslike fashion. "In the past 15 years," Jonsson said in a 1974 interview, "I've given away more money than I've made. You learn philanthropy is a business that takes some doing. You can't waste money. You have to look at the investment and see where you get the greatest return."

At the Jonsson Hospital dedication, special recognition was also given to Dr. Frank H. Kidd Jr., a long-time Baylor physician who served as chairman of the professional division of the 1967 fund drive for the Jonsson Hospital and in the same capacity in the 1957 campaign that financed construction of the Women and Children's Hospital. During the two campaigns, the Baylor medical staff contributed more than $1 million toward the expansion projects under Dr. Kidd's leadership. In both campaigns, the announcement at the first general campaign meeting that the medical staff and Medical Center employes had already pledged more than their goals was a major stimulus to the fund-raising drives' overall success.

Because of the restricted amount of land for the Jonsson Hospital—it had to fit into the space between the Truett and Hoblitzelle Hospitals—the new facility was designed with "double corridor" patient floors, rather than the single corridor that had always been used before. With the "double corridor" design, all patient service functions were located within double parallel corridors, with patient rooms on either side. The new hospital also provided a new and larger Department of Emergency Services and a new Department of Physical Medicine and Rehabilitation. In addition, it housed a 20-bed day hospital for surgical patients whose stay required less than a day, and four intensive care units, including one medical, two surgical and one coronary care unit. A fifth unit, for intermediate coronary care, was added in May 1972.

At the time the Jonsson Hospital was being built, other remodeling and expansion programs were also carried out at Baylor. Dallas businessman Ralph W. McCann Sr. and his wife, Thelma, donated the funds for the establishment of the McCann Department of Electrocardiography and Electroencephalography, greatly increasing Baylor's capabilities in detecting and diagnosing heart and brain disorders. New facilities were also provided for the inhalation therapy and pulmonary laboratory, an expanded chemistry lab, new mycology lab, new center for immunological study, expanded endocrine lab, a processing area for photographs taken by a new electron microscope, an enlarged 28-bed post-anesthesia recovery unit and an expanded medical records department.

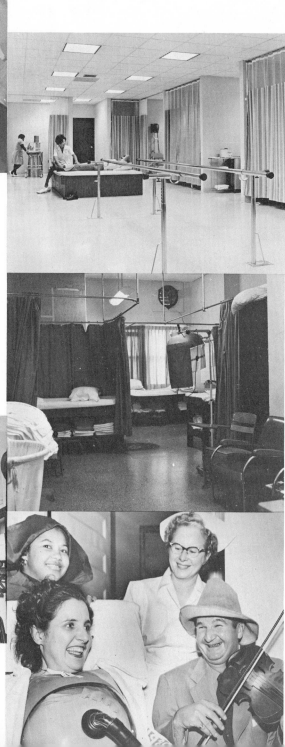

Baylor University Medical Center has one of the world's largest and most comprehensive departments of physical medicine and rehabilitation, and, through the years, the growth has been made possible through a series of gifts from the late Grady H. Vaughn Sr., above, and his family. With the opening of the Jonsson Hospital, the Vaughn Department of Physical Medicine, top photo, at right, was moved to new and expanded quarters in the Jonsson Hospital from its former location in the Truett building.

During the 1950s, polio victims greatly increased the number of patients at the Department of Physical Medicine and Rehabilitation. Patients at Baylor's polio clinic, above and at right, are entertained by country musicians during a Halloween party on October 31, 1952.

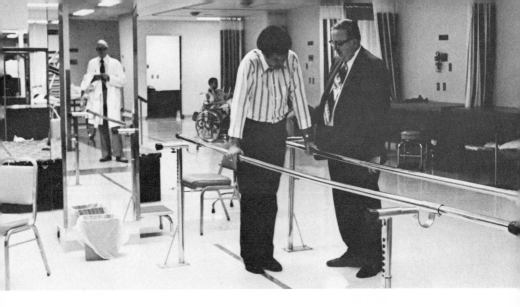

Dr. E. M. Krusen, at right, above, the first specialist in physical medicine in the North Texas area, aids a patient as he tries to walk with the use of the parallel bars in the Vaughn Department of Physical Medicine and Rehabilitation. When Dr. Krusen first arrived in Dallas in 1950, many of the patients he cared for were polio victims, bottom photo, at right. Through the years, equipment for the treatment of the disabled has greatly advanced, as the hydrotherapy room, top photo, at left, and the Hubbard tanks, bottom left, show.

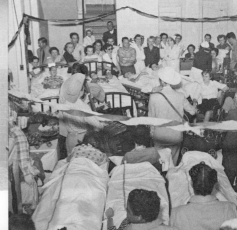

Hospital Renamed

With the dedication of the Jonsson Hospital, the Women and Children's Hospital also was formally renamed to acknowledge a $500,000 gift from the Hoblitzelle Foundation in honor of veteran Dallas businessman and show business entrepreneur Karl Hoblitzelle and his wife, Esther. Thereafter, the hospital would be known as the Karl and Esther Hoblitzelle Hospital and would be open to general medical patients, as well as maternity, obstetrical and pediatric patients.

The name Karl Hoblitzelle is to theatrical circles in the Southwest what Henry Ford is to the American automobile industry. Before Hoblitzelle organized his Interstate Circuit for vaudeville acts in the early 1900s, there simply was not much "live" theatre in this part of the country. From this start sprang the Interstate Theatres chain and a far-reaching network of affiliations in such diversified fields as banking, insurance, utilities, education and medical research.

The youngest of 13 children of a Missouri farmer, Hoblitzelle went to work at an early age to help support his family. His daily routine during the crop season was to get up at 2 a.m. and drive to the produce market in St. Louis to sell vegetables off the family farm, then return home to peddle his remaining wares house to house.

After a time, the work proved too much for the rather frail youth, and he took a job as office boy for Isaac Taylor, the man in charge of the planning and construction for the 1900 St. Louis World's Fair. His subsequent association with concessionaires at the big exposition led to the idea of starting a vaudeville circuit operating theatres in Dallas, Houston, Fort Worth, Little Rock, Hot Springs, Shreveport and Birmingham.

Soon after that, Hoblitzelle adopted Texas as his home state and spent the rest of his life contributing to the strengthening of its educational, scientific, humanitarian and charitable institutions. In 1920, he was married to the former Esther Thomas, a talented actress and singer, and together they established the Hoblitzelle Foundation to administer their gifts to many Texas causes, including Texas A&M University, the Texas Research Foundation and the Southwestern Medical Foundation.

Hoblitzelle summed up his philanthropic philosophy by saying: "I believe that we have an obligation to create wealth, however much or little, to get beyond the supply of our necessities so as to use that wealth in a very creative way to add to the happiness of our fellow men."

Karl Hoblitzelle did create great wealth, and he did use it in a most creative way for the betterment of his fellow men. And if human health can be equated with human happiness, one of his most impressive contributions was his gift to Baylor. He died in 1967 at the age of 87 (Mrs. Hoblitzelle died in 1943) but the hospital that bears their names stands as a living symbol of their vision and generosity.

Emergency Services

In April 1967, the Zale Foundation contributed $180,000 to the Medical Center for the establishment of a new Department of Emergency Services, which was to be located on the lower level of the Jonsson Hospital. The Emergency Department was officially moved from the first floor of the Veal Hospital to its new quarters in June 1970—a move that involved a great deal more than a mere change of location. It also marked the turning point in the whole system for delivering emergency care at Baylor.

Prior to the move, for as far back as any one can remember, the emergency room had been a kind of "stepchild," not only at Baylor, but at virtually all hospitals around the country. It was located in a cramped 1,500-square-foot area in the Veal building, and, until 1967, it had no full-time staff other than nurses and a few dental school students who worked there at night. If a patient needed a physician, the nurses could only resort to the telephone, making call after call until a doctor could be located. Even the services of medical residents or interns were rare. Visitors had to wait in the corridor just outside the treatment rooms, and there was little privacy in the area.

But by the late 1960s, the number of patients utilizing the emergency room had jumped drastically, to almost 23,000 per year. This increase caused Baylor to take a fresh look at the services available for emergency cases. The result was a contract with the Lakewood Medical Clinic to provide round-the-clock physicians for the emergency room. By 1971, emergency services had been designated an entirely separate department with its own director, Dr. LeWayne Lambert; assistant director, Dr. Leonard Riggs, and a separate staff of employes.

Today, under Dr. Riggs' direction, the Emergency Department functions as a complete "mini-hospital" within the Medical Center. It contains 21 observation-treatment rooms with 6,000 square feet of floor space, employs 17 nurses and 23 other support personnel and is staffed by 30 physicians, one of whom, along with one intern, is on duty at all times. It is equipped with sophisticated cardiac monitoring equipment, its own x-ray rooms and a pneumatic tube system that links it with Baylor's laboratories and allows test results on emergency cases to be received within 30 minutes.

The department's caseload now stands at almost 40,000 patients per year, and there are no restrictions on who can be treated on an emergency basis. But, based on Baylor's experience, Dr. Riggs does not believe misuse of the emergency system is as widespread as some authorities contend today. "Two to five per cent of the patients who come here are life-threatening emergencies," he says. "Another 70 per cent can be classified as urgent, and only about 25 per cent could have been taken care of elsewhere."

Radiology Expands

A $350,000 gift from Mr. and Mrs. Herman W. Lay during the Jonsson campaign made possible a much-needed expansion of the Medical Center's Radiology Department. At the time, Lay was chief executive of Frito-Lay and a member of the Baylor Board of Trustees.

Although radiology is now regarded as one of the more important functions of the modern hospital, it had a humble beginning at Baylor, as it did in most hospitals across the country. The Baylor department was started in a small basement room of the Veal Hospital by Dr. James M. Martin, who is considered the father of radiology in the Southwest and who equipped the room at his own expense.

Born in 1867 in a log cabin on a Missouri farm, Dr. Martin first became interested in radiology in 1902 while working as a general practitioner in Hillsboro, Texas. He built his first x-ray machine there, using a wall plate to produce electrical current and a static machine to produce low-voltage x-rays, and began studying the effects of "electro-therapeutic" treatment on skin cancers. After taking a correspondence course on x-ray methods, he constructed a more sophisticated machine with which he could make "skiagraphs" of any part of the body. When he delivered an illustrated lecture on the treatment of skin cancers by x-ray before the Texas Medical Association, he stirred the interest of the Baylor College of Medicine and was offered a post on the faculty—without pay, of course. For a time, he made the 120-mile round trip from Hillsboro to Dallas once a week to lecture to the

195

senior class, but in 1906, he moved to Dallas, arriving in a two-cylinder Ford with $200 in his pocket. During the same period, he established the Radiology Department at Texas Baptist Memorial Sanitarium, equipping it with his own homemade apparatus, including wooden x-ray tables built in his woodworking shop.

Dr. Martin remained the only radiologist in Dallas, until his son, Charles L. Martin, received his M.D. degree from Harvard and joined his father in practice. By the 1920s, when the younger Dr. Martin assumed the helm of Baylor's Radiology Department, far-reaching changes were taking place. The old easily-broken glass plates used for x-ray negatives were replaced by film and the use of x-rays in diagnosing all sorts of physical disorders became more widespread. In 1931, the younger Dr. Martin set up a charity tumor clinic at the hospital. Later in that decade, the Radiology Department was moved to the fourth floor of the children's wing, where space was available for a waiting room, secretary's office, examining room and a small operating room for biopsies, electro-surgery and low intensity radium needle implants. Enough equipment was purchased to perform x-ray therapy, fluoroscopy and diagnostic radiography in separate rooms, and a portable x-ray machine was obtained for use in the wards. In 1940, the Martins left Baylor and started their own independent radiology practice in a building adjacent to Gaston Episcopal Hospital.

By the time Dr. Jerry E. Miller arrived at Baylor in 1949 to become chief of radiology, the department had been moved to the first floor of the Veal Building, where it occupied three small rooms. Under Dr. Miller, a 1938 graduate of Baylor College of Medicine who had completed his residency at Cleveland (Ohio) City Hospital, the department began adding the new super-voltage radiation therapy machines that would become a major weapon against cancer, as well as improving its capabilities in diagnostic radiology. During his years as chief, the department moved out of the Veal building into new quarters in the Truett Hospital. "As soon as I got to Baylor, medical technology began to explode," Dr. Miller recalls, "but we succeeded in keeping up-to-date." In 1966, Dr. Miller resigned his post at Baylor and became chief of radiology at St. Paul Hospital. His leaving accompanied one of the remarkably few real controversies Baylor has experienced in recent years, compared with the many external pressures which have troubled other progressive medical centers. With the advent of Medicare, several of the "hospital-based" specialty groups advocated that their services be billed to the patient directly by the physician instead of being billed by the hospital, as had been done in the past. Dr. Miller, as chairman of the Board of Chancellors of the American College of Radiology, was committed to making this change without delay. But Baylor's trustees, medical leaders and administrative officials believed that the changes should be approached gradually to minimize the risk of adverse patient relations.

Succeeding Dr. Miller was Dr. A. D. Sears, a graduate of the University of Texas Southwestern Medical School who had served both his internship and residency at Parkland Hospital in Dallas and who continues to serve as Baylor's chief of radiology today. Under his leadership, Baylor implemented the concept of "separate billing" by radiologists steadily and smoothly. The Radiology Department's programs and staffing had been affected for about a year by the controversy, after which the momentum accelerated.

The 1970 radiology expansion program more than doubled the space allotted to radiology—from 6,000 to 15,000 square feet. It also increased the number of x-ray rooms from seven to 17, including completely new areas for gastrointestinal studies and urological procedures and three suites for vascular radiology. A

197

special room was also built to house a new EMI brain scanner, the first such instrument in North Texas, and the new space permitted the purchase of seven new automatic x-ray film processors, capable of developing films in 90 seconds. The first automatic film processor at Baylor—and one of the first to be used in the United States—had been purchased in 1956 to replace an antiquated system in which radiologists had to hand-process their film in a darkroom.

The Department of Radiology now has a staff of 16 radiologists and performs more than 140,000 diagnostic procedures annually.

Nuclear Medicine Grows

In the mid-1950s, the Division of Nuclear Medicine at Baylor was such a small operation that its equipment was located in the same departmental space with radiology. At that time, Baylor had only one rectilinear scanner, a relatively primitive forerunner of the modern disease-detecting devices that would be developed later, and it was used to perform only two or three scans on an average day. In the Fifties and Sixties, scanning techniques were limited to inserting a radioactive substance into the body to allow an x-ray picture to be made of a certain organ to determine whether or not the organ was diseased. By the early 1970s, however, a technological revolution that would dramatically increase medical capabilities in disease diagnosis was rapidly unfolding, and Baylor's Division of Nuclear Medicine quickly began to grow and add new equipment.

In 1972, when Dr. Herbert Steinbach, who had done his radiology residency at Baylor in 1964, became director of nuclear medicine, the division was moved to a 1,900-square-foot area of its own, although it remained—as it does today—an integral part of radiology. The division then had two rectilinear scanners and a Dynapix scanner. Shortly after the move,

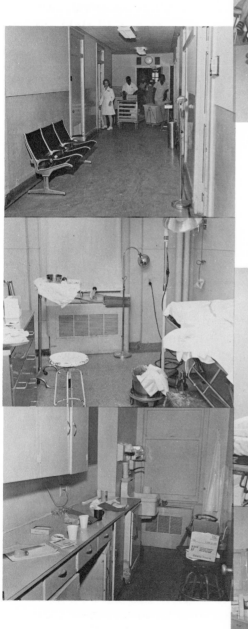

In June 1970, the Department of Emergency Services at Baylor was moved from its old location on the first floor of the Veal Hospital, as shown in photos at left, into new and expanded quarters, photos above and below, in the newly completed Jonsson Hospital. The relocation of the Emergency Department was made possible with a gift from the Zale Corporation.

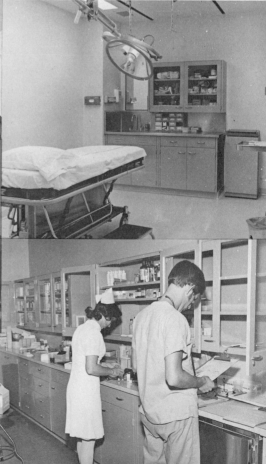

an Anger camera was added. With this new scanning instrument, nuclear medicine soon "came of age" at Baylor, and the patient caseload was doubled within a period of just three months.

By 1978, another scanning technique—the use of sound, instead of radioactive materials—was beginning to become known in medical circles. At Dr. Sears' suggestion, Dr. Steinbach attended a Society of Nuclear Medicine meeting in Boston in July of that year to study the use of "ultrasound" in scanning procedures. Although skeptical at first, Dr. Steinbach became completely intrigued with the new technique and spent his entire stay in Boston working with the unit there. On his return to Dallas, he purchased a Picker ultrasound unit and became the first radiologist in Texas to utilize the equipment. Ultrasound is used primarily in scanning for abdominal problems and to pinpoint the size and location of the fetus in the uterus.

No sooner had Baylor implemented the use of ultrasound, however, than still another new scanning technique—this one with the capability of photographing the entire human organism—was introduced. Known as the computerized axial tomographic (CAT) scanner, it outperformed any other scanning device known to medical science, with the capability of scanning one whole section of the human body in 20 seconds. And in July 1976, the first CAT scanner in North Texas was installed at Baylor.

Today, Baylor's Division of Nuclear Medicine is located in a 5,000-square-foot area in a wing between the Veal and Jonsson Hospitals, and it encompasses all three modalities of diagnosis—nuclear medicine, ultrasound and CAT scanning. Its equipment includes four diagnostic ultrasound units, five Anger cameras, one rectilinear scanner and one CAT scanner. Together, these "miracle machines" are used to perform more than 16,000 diagnostic procedures in a single year.

No Time to Stop

By the early years of the 1970s, Baylor had taken giant strides in many directions—constantly building upward and outward, shuffling departments, tearing out, renovating, restructuring, adding to equipment and services. But even now, there was no stopping place in sight.

Less than two weeks after the Jonsson Hospital opened, executive director Powell received a fitting tribute from fellow hospital administrators across the nation—the Gold Medal Award for Excellence in Hospital Administration, given by the American College of Hospital Administrators and representing the highest honor Powell's profession can bestow. Just a month prior to the award, he had observed his 25th year at Baylor—a quarter-century that had witnessed more growth than most observers would have dreamed possible in the mid-1940s when he had first arrived on the scene.

Powell had promised the fund-raisers at the victory luncheon celebrating the conclusion of the Jonsson campaign that "We will build the finest medical and surgical hospital in the world." And, truly, the Jonsson Hospital had lived up to that advance promise.

It was an achievement that would have been sufficient to satisfy many administrators. But there was no stopping place in sight for Boone Powell, either. As everyone at Baylor knew, he was not nearly through building yet.

XII

New Plateaus

Collins Hospital

Carr P. Collins Sr.—who celebrated his 86th birthday as this book was being written—gained a reputation during his long career in the fields of insurance, investments, manufacturing and real estate development as one of the most astute businessmen in Texas. A self-made millionaire who got his start delivering groceries in a horse-drawn wagon for $2.50 a week, Collins went on to head Fidelity Union Life Insurance Company, which he helped found in 1928 and which he built into the fourth largest insurance firm in Dallas operating nationwide. He also engaged in such diverse business activities as the development of the huge Plymouth Park area of Irving, at one time the largest air-conditioned housing development in the country, and the organization of the highly successful Vent-A-Hood Company of Dallas, a manufacturer of kitchen appliances.

Collins, a native of Tyler County, has also devoted much of his time to civic, charitable and humanitarian causes. An ardent Baptist, he served at various times as vice president and director of the Baptist Foundation of Texas, director and member of the Executive Committee of the Southern Baptist Convention and deacon of the Park Cities Baptist Church. He has been elected to two terms on the Board of Trustees of Baylor University Medical Center—the first time in 1924 and again in 1958. During those years of service, he became one of the institution's most faithful and enthusiastic supporters. A man of conviction and decision, capable of quick analysis and immediate action, Collins not only gave a large share of his own wealth to Baylor, but was instrumental in securing many contributions from others.

In 1968, the veteran trustee made a donation of $1 million to the Medical Center—an act of benevolent generosity that was destined to bring a new kind of hospital facility to Dallas and the Southwest. When the 300-bed Carr P. Collins Hospital was dedicated on January 6, 1972, it represented the latest concept of integrating acute hospital care with specialized rehabilitation programs for patients.

The seven-story hospital had been in the planning stages since August 1967, when the Medical Center's Board of Trustees formally decided that Baylor needed a rehabilitation hospital. From the time of the initial discussions, Collins liked the idea and, during that August meeting, he volunteered to assist both with the planning and financing of the project. "It is my hope that patients of this new hospital will again discover the rewarding joys of a satisfying life by overcoming the limitations resulting from injury or illness," Collins said in making the initial contribution for the hospital. By the time the gift was announced during the winter of 1968, contracts had already been approved with Thomas E. Stanley, Architects-Engineers, for designing the facility, and Hayman-Andres General Contractors, for the actual construction. It was announced at that time that the hospital, to be constructed with a 550-car underground parking garage, would be located across the street from the Jonsson Hospital on Junius Street and connected to the rest of the Medical Center complex by an elevated walkway.

Because the hospital was to be used primarily for rehabilitation services, careful attention was given to every facet of its planning, design and construction. And while special amenities for the handicapped are more common in publicly-used buildings today—and, indeed, are required by law in many instances—it was unusual in the 1960s for an institution to take the initiative in providing such facilities—a fact that drew recognition in a major article in *Southern Hospitals* magazine. The hospital's unique features grew out of the suggestions of a committee of Baylor physicians, which toured other rehabilitation centers across the country, and a committee composed of former rehabilitation patients. Some of the features included: the use of ramps, rather than steps, at patient entrances; the use of extra space for patient mobility; specially-designed desks and lavatories with open space beneath to allow greater accessibility by wheelchair patients; larger shower facilities with floors level with the rest of the room, permitting easy access by wheelchair; and wall-mounted grab bars located around the circumference of each bathroom. To help bridge the gap between acute treatment and the return home, each patient was to receive his own rehabilitation program, in which nursing, physical therapy, occupational therapy and other services were to be coordinated.

Psychiatric Units

With the opening of the Collins Hospital, Baylor also established its first specialized unit for psychiatric patients. This 46-bed unit, designed with the advice of the Medical Center's psychiatric staff, other members of the medical staff and the assistance of an architect from the National Institutes of Health in Bethesda, Maryland, was located on the second floor of Collins and was named in honor of William K. and Peggy Manning, long-time Dallas residents who contributed the funds.

In the original unit, both adult and adolescent patients were admitted. However, it was ultimately determined that the patient load would have a maximum of 25 per cent adolescents, so 11 of the 46 beds

Carr P. Collins Sr., a self-made millionaire and long-time Baylor trustee, made a $1 million gift in 1968 to the Medical Center that would make possible a new hospital in 1972. Construction on the hospital and its adjoining 550-car underground parking garage began in 1969.

The new 300-bed Carr P. Collins Hospital was dedicated on January 6, 1972. Later, Collins made another substantial gift to the Medical Center to complete the top three floors of the hospital, which had been reserved for expansion.

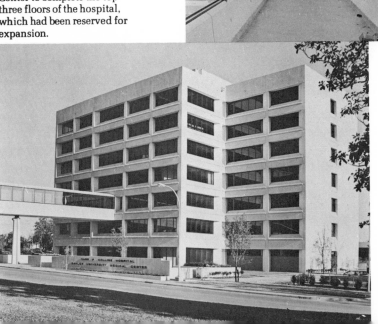

were designated for that purpose. But by 1977, the waiting list for beds in the unit had grown so lengthy—especially for teenage pyschiatric patients—that another 54-bed unit was opened on the fifth floor of Collins. Together, the second and fifth floors form a comprehensive, short-term acute care psychiatric facility for adult and adolescent patients, who are admitted by members of the medical staff of the Medical Center's Department of Psychiatry and whose stays range in duration from three weeks to six months. Patient care is provided by a treatment team composed of physicians, nurses, occupational therapists and social workers, as well as a full-time teacher from the Dallas Independent School District for adolescent patients. Dr. Sam Neely serves as full-time medical director of the psychiatric units.

The establishment of the first psychiatric unit at Collins in 1972 represented an important milestone for psychiatry at Baylor. Before that time, Baylor had no beds specifically designated for psychiatric patients, and members of the psychiatric staff served primarily as consulting physicians. Patients admitted with psychiatric conditions had to be transferred from Baylor or hospitalized under special limitations.

In the early days of Baylor College of Medicine, the school's founder, Dr. Rosser, had taught clinical medicine and mental and nervous diseases. It is presumed that Dr. Rosser, who served as superintendent of the North Texas Hospital for the Insane in 1895, treated persons with mental disorders at the Texas Baptist Memorial Sanitarium, since there were no other facilities available for them in the city. In 1918, Dr. James J. Terrill became chairman of the Department of Psychiatry at the medical college and headed the psychiatric service at the sanitarium. A year earlier, in 1917, Dr. Terrill had founded Timberlawn Psychiatric Hospital, the first facility of its kind in Dallas. In 1932, Dr. Guy Witt assumed chairmanship of the medical college's Department of Neuropsychiatry (the name having been changed in 1920) and, in 1947, became chief of the psychiatric service at Baylor Hospital, a position in which he continued to serve until 1955.

Through the years, treatment for psychiatric patients has moved in many directions with what now appear to be some rather unusual developments. Psychotherapy or "talk" with the patient has always been the primary mode of therapy, especially since the work of Sigmund Freud, but at various times other modes of treatment have been introduced. The most popular treatments included sleep therapy, hormone therapy, various kinds of physical manipulation (cold packs, wrapping in sheets, swirling in tubs of water and confinement in darkened rooms). Syphilitic infections of the nervous system resulting in mental illness were treated by artificially raising body temperature to high levels by infecting the patient with malaria, using typhoid vaccine, or placing the patient in a "hot box" for controlled periods of time, among others. The 1930s brought numerous innovations in quick succession. Among them were convulsive treatment by chemical injections (1934), insulin therapy (1936), and electro-convulsive treatments (1937). Psychosurgery, including such techniques as the lobotomy, were used extensively in the 1950s. The same decade saw the introduction of many new drugs for the treatment of mental disorders, and drug therapy grew rapidly in popularity. Drugs are still widely used today, in conjunction with the current major form of treatment—psychotherapy.

In 1955, Dr. Perry Talkington became Baylor's chief of psychiatry, and it was under his leadership that the direction of the service began to change. In 1963, Dr. James K. Peden, who was to succeed Dr. Talkington as chief in 1968, served as chairman of a long-range planning task force on psychiatry and neurology that recommended the establishment of an active Department of Psychiatry within the framework of the hospital staff and development of a specialized unit for psychiatric inpatients. The realization of these goals became possible with the completion of the Collins Hospital. Dr. Peden, who continues as chief of the department today, is a 1939 graduate of Baylor College of Medicine. He taught anatomy at the college until it moved to Houston in 1943, then assumed a teaching position at the new Southwestern Medical School. He received his psychiatric training at the Illinois Neuropsychiatric Institute, Timberlawn Psychiatric Hospital, and the Hospital of the University of Pennsylvania before joining the Baylor staff in 1952.

Continuing Education

Almost daily during the 1970s, medical research is producing new and important information on the diagnosis and treatment of the ailments that afflict mankind. With medical research projects mushrooming, it is now estimated that scientists are producing more medical knowledge in a month than anyone could read and absorb in a lifetime. Because of this situation, Baylor officials recognized early in the decade that one of the greatest challenges facing medicine and its related professions was in cutting the time lag between the discovery of new information and its ultimate application to the care of patients. In fact, meeting this challenge was one of the major concerns of the Medical Center's long-range planning program that had begun in 1963.

Nearly a decade later, Baylor was to meet the challenge head-on with the establishment in 1972 of the A. Webb Roberts Center for Continuing Education in the Health Sciences. Sponsored at first by Baylor and later co-sponsored by the University of Texas Health Science Center at Dallas, the new educational center was comprised of the Beulah Porter Beasley Memorial Auditorium, completed in 1972 with a

$300,000 gift from the late Mrs. Beasley's husband, Dallas insuranceman Theodore P. Beasley; a 25,000-volume medical library which receives and files some 700 scientific journals each month, and adjoining lecture rooms for classes and seminars.

The $1 million endowment necessary to make the center a full-time operation was contributed by A. Webb Roberts, wealthy Dallas banker and real estate developer for whom the center is named. The youngest of seven children of a small-town merchant and a native of Ball Ground, Georgia, Roberts was content to run a general store for his father for a short time after college, but later came to Texas to strike out on his own. During World War II, he served as Texas-Oklahoma regional director of the federal War Production Board's government division, and it was through this experience that he developed an interest in the humanitarian aspects of hospitals. Quiet and unassuming, Roberts nevertheless made a reputation for himself as a zealous and dedicated worker. His gift to Baylor was in memory of his mother, Georgia Coggins Roberts, whom he describes as a "devout Christian" and a woman of exceptional wisdom, to whom hundreds of Georgia mountain folk turned for advice and counsel during Roberts' boyhood.

The Roberts Center not only allows Baylor to provide for the continuing education of its own staff, but also offers an opportunity for medical personnel throughout the Southwest to participate in continuing education programs. Established with the philosophy that "excellence is achieved through a concept of shared resources," the Roberts Center has put that philosophy into action through one-day seminars, intensive four- and five-day review courses, off-campus seminars, the printing and distribution of materials and handbooks for the courses, closed-circuit television with talk-back capabilities, a video-cassette library lending system, grand rounds, preceptorships, coordination with other continuing education centers

209

in Texas, and the preparation of a semi-monthly calendar of all continuing education activities in the region which is mailed to about 6,000 health care professionals.

The inaugural program for the center, entitled "Great Ideas in Surgery," was presented November 3 and 4, 1972. Conceived and organized by Dr. Robert S. Sparkman, chief of the Department of General Surgery at Baylor, the program featured nine speakers, all of whom had made monumental contributions in surgery or their related fields. Speakers included Dr. Warren H. Cole of Asheville, North Carolina, who developed the first method of x-ray examination of the gallbladder; Dr. Michael E. DeBakey of Houston, world-famous cardiovascular surgeon; Dr. Lester E. Dragstedt of Gainesville, Florida, a world authority on normal and abnormal physiology of the stomach and duodenum; Dr. John E. Gibbon Jr. of Media, Pennsylvania, creator of the heart-lung machine; Dr. Charles A. Hufnagel of Washington, D. C., first surgeon to implant an artificial heart valve; Dr. Charles B. Huggins of Chicago, a Nobel Prize winner for development of the treatment of malignant disease by alteration of the hormonal environment; Dr. David M. Hume of Richmond, Virginia, who contributed greatly to the study of organ rejection in transplant patients; Dr. Alton Ochsner of New Orleans, a specialist in broncho-pulmonary surgery; and Dr. Owen H. Wangensteen of Minneapolis, a noted educator and specialist in intestinal obstruction. Manuscripts presented at the Roberts Center during the original program are subsequently being edited by Dr. Sparkman for publication in *The American Journal of Surgery*.

In the years since that first program with its prestigious participants, more than 42,000 physicians, nurses and allied health personnel have been registered at the hundreds of various programs conducted at the center. The overwhelming success of the center's program can be credited to the fact that it was established with a permanent staff and budget for planning, promoting and operating educational activities.

Administering the center is Dr. George Race, who was appointed on January 1, 1973, to the dual posts of dean of continuing education of the Roberts Center and associate dean of the UT Health Science Center. Dr. Race's appointment was made jointly by Boone Powell and Dr. Charles C. Sprague, health science center president. In addition to the Roberts Center positions, Dr. Race serves as director of Baylor's laboratories and chief of the Medical Center's Pathology Department, posts he has held since 1959.

In Powell's words, "The A. Webb Roberts Center is one of the most far-reaching advancements Baylor University Medical Center has ever made. It has showcased the Medical Center and has brought recognition to it from all parts of the globe by serving as an inspirational vehicle for physicians and other health personnel to do a better job for their patients and themselves."*

Medical Education

Although it has been more than three decades since the Baylor College of Medicine moved away, Baylor University Medical Center remains a major teaching facility for physicians, nurses and other allied health personnel, and it continues today to pursue its traditional commitment to education as a major objective, not only in the A. Webb Roberts Center but throughout the Baylor complex.

Dr. Ralph Tompsett came to Baylor in 1957 to become chief of the Department of Internal Medicine and Baylor's first full-time director of Medical Education. He replaced Dr. Paul Thomas, who had been the voluntary chief of internal medicine and who was

*See Appendix H

A. Webb Roberts, Dallas banker and real estate developer, contributed $1 million to Baylor for the creation of a continuing education center. The center, known as the A. Webb Roberts Center for Continuing Education in the Health Sciences, was completed in 1972.

Dr. George J. Race, left, dean of continuing education at the Roberts Center, and A. Webb Roberts, the center's benefactor, attend a seminar at the facility.

A. Webb Roberts was an honored guest at the first program presented at the Roberts Center. The seminar, entitled *Great Ideas in Surgery*, was held November 3 and 4, 1972.

Dr. Robert S. Sparkman, center, introduced heart surgeon, Dr. Michael E. DeBakey, left, of Houston, as a speaker for *Great Ideas in Surgery*. Dr. LeRoy J. Kleinsasser, right, is Baylor's former director of Surgical Education.

In November 1976, Dr. Milford O. Rouse, left, above, a gastroenterologist and longtime member of the Baylor staff, endowed the Milford O. Rouse Lectureship in Digestive Diseases and Nutrition, which is held annually at the A. Webb Roberts Center. With Dr. Rouse are Dr. Ralph Tompsett, second from left, chief of internal medicine; Dr. J. L. Matthews, third from left, associate dean of the Roberts Center; and Dr. Daniel Polter, director of gastroenterology.

Dr. Robert S. Sparkman serves as chief of the Department of General Surgery at Baylor and director of Surgical Education.

Dr. Ralph Tompsett is chief of internal medicine at Baylor and director of Medical Education.

chairman of the search committee responsible for Dr. Tompsett's selection. At the time he came to Baylor, Dr. Tompsett was already well-known in the field of infectious diseases and had established himself as an outstanding clinician at New York Hospital and Bellevue Hospital in New York City. During World War II, he had served as ward officer and chief of the General Medicine Section in the Ninth General Hospital in the Southwest Pacific Theater. His ability as a teacher had been proven at teaching posts in medicine and pharmacology at Cornell University Medical School, his alma mater, and he had gained experience in administration as director of student and personnel health at New York Hospital.

"We saw in his credentials a man who had the experience we needed to direct medical education and to be chief of internal medicine," Dr. Thomas recalls. "In our interviews, he demonstrated an exterior calm, an unpretentiousness and an honesty that captured our confidence."

When Dr. Tompsett assumed the positions, the internal medicine staff at Baylor was considered strong, and the level of medical practice was excellent, but the educational program in the department was at its lowest point since the Baylor College of Medicine moved to Houston. Nationally, the competition among hospitals for interns and residents was very stringent, and many house staff positions throughout the country were vacant—especially in educational programs not conducted by a medical school. Hospitals such as Baylor were approved for large numbers of interns and residents, but it was difficult for them to attract students for the positions and even more difficult to attract those with the better academic records.

On the national scene, it was also evident, both from a practice and from an educational standpoint, that an upsurge was occurring in the development of medical subspecialties. At Baylor, however, there were few subspecialists and only one hospital-based internist, the cardiologist in charge of the cardiology laboratory.

To strengthen medical education at Baylor and to attract a large number of subspecialists, Dr. Tompsett worked closely with Baylor's Medical Education Advisory Committee, effectively chaired for a long period of time by Dr. Milton V. Davis, and other physicians committed to the development of the teaching programs. The committee felt that a multifaceted approach was needed to develop medical student activities, improve the house staff programs and increase the level of attending staff expertise in general internal medicine and the subspecialties, while strengthening the clinical and basic science teaching in the educational program and pursuing the active recruitment of interns.

In Dr. Tompsett's twenty-one year period of leadership, the department's staff has grown from 116 members to 202 members. Eight subdivisions have been developed within the department and are staffed with physicians with offices and laboratories in the department. These include:

Subspecialty	Hospital-Based	Others
Cardiology	7	5
Endocrinology	2	-
Gastroenterology	3	10
Hematology-Oncology	9	3
Infectious Diseases	1	-
Nephrology	2	7
Pulmonary	3	3
Neurology	1	3

A ninth division, rheumatology, is formally organized with five physicians, and a rheumatologist is being sought to serve as its full-time director.

Since 1957, the average daily patient census in the Department of Internal Medicine has increased from 121 to 270. The house staff in the department has grown from four to 24, plus 20 residents from other departments who rotate through the department on a first-year basis. Fellowship programs with 10 fellows have been developed in the medical subspecialties. The clinical clerkship, in which third-year medical students from the University of Texas Southwestern Medical School rotate in internal medicine at Baylor, has increased from nine students to 60 students, and approximately 150 other students come from Southwestern in their second or fourth years of medical school.

In recent years, similar advancement has occurred in Baylor's Department of General Surgery under the leadership of Dr. Robert S. Sparkman. As chief of this service, Dr. Sparkman succeeded Dr. J. Warner Duckett, who was responsible, in part, for the early growth of heart surgery at Baylor and who was chairman of the Medical Board from 1956 until 1967.

Dr. Sparkman received his M.D. degree from Baylor College of Medicine and had done postgraduate work at Baylor Hospital and Cincinnati General Hospital when he was called to active duty in the Army Medical Corps in 1940. On duty in the Southwest Pacific, he served as chief of surgery at the First Evacuation Hospital and the 248th General Hospital, where he held the rank of commanding officer for a time. At the end of World War II, Dr. Sparkman, who had achieved the rank of colonel, returned to Dallas and became active on Baylor's medical staff. In 1968, he became voluntary chief of the Department of General Surgery and, in July 1969, was appointed part-time chief, although he has devoted full-time to the position while maintaining an active private practice and extensive writing activities.

During his ten years as chief, the Department of General Surgery has grown rapidly in national stature and in size. Virtually every national leader in surgery and many international leaders have visited Baylor and have participated in programs Dr. Sparkman has planned and conducted. His organizational talents have been particularly evident in the teaching program, where the number of general surgical residents has increased from five to thirty. He has stimulated gifts of more than $500,000 in endowment for the educational activities of the department and has still further plans for insuring the future financing of the department in years to come. Although in Baylor's medical staff organization, general surgery and the ten surgical specialties—colon and rectal surgery, oral surgery, neurosurgery, ophthalmological surgery, gynecological surgery, orthopedic surgery, otolaryngology, plastic surgery, thoracic surgery and urological surgery—are organized in separate departments, Dr. Sparkman is influential among them and serves as chairman of the committee which coordinates surgical policies and resources. This coordination is especially important at Baylor since it ranks third among all hospitals nationally in the number of surgical procedures, with more than 23,000 each year, and since high percentages of Baylor's surgical procedures are unusually intricate.

Peripheral vascular surgery is a subspecialty that has remained within the Department of General Surgery and has gained a national reputation. Dr. Dale Austin and Dr. Jesse Thompson were recognized in the early 1950s for their successful results in carotid artery surgery, and this laid the foundation for the large volume of this surgery performed at Baylor today, the attraction of other vascular surgeons and for the development of many specialized services for patients suffering strokes, including a laboratory for vascular diagnosis. In February 1978, a national vascular surgical society was established in Dr. Thompson's honor.

As the teaching environment at Baylor was upgraded and as recruitment programs were enhanced significantly by the efforts of Dr. Merrick Reese, who became director of intern recruitment in 1967,

Baylor's medical educational programs have grown steadily in number and quality. All of the 150 positions are filled each year, and there is competition for these appointments among the top students in medical schools. Full residency programs are conducted at Baylor in internal medicine, general surgery, obstetrics-gynecology, pathology, diagnostic radiology, radiation therapy, physical medicine, colon and rectal surgery, physical medicine and rehabilitation and oral surgery. There are fellowships in cardiology, cardiovascular and thoracic surgery, gastroenterology, infectious diseases, pulmonary medicine, rheumatology and vascular surgery. Residencies are sponsored jointly with Southwestern Medical School in orthopedic surgery, plastic surgery, thoracic surgery, urology and anesthesiology. Residents in psychiatry are assigned to Baylor from Timberlawn Psychiatric Hospital.

Baylor places high priority on its educational programs as a means of preparing physicians for society. However, the strengthened teaching programs have also added many dimensions to the Medical Center's ability to serve patients. Young physicians in training are continually available to provide many specific services and safeguards for patient care. Teaching is also intellectually stimulating to the attending physicians, and the programs aid them in keeping their own knowledge current. These and many other intangible factors greatly enrich the quality element in all facets of the Medical Center, and the ultimate benefit is to its patients.

Clinical Education

The educational programs for nurses and other professional and technical specialists provide similar values. The Medical Center is the primary site for the clinical experience for the Baylor University School of Nursing. The school, which has an enrollment of 400 and graduates about 100 students per year, is academically accountable to Baylor University but is the financial and administrative responsibility of the Dallas Board of Trustees.

In addition, the Medical Center provides a clinical site for El Centro College's associate degree program in nursing education and for the vocational nursing program sponsored by the Dallas Independent School District. Other educational programs in nursing include post-graduate courses for operating room nurses and nurse anesthetists, as well as a refresher class for inactive registered nurses.

But educational programs at the Medical Center are not limited to physicians and nurses alone. Baylor sponsors schools in histologic technique, medical technology and radiologic technology. The Medical Center also receives students in occupational therapy and physicial therapy from many universities and conducts a dietetic internship, a pastoral care internship, a pastoral care residency and an administrative residency, which are all fully accredited.

The pastoral care internship and residency programs were started in 1974 by Baylor Chaplain Joseph E. Gross to provide practice experience for students studying for the ministry and pastors who wish to enhance their pastoral care and counseling skills through a supervised continuing education program.

The administrative residency is a one-year program for persons who have fulfilled the post-graduate academic requirements for a Master's Degree in Health Care Administration. The program has graduated 63 since it began in 1947, more than any other residency in the nation. The graduates occupy a wide variety of important positions in hospitals, planning agencies, consultant firms, and other health-related organizations throughout the United States and Canada, and include the chief executive officers of many leading institutions and of the Blue Cross plan of one state. Many of them have received wide recognition in hospital associations and in their professional societies. The present board chairman, Ray Woodham, and chairman-elect, Chester Stocks, of the American College of Hospital Administrators are both alumni.

Special Care Nursery

With a long-standing reputation as a progressive innovator in newborn care, Baylor added another in its lengthy list of accomplishments in this field in June 1973 with the opening of new admission and special care nursery units on the first floor of the Hoblitzelle Hospital.

Developed by Baylor officials, with assistance from the hospital planning department of Ross Laboratories, in response to the many scientific breakthroughs in newborn care that had begun in the 1960s, the nurseries represented the culmination of several years of work on the part of Baylor's Departments of Pediatrics and Obstetrics-Gynecology.

In the 1960s, extensive research had revealed that close observation of the newborn was vital in the first few hours of life and that the chance of survival was greater for critically ill newborns if they could receive care in the same place where they were delivered. As these new ideas were emerging, obstetrician-gynecologists were gaining new knowledge in the detection of high-risk pregnancies, new equipment was being developed to determine the health of the fetus before birth, and a new pediatric subspecialty— neonatology—was forming that would concentrate its full efforts on the care of sick and premature newborns. As Baylor's physicians became acquainted with these innovations, they wanted to develop a new system of nurseries, so that they could better serve the newborns at the hospital. Therefore, with the completion of the new units at Baylor, newborn infants could be placed at first in the admission nursery for a period

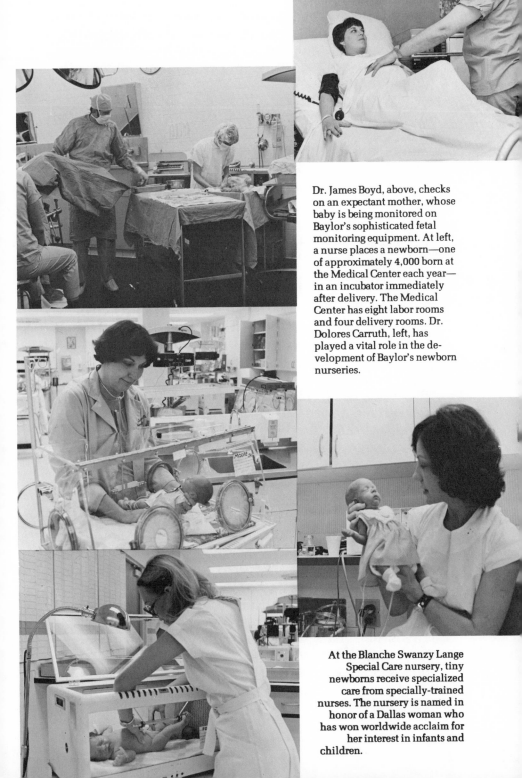

Dr. James Boyd, above, checks on an expectant mother, whose baby is being monitored on Baylor's sophisticated fetal monitoring equipment. At left, a nurse places a newborn—one of approximately 4,000 born at the Medical Center each year—in an incubator immediately after delivery. The Medical Center has eight labor rooms and four delivery rooms. Dr. Dolores Carruth, left, has played a vital role in the development of Baylor's newborn nurseries.

At the Blanche Swanzy Lange Special Care nursery, tiny newborns receive specialized care from specially-trained nurses. The nursery is named in honor of a Dallas woman who has won worldwide acclaim for her interest in infants and children.

of eight to twelve hours of constant monitoring in a controlled environment by specially trained nurses, and then be moved, depending on their conditions, to one of three other units—the well baby nursery, the premature nursery or the newborn intensive care unit located adjacent to the admissions nursery.

Baylor's progressive attitude in the care of newborns dates back to 1908, when Dr. Hugh Leslie Moore, the first pediatrician in the State of Texas, made his way to Dallas to set up practice. Dr. Moore had been a rural practitioner at Van Alstyne in Grayson County when he took an interest in pediatrics and decided to study the new specialty in both England and Germany. Armed with the new knowledge that resulted from these studies, Dr. Moore joined the staff of Texas Baptist Memorial Sanitarium. He found the children of Dallas suffering from many disorders that could not then be successfully treated. Such widespread childhood diseases as pneumonia, polio, tetanus, whooping cough, and even common diarrhea, usually simply had to be allowed to run their course, while the physician made the patient as comfortable as possible and hoped for the best.

During those early days in Dallas, Dr. Moore found that the only way he could keep a premature or sick infant warm was to place the child in a tub or other large container lined with blankets and heated with hot bricks. But even in these primitive circumstances, he did his utmost to meet the needs of all the sick children in the city, caring for private patients at the sanitarium, and for those who could not afford hospital care, at their homes. With the help of Mae Smith, a dedicated visiting nurse, Dr. Moore established the Dallas Baby Camp on Oak Lawn Avenue in 1913, after Miss Smith had became appalled at the number of cases of infantile diarrhea she saw on her visits to indigent homes. She managed to scrape together enough money to buy two large Army tents and set them up to serve as a makeshift facility for sick babies. Again, the only method of keeping the infants warm was in homemade tub incubators. She and Dr. Moore treated the babies with a "protein milk formula" that was later recognized as the answer to the greatest health problem facing young children at that time—dysentery.

By 1920, the sanitarium had acquired its first Hess incubator, a large, tub-shaped container heated by hot water that circulated between its inner and outer walls. In 1929, the Bradford Hospital for Babies was established on Maple Avenue, to be followed in the early 1940s by the Texas Children's Hospital and the Freeman Memorial Clinic. Dr. Moore served as head of pediatrics at all these institutions, while continuing to serve as head of pediatrics at Baylor, until 1946, when he resigned his Baylor post to be succeeded by his son, Dr. Robert L. Moore. (The elder Dr. Moore's grandson, Dr. Hugh Leslie Moore II, is also a pediatrician currently on the Baylor staff.)

Dr. Robert Moore served as chief of pediatrics at Baylor during an important transitional period in infant and child care. It was a time in which medical science progressed from the point of merely being able to support a critically ill newborn or small child to the point of being able to combat childhood diseases through the use of antibiotics and other new drugs. Incubators steadily improved also, even though such mysterious disorders as hyaline membrane disease, a respiratory ailment, continued to be almost 100 per cent fatal in newborns.

Dr. Robert Moore had become interested in medicine in general and pediatrics in particular as a boy, when he often accompanied his father to the sanitarium and on house calls. He received his M.D. degree from Johns Hopkins Medical School and served his residency in pediatrics at St. Louis Children's Hospital and Johns Hopkins. But his father imparted more to his son than a love of medicine alone. He also instilled him with a "cooperative spirit" in promoting the progress of pediatrics throughout the City of Dallas. "My father never thought of another pediatrician as competition," he explains. "In fact, at one time, about three-fourths of the pediatricians in Dallas had gotten their starts in my father's office. He would give them free office space to allow them to get their practices established, and, in return, they would help him when he got too busy. He was looked up to and loved by every one, and that has a lot to do with how well Dallas pediatricians get along with one another today."

This same "cooperative spirit" made it possible to maintain a close working relationship between the Department of Obstetrics-Gynecology and the Department of Pediatrics at Baylor—a closeness that has prevailed over the years, and without which the Medical Center's reputation for excellence in newborn care might have been impossible. Such cooperation made Baylor's Women and Children's Hospital a reality in 1959 and brought about a smooth transition when pediatrics was reduced in emphasis at Baylor in 1967 (except for newborn care) to make possible the concentration of the city's medical resources for children at the new Children's Medical Center on Harry Hines Boulevard.

In 1968, when Dr. Floyd Norman became Baylor's chief of pediatrics, advances in newborn care began to come even more rapidly in the first stage of a technological revolution that would burst into full bloom in the 1970s and make possible the saving of countless infant lives—lives that were beyond saving just a few years earlier. The 1960s brought special intensive care units for newborns and vastly improved incubators, equipped with total life support systems for premature or ill newborns. The period also brought fetal monitoring during high-risk pregnancies, a new type of ventilator that has proved remarkably effective in helping infants with hyaline membrane disease to survive the crisis period, the ability to do laboratory tests and monitor blood gases (carbon dioxide and oxygen) in small amounts of blood, and the new specialty of neonatology. Other advances during this era included the development of sonography and ultrasound devices to determine fetal position and fetal age; amniocentesis, a test in which fetal fluid is removed by a large needle inserted into the expectant mother's abdomen to determine certain birth defects before birth and to determine if the fetal lungs have matured before delivery by caesarean section.

Meanwhile, far-reaching changes were also taking place in the field of obstetrics, too. Obstetricians developed the capability of identifying potential high-risk mothers—those with diabetes, hypertension, toxemia, kidney disease and heart disease—early in pregnancy, so that both the mother and her unborn infant could receive proper care during the course of the pregnancy. High-risk centers were established for these mothers, in which proper care facilities could be concentrated. Obstetricians also began using a new epidural-type anesthesia to allow the mother to remain conscious during delivery and to avoid anesthetic depression of the baby. At Baylor, nursing standards for obstetrical care, particularly with regard to post-delivery care of new mothers and their newborns, received major attention and were improved. Early in 1968, a new serum called RhoGAM became commercially available, and since that time has virtually wiped out the once-dread Rh disease, an anemic and potentially fatal condition in newborns, sometimes caused when an Rh-negative mother gives birth to an Rh-positive baby. But even before that, the director of microbiology at Baylor, Dr. Sol Haberman, with the assistance of Dr. E. B. Mendel, an obstetrician-gynecologist, produced enough of a RhoGAM-like serum to save the lives of more than 140 infants who would otherwise have been born with Rh disease. (It was not the first time that Dr. Haberman had moved a step ahead of the times; in the 1940s, he had also made penicillin in his laboratory before it became commercially available, thereby saving numerous other lives.) These and many other advancements evolved at Baylor under a series of dedicated and innovative chiefs of obstetrics-gynecology, including Dr. W. K. Strother Jr., who held the post from 1947 to 1968; Dr. Oran Prejean and Dr. William Devereux, who volunteered to jointly serve until a replacement could be found for Dr. Strother; and Dr. Reuben Adams, who accepted the post in 1970 and serves in that position today.

With these developments and others, newborn care began evolving into one of the most complex medical disciplines, requiring the close team work of pediatricians, obstetricians, and specially-trained nurses to insure that each newborn was to be given the best possible chance for life. By early 1970, Dr. Norman was actively upgrading the nursery facilities at Baylor and implementing the many new concepts in newborn care that had become available. Toward that end, he invited Dr. Dolores Carruth, then a neonatologist at the University of Texas Southwestern Medical School who had been involved with neonatal intensive care at Children's Medical Center, to evaluate the nursery and equipment needs at Baylor. Dr. Carruth's recommendations led to the establish-ment of the admission and special care nursery units in 1973. Prior to that time, the typical hospital nursery had been little more than a large open room. But Baylor architect George Mills and consultant Michael Tyne of Ross Laboratories designed the nurseries with special utility fixtures and allotted 25 square feet of space per infant in the regular nurseries and 60 square feet per infant in the intensive care unit, where more space was necessary to accom-modate incubators, respirators, monitors and other specialized equipment.

In 1975, Baylor's eight-bed special care nursery was dedicated in honor of a a Dallas woman who has won worldwide acclaim for her interest in infants and children, Blanche Swanzy Lange. Mrs. Lange is the wife of Dr. Frederick M. Lange, president of the Dallas Community Chest Trust Fund, whose efforts have made possible many advancements on the Baylor campus. Also in 1975, Dr. Carruth became director of neonatology at Baylor.

Under the leadership of Dr. Percy Luecke Jr., the current chief of pediatrics; Dr. Adams; and Dr. Carruth, the Medical Center has continued to maintain its reputation as one of the outstanding referral centers for newborn care in the Southwest. According to standards set by the National Committee on Perinatal Health, Baylor will qualify as a Level III obstetrical unit, the category for the best-equipped medical facilities dealing with pregnancy and infant care. The Medical Center has also established an outreach program on newborn care for other hospitals in Texas with a grant from the Regional Medical Program of Texas. Through the program, Baylor physicians and nurses engage in educational programs at the hospitals and aid physicians in transferring sick or premature newborns to Baylor for treatment that is unavailable at their own facilities.

Baylor Medical Plaza

As early as the late 1940s, there had been interest among some Baylor physicians in erecting a doctors' office building convenient to the hospital. But when the idea was first proposed, financing priorities did not allow any construction funds for that purpose. Many years were to pass before the idea could be consummated, and in the meantime, several large commercial office structures were to arise near the Baylor complex, and a number of physicians built offices of their own. Still, the idea of an office building that would be an integral part of Baylor itself continued to resurface from time to time and never completely died out. Over the years, as changes took place in East Dallas, many of the commercial offices began to change ownership. And often the new owners were less responsive to the needs of the medical community than their predecessors had been. At that point, some physicians began to move out of the immediate area, and Baylor officials realized that the old idea of building the Medical Center's own office structure for physicians was becoming more and more an essential ingredient in Baylor's continued growth and progress.

And so, on July 2, 1971, the Board of Trustees approved construction of a medical plaza building which would encompass both office facilities for physicians and other services. Shortly after this action, Carr P. Collins Sr. presented Baylor with his second million-dollar contribution—this time to make a 25-year-old idea which Collins had advocated and supported a bright reality.

In August 1972, the building that had housed the Wadley Blood Center, located between Gaston Avenue and Junius Street across from the Hoblitzelle Hospital, was demolished to make way for the Medical Plaza, and the blood center was moved to a new location on Harry Hines Boulevard. A short time later, two other substantial contributions—one from Albert S. Barnett, an internationally-known Dallas cotton broker, and another from Texarkana philanthropist J. K. Wadley— were received for the construction project. Consequently, the twin 10-story towers of the Medical Plaza are named the Albert S. and Velma Barnett and the J. K. and Susie L. Wadley Medical Towers.

Designed by Thomas E. Stanley Architects and built by the Hayman-Andres Construction Company, the $14.5 million plaza encompasses not only the two towers, but a base building measuring approximately one block in length and a 360-car underground parking garage. The plaza was designed with the help of a building committee from the medical staff to insure that it would meet the needs of physicians officing

In 1972, the Wadley Blood Center on the Baylor campus was torn down to make way for a new development, the Baylor Medical Plaza. Shown at the demolition site is Boone Powell, left, and Dr. Norwood Hill, then medical director of the blood bank.

Construction on the new Medical Plaza began in September 1971 and was completed in December 1973. The twin towers of the plaza—named in honor of J. K. and Susie L. Wadley and Albert S. and Velma Barnett—added a new dimension to the Baylor University Medical Center campus. The primary purpose of the plaza is to provide convenient and attractive office spaces for the physicians who practice at Baylor.

there. Construction began in September 1971 and was completed in December 1973. On March 31, 1974, offices in the Barnett Tower were occupied by the first 21 physicians. Dr. James T. Boyd, obstetrician-gynecologist, had signed the first lease on February 1. (By July 1978, there were 210 physicians with offices in the two towers.)

The primary purpose of the Baylor Medical Plaza is to provide doctors with convenient and attractive offices adjoining the Medical Center and offering immediate access from the office to patient's bedside, surgical suite or emergency room. But the Plaza also serves numerous secondary functions. Besides its 250 office spaces for physicians, the towers also house a diagnostic and treatment center, buffet restaurant, delicatessen, barbecue restaurant, pharmacy, post office, florist, barber and beauty shops, optical shop, various other retail businesses—and even a 75-room hotel. The plaza's services are provided through three wholly owned subsidiary corporations of the Medical Center: Baylor Medical Plaza, Inc., Baylor Medical Plaza Services Corporation and BMP, Inc. Any operating surplus from the corporations is channeled back into teaching, research and charitable activities of the Medical Center. (The Medical Center also started its own construction firm, Gaston Construction Company, in 1972.)

The hotel, an unusual amenity for a hospital, provides accommodations for patients who do not require actual hospitalization, but who need to be close to their physicians; patients' families and guests attending the many seminars and teaching programs at Baylor. It also serves as a high-risk maternity unit for expectant mothers. In 1977, Belinda Bennett, a young expectant mother from the Pleasant Grove section of Dallas, made news when she was the first pregnant woman to be a guest at the hotel while awaiting the birth of her second child at the Hoblitzelle Hospital. Classified as a high-risk pregnancy patient because of a condition called placenta praevia, Mrs. Bennett was required to lie flat on her back much of the time for several weeks prior to delivery, and it was necessary for her physician and labor room nurses to examine her several times each day and for her vital signs to be closely monitored during this period. While her home was only about 15 minutes away from Baylor, this was considered too far for safety, so Mrs. Bennett registered as a guest at the hotel. Here, all the necessary medical precautions could be taken, but her daily room rate was only $29 as compared to $79 for a semi-private room in a hospital at Baylor. This charge covered her private two-bed room with adjoining private bath, telephone, television and daily maid service, plus three meals a day and twice-a-day examinations by labor room nurses. What's more, visitors were not restricted, and Mrs. Bennett's doctor's office was just a short elevator ride from her bedside.

By constantly branching out into new fields of endeavor, continually adding new services and refining old ones, and by never losing sight of the welfare of the individual patient, Baylor has moved to a unique position among American health care facilities.

In Dallas and many other cities, the 1970s saw inner-city problems swell to monstrous proportions and inner-city decay and decline reach their worst point in the nation's history. But by its example of industry, enthusiasm and innovation—and, indeed, by its very presence—Baylor pointed the way toward inner-city revival and revitalization in Dallas. And, as Baylor entered the final third of the decade, it had become increasingly obvious that the rest of Old East Dallas was about to follow the Baylor example. Although the odds had seemed hopelessly stacked against it only a few years earlier, East Dallas was coming back. New middle-class families of "urban pioneers" were moving in; rundown houses were being refurbished; new businesses were opening and old businesses were looking more prosperous; property values were rising;

a new spirit of community pride and community involvement was forming. A modern-day Renaissance was happening.

And Baylor, more than any other institution in Dallas, had led the way.

XIII
Special Challenges

Malpractice Crisis

The mid-1970s were characterized by much more than advancements in medical technology and the construction of new buildings. For Baylor and countless other health care facilities across the country, it was also a time of pressure to rival any period in their history. There were dilemmas such as the malpractice "crisis" with such profound social, political and economic implications that they threatened the very existence of America's traditional health care system. And even as this book went to press, the difficulties were far from over.

The roots of the malpractice dilemma are difficult to trace down—much less to analyze—even now. Some of them undoubtedly grew out of legitimate deficiencies in patient care and a gradual loss of closeness and communication between doctor and patient. Others sprang from public reaction to the spiralling cost of health care. Still others sprouted amid the private citizen's growing resentment toward being dependent upon the "system"—or, more correctly, a whole phalanx of "systems," one of which he saw in the health care industry.

Increasingly, citizens expressed their dissatisfaction and lack of understanding by filing lawsuits asking for massive awards. The million-dollar lawsuits filed and the cases with large judgments and settlements received wide publicity, and this stimulated many more people to seek legal redress for their claims. A phenomenon, known as the "Dr. Marcus

Welby syndrome," led patients to expect optimal results from medical care, and this was believed to be a factor in many lawsuits. The prospect that insurance companies would settle claims readily to avoid legal costs was also a factor.

The manufacturers of all types of products and services were being sued. Doctors and hospitals were particularly vulnerable, because they deal daily with people who have residual disability, and the medications and techniques they use involve risk. Some attorneys, sensing a bonanza, generally allowed themselves to be retained on contingency fees in malpractice suits, which meant that their clients could file suits without having to pay an initial legal fee.

Some major liability insurance carriers stopped writing medical professional liability policies altogether. Those remaining in the field raised their rates by incredible proportions and accepted no new policyholders, leaving many physicians and hospitals without coverage. The anxiety among physicians and hospitals about loss of coverage led to a climate of panic. In a few cases, hospitals and physicians sued each other over the way claims were settled, and, in many more instances, their relationships became strained.

Across the United States, doctors were staging work stoppages and slowdowns in efforts to obtain legislative relief and to arouse public awareness of the problems. In Fort Worth, anesthesiologists—among the hardest-hit groups of physicians—limited their cases to emergency or "urgent" surgeries. Dallas anesthesiologists debated whether they should do the same but decided against it.

The malpractice epidemic spread through the nation, beginning in a few states with especially liberal concepts of liability, such as those that place the burden of proof on the hospital or physician. The turning point in Texas was the Supreme Court decision in 1971 overturning the "charitable immunity" exemption for nonprofit hospitals, which allowed both the hospital, as well as the physician, to be sued. During the two-year period between 1972 and 1974, malpractice suits totalling some $50 million were filed against physicians and health care institutions in Dallas County.

At Baylor, the premiums quoted for malpractice coverage soared from just $78,000 in 1974 to $903,000 in 1975, to $1.5 million in 1977, and the level of coverage was actually reduced during that period. This occurred even though over the years until 1975 Baylor had paid only $74,000 in claims, and its reserves for all unsettled claims amounted to only $106,000.

As the Texas Legislature sought ways to resolve the situation, Baylor took positive action on its own by developing innovative self-insurance methods for its general and professional liability coverage. Before the end of 1977, the Church University Insurance Company, a wholly-owned, Bermuda-based subsidiary of the Medical Center, was operational for providing both professional and general liability coverage for Baylor.

The Cost Crunch

Even with a workable resolution to the malpractice crisis, however, other problems for Baylor and the health care industry, in general, intensified. By 1974, the nation's annual health care bill totaled in excess of $100 billion. Yet large segments of the country's population were not receiving adequate health care, and health care facilities and manpower were considered maldistributed. To help remedy this problem, the National Health Planning and Resources Development Act was approved by Congress in 1974 and signed by President Gerald Ford in 1975. By virtue of the act, other regulatory agencies for health care institutions were created at the statewide level—

the Texas Area Five Health Systems Agency, now in the process of developing an overall plan for the health care needs of the three million residents of the 19-county North Texas area, and the Texas Health Facilities Commission, which has the power to approve or disapprove all expenditures in excess of $100,000 by any health care facility in the state.

But even with the imposition of these strict new state and federal requirements with the dual purpose of better distributing health resources, while holding down capital expenditures, another problem of national importance was confronting the health care industry—the issue of rising costs.

From the 1940s until the early 1970s, federal policy had placed high priority upon improving the quality of health services and extending convenient access to modern scientific services to all communities and to all groups. This policy was heavily supported by grants for research, training, and facilities which produced a burgeoning system under enforced higher standards, a system which is costly to maintain. It also increased public expectations, and the motto that "health care is a right" went unchallenged for many years. National expenditures for health multiplied due to inflation in the general economy, the even faster rise in cost of new technology, the vast expansion of facilities with some overcapacity due to geographic shifts in population, and the public's tendency to use more services as their insurance (or Medicare/Medicaid) coverage improved. In addition, the cost of complying with numerous new federal and state regulations and higher accreditation standards became a substantial expense item in themselves for health care institutions.

In the early 1970s, the federal government and many economists, in a reversal of the goals, adopted cost containment as the new priority. The budgetary impact of the rising cost of the Medicare and

Medicaid programs, plus the realization that any national health insurance program adopted would escalate the demand for and cost of services, became a national concern. As a result, powerful forces within the federal government began advocating regulatory and economic control measures for the health care industry.

President Ford sought a seven per cent limit on allowable routine care costs for Medicare, and, as the nation's annual health care bill soared to $140 billion in 1978, President Jimmy Carter proposed to limit all hospitals to revenue increases of no more than nine per cent—a proposal still being debated in Congress as of this writing. If approved, most hospital administrators believe the Carter proposal would severely handicap the private system of health care delivery in America, particularly in specialized referral hospitals like Baylor and hospitals heavily involved in community service.

Always concerned about the costs it must pass along to its patients, Baylor has for years been actively engaged in a broad-based program of cost control, but many inflationary trends are beyond the control of any single institution, no matter how large or how well-intentioned. Baylor's fuel bill, for example, jumped from $168,000 in 1973 to an estimated $1.4 million in 1978, an increase of 713 per cent in five years, or more than 142 per cent per year. Electricity bills during the same period rose from $229,200 to an estimated $700,000, an increase of 215 per cent. Within just two years, from 1976 to 1978, the price paid by Baylor for pacemakers rose 200 per cent; for intravenous (IV) fluids 106 per cent; for insulin 226 per cent; for streptomycin 79 per cent; for coffee 295 per cent. Within that same two-year period, the costs of some types of hospital equipment have doubled and even tripled.

Some of the savings effected by the Medical Center during this era of rapidly escalating costs—

savings undertaken at Baylor's own initiative—have been considerable. A joint purchase program with other area hospitals in the Dallas Hospital Council resulted in a $100,000 saving on the purchase of IV solutions over a three-year span. A new type of x-ray camera, which uses less expensive grades of film, has resulted in an annual saving of $25,000. Group purchase of x-ray film saved another $20,000 per year. The purchase of a photo monitor for use with the EMI head scanner in the Baylor Radiology Department has made possible an annual saving of nearly $13,000. In-house production of a certain type of antibody preparation has saved approximately $9,000 each year. And the list goes on and on.

A Specialty Center

By the mid-1970s, Baylor was deeply involved in yet another long-range planning program to establish the general goals of the institution over the next 10 years. Among the goals outlined for the Medical Center was the development of what has become known as the "centers within a center" concept. Under this concept, specialized care would be provided at separate facilities to patients suffering from such illnesses as cancer, heart disease and arthritis. But since these facilities would remain within the physical confines of the Medical Center, they would be able to draw on all its vast resources whenever necessary.

Without the size and stature Baylor had achieved by this time, however, the establishment of such specialized centers would not have been possible. During the 1960s and 1970s, new equipment and techniques to increase the accuracy and speed of diagnosis and give the physicians more options in combating serious diseases had come in rapid-fire succession, and frequently Baylor had been the regional pacesetter in initiating these innovations.

Meanwhile, integral parts of the Medical Center's overall structure—such important support facilities as the laboratories, radiology, nuclear medicine and physical medicine—had been carefully developed throughout the years and were available as resources for the now envisioned specialty centers.

To facilitate the expanded activity in specialized areas during the last half of the 1970s, Baylor's management staff was again reorganized to meet the accelerated pace of change and progress. Effective January 1, 1975, Powell became director of the Medical Center with primary responsibility for long-range planning and development, and Hitt was named executive director with the responsibility for overall management, organization, policies, planning and financing for current operations and programs. The Powell-Hitt team was to fulfill the dual needs of Baylor by effectively executing plans for the future, while still maintaining the institution's standards of excellence for the present.

As part of the reorganization, two new associate executive director positions were created and filled by Howard Chase and Richard H. Malone. Chase was named to head a team of four associate directors in supervising the various departments providing diagnostic and therapeutic services, administrative services and the physical plant. Malone's responsibilities included direction and coordination of the administrators of the individual hospitals and of the executives working with medical staff activities, medical education, medical records and public relations.

In the years since 1968, Baylor had added $25 million worth of new equipment and facilities, and, by 1975, another $10.4 million in future construction projects had been approved. To make these projects—including implementation of two "centers within a center" concepts—become realities, Baylor launched a massive communitywide fund drive under the leadership of William H. Seay, president and chairman of the board of Southwestern Life Insurance Company. The proceeds would finance buildings for a cancer center, heart center and education center (later named in honor of oilman Harry W. Bass) and would allow the completion of the top three floors of the Collins Hospital, which had been set aside for expansion when the hospital originally opened. More than $7 million was eventually raised in the fund-raising drive—the original goal had been $4 million—and almost $750,000 of that amount was contributed by the Baylor medical staff, in a campaign headed by urologist, Dr. Elgin W. Ware Jr.

Sammons Cancer Center

As the fund-raising drive began in April 1976, the cancer center envisioned by Baylor was already well on its way to reality. Charles A. Sammons, the largest single contributor in Medical Center history, had already given $1 million as a "challenge gift" toward the new facility's construction, and a site had been selected next to the Collins Hospital on Junius Street. By January 1977, the five-story Charles A. Sammons Cancer Center was receiving its first patients.

The man whose philanthropy paved the way for the center was born at Ardmore, Oklahoma, in 1898, when it was still Indian Territory. Orphaned at age 12 and sent to live with an aunt at Plano, near Dallas, Sammons earned his keep doing farm chores and odd jobs. At 19, after organizing a successful laundry business at Plano, he moved to Dallas to become a hay and grain merchant, and has been self-employed ever since. He went broke twice and had to start over, but in 1928, he entered the insurance business, forming a mutual company with two partners. Ten years later, he founded Reserve Life Insurance Company, which has grown into one of the giants of the local insurance industry, with diversified operations in such fields as

In January 1977, the Charles A. Sammons Cancer
Center, above, located adjacent to the Collins
Hospital at Baylor, was receiving its first patients.
The new center, which houses the Department of
Radiation Therapy, the Division of Medical Oncology-Hematology and the Division of Surgical Oncology, was built with a million-dollar challenge gift
from businessman Charles A. Sammons, right, and
other contributions from a community fund drive. In
the Department of Radiation Therapy, photos below,
radiotherapist Dr. Felix J. Vendrell, center, holds a
conference on a patient; the patient is then marked
by a dosimetrist at the point where the radiation is to
be given; and treatment is administered on one of
several therapy units at the center.

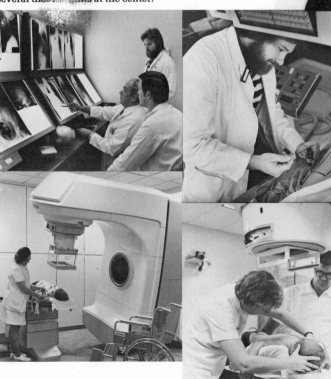

241

advertising, printing, radio stations, travel, oil field equipment, imports and hotels.

As a businessman, Sammons demonstrated his ability to see potential in uncultivated fields time and again. As a philanthropist, he is unassuming and tends to downplay his contributions. He became interested in health care through his company's hospitalization insurance program, and says: "When I made my initial gift to Baylor, I had no personal experience with cancer, but later two of my sisters died with malignancies. I don't deserve any particular credit for the charitable corporate gifts. They're probably on the low side of what they should be."

For more than three decades before the new cancer center was completed, Baylor had provided an extensive program of diagnosis and treatment of tumors, made possible largely through Sammons' generosity. But during the 1970s, it became increasingly apparent that cancer patients could receive even better care if all the specialists dealing with the disease and the technological equipment used to treat it could be concentrated in a single facility. With this in mind, a committee of Baylor medical staff members and administrators was formed in May 1973 to begin planning what would become the Sammons Cancer Center, now a 51,440-square-foot building housing the Division of Radiation Therapy, the Division of Medical Oncology-Hematology and the Division of Surgical Oncology.

"We had no preconceived ideas of what the building should look like, and we could find no other comparable cancer centers to serve as models," noted Glen Clark, the administrator in charge of planning the project. "The departments analyzed their space requirements and the architect developed proposed layouts that were revised and approved by both the medical specialists and the planning committee."

Dr. Marvin J. Stone, an associate professor of internal medicine at the University of Texas

Southwestern Medical School and a specialist in oncology and hematology, was named director of the center. A graduate of the University of Chicago School of Medicine, he served an internal medicine residency at Barnes Hospital in St. Louis and at Parkland. After additional training at the National Institutes of Health at Bethesda, Maryland, and Southwestern Medical School, Dr. Stone remained on the faculty at Southwestern, where he distinguished himself in the fields of hematology, medical oncology and immunology. At Baylor, he also serves as chief of oncology and director of immunology, and is the first individual in Medical Center history to hold these posts. The author of 35 scientific papers on cancer, Dr. Stone continues to serve at Southwestern Medical School as a clinical professor of internal medicine.

As a comprehensive diagnostic and treatment facility, the Sammons Cancer Center offers a "multidisciplinary approach" to patient care, in which various specialists pool their knowledge to plan the best possible course of treatment for each patient. Besides consolidating resources for cancer patients, the center also offers community and regional programs of cancer detection education, research and education programs in coordination with the University of Texas Health Science Center and other institutions, new clinical research projects in the cancer treatment field, and consultation and evaluation for patients referred to the center by private physicians. In addition, the center provides vital training programs for health care professionals—physicians, residents and medical students—in cancer diagnosis and treatment. "The value of the team approach in cancer care has become clearly evident during the past decade, particularly in certain blood cancers such as Hodgkin's disease and acute leukemia," Dr. Stone says. "Many patients with these diseases are alive and well years after the discontinuation of treatment, and it is felt that the multidisciplinary approach will pay handsome dividends for persons with other types of cancer, too."

At Baylor, Dr. Richard E. Collier has watched the evolution of cancer diagnosis and treatment since the early 1950s, when he served his radiology residency there and later became director of nuclear medicine. Today, he serves as director of the Division of Radiation Therapy, a post he has held since 1967. "While much of the public still looks upon radiation therapy as a last resort, this is far from the truth," he says. "It is the prime treatment for some cancers, is also used before and after surgery to enhance surgical treatment, and to relieve such symptoms as pain, hemorrhage or cough in patients who are incurable. There's a great deal of satisfaction in helping people prolong their useful lives. Some patients I treated when I was a resident here have come back for their 20-year checkups."

An average of 150 patients per day are examined and treated in the Charles and Elizabeth Prothro Department of Radiation Therapy on the first floor of the Sammons Center, where the equipment is far more sophisticated and techniques far more precise than they were when Dr. Collier first began his Baylor career. When today's patient receives radiation therapy, his treatment plan is set up with the aid of a computer and a treatment simulator, allowing doctors to determine at exactly what point in the body the radiation should be delivered in order to be most effective. Depending on the type and extent of the disease, the patient is treated on one of a variety of machines using cobalt, cesium, 250-kilovolt x-rays and 150-kilovolt x-rays. Equipment in the department also includes a four-million-volt linear accelerator donated by Fort Worth businessman, Lee Paulsel, and his wife, Patricia, as well as the only 18-million-volt linear accelerator in North Texas, made possible by a gift from Wichita Falls businessman Charles Prothro and his wife, Elizabeth. The latter machine is especially effective in treating either large sections of the body or tumors located in deep or inaccessible spots, since it can penetrate deeply without harming healthy body tissues or treat wide surfaces without penetrating underlying organs. More than 70 truckloads of concrete were used to build the fortress-like structure that houses the huge machine, with walls up to seven feet thick shielding its radiation emissions.

In the Division of Medical Oncology-Hematology on the second floor of the center, patients with cancer and blood diseases receive chemotherapy. In keeping with the multidisciplinary approach, this type of treatment with chemical compounds is often administered in combination with radiation therapy or following surgery. Heading the division is Dr. Merrick Reese, a consulting hematologist and oncologist at Baylor since 1967. Ten years ago, Dr. Reese says he worked under a double handicap—using only limited tools and seeing patients only after their disease had reached an advanced stage. Now, however, with the advancements in cancer treatment represented in the Sammons Center, Dr. Reese can say confidently: "Cure is now a realistic expectation in many patients." This specialized division has received $100,000 in support from the Leukemia Association of North Central Texas.

The Division of Surgical Oncology, specializing in the removal of both benign and malignant tumors, is located on the center's third floor and is headed by Dr. Billie L. Aronoff, a specialist in surgical oncology for 36 years. It is equipped with two treatment rooms for minor surgical procedures, five examining rooms, special chairs for examination of the head and neck areas, tables designed for pelvic and rectal examinations and a recovery suite.

Dr. Aronoff's interest in cancer treatment dates back to 1942, when surgical oncology was a challenging new field and cancer was not yet recognized as the massive health threat it is today (the second leading cause of death among diseases in the U.S., with 365,000 fatalities per year). After first joining Baylor in 1941, Dr. Aronoff served in World War II, during which progress in surgical oncology was greatly accelerated by new techniques, and returned to Baylor in 1945. Within his division at the Sammons Center, he and his staff have at their disposal today revolutionary equipment that was undreamed of in the 1940s—machines such as the colposcope, nasopharyngoscope and colonoscope, all of which enable a surgeon to look inside the human body and perform a biopsy to obtain tissue for examination without making an incision.

On the fourth and fifth floors of the center are an immunology laboratory, a skin testing laboratory and other facilities. The basement contains a computerized medical records department and a machine shop where special treatment devices for patients are fabricated. In addition to providing educational, research and patient services, the center also hosts frequent medical conferences. A Tumor Registry with complete, continuing records of all cancer patients treated at Baylor is also maintained at the center to allow evaluation of the long-term results of treatment.

Hunt Heart Center

Less than a year after the official opening of the Sammons Center, Baylor dedicated another specialized medical facility—this one for heart disease, the number one cause of death in the United States and either a primary or secondary diagnosis for more than 6,500 patients entering Baylor each year.

Made possible by a substantial gift from Hunt Oil Company and members of the family of the late H. L. Hunt, the facility was named the H. L. and Ruth Ray Hunt Heart Center. It occupies the first three floors of the Wadley Tower in the Baylor Medical Plaza and provides a comprehensive approach to the diagnosis, treatment and rehabilitation of patients with a wide range of cardiac diseases.

Although he was born in Illinois, the colorful Hunt became a living symbol of the Texas oil millionaire after he became one of the world's wealthiest individuals as a result of the East Texas oil boom of the 1930s. A self-made man who had worked as a cowboy, lumberjack and laborer, Hunt became a nervy, gambling "wildcatter" after he saw his first oil well in 1921, trading in oil leases and drilling his own exploratory wells. Among the first to realize the vast potential of the huge East Texas field, Hunt bought the Daisy Bradford No. 3 in Rusk County, Texas, in 1930, using a new method of financing he had devised himself. That well became the discovery well of the then richest petroleum pool on earth, and, by the time of his death in 1974, Hunt had become one of the most famous figures of the Twentieth Century.

His unpretentious wife, Ruth, who has remained active in Hunt Oil Company since her husband's death, also served quietly for years as a Medical Center volunteer, working as a hostess at the information desk in the Truett Hospital and staying overtime with hospital chaplains to visit the sick and lonely. "There is no reason for anyone to become bored with life when there are so many needs to be met," Mrs. Hunt says. "I loved working in a hospital as much as anything I've ever done. If I had my life to live over again, I'd be a nurse." The gift that made the Hunt Heart Center possible will benefit more patients by far, however, than Mrs. Hunt could ever have helped personally as a nurse.

Director of the heart center is Dr. John W. Hyland, a graduate of the Washington University School of Medicine in St. Louis who came to Baylor in 1962 after serving a research fellowship in cardiology at Harvard Medical School. Under his leadership, the Department of Cardiology was organized at that time, and, since then, its history has been one of outstanding progress in the treatment of heart disease. In 1967, when Baylor's coronary care unit first opened, it had only four beds; today, it has 15, plus an additional 12 beds in a post-coronary care unit established in 1972 for the intermediate care of heart patients between the critical and rehabilitative stages of their illness. Since 1963, the number of electrocardiograms, the most basic test to determine the patterns of electrical impulses produced by the heart, has increased from 12,000 to more than 43,000 annually, and the number of cardiac catheterizations has risen from 116 to almost 1,500 per year.

Just 15 years ago, according to Dr. Hyland, a diagnosis of heart disease consisted primarily of a physician listening to a patient's chest, looking at his electrocardiogram and saying, "I believe it's so and so." And after the diagnosis, treatment possibilities were extremely limited. "But now," he says, "technological advancements allow precise diagnosis and effective treatment in a high percentage of even the most difficult cases."

It was, in fact, technology coupled with larger and larger patient loads that made it necessary several years before the heart center opened to appoint a task force to chart the future of Baylor's entire cardiac treatment program. Out of this task force of physicians, surgeons and administrators came the proposal in 1974 that a separate center be established with the objectives of providing more and better diagnostic care and facilities, offering uniform care for many types of cardiac patients, coordinating and unifying diagnostic procedures, maintaining careful statistics on various cardiovascular conditions, enhancing possibilities for clinical research by properly supporting dedicated scientists and technologists and providing expertise in the development of medical electronics and computer technology.

In recent years, spin-off technology from space exploration and nuclear experiments has greatly influenced the progress of diagnostic medicine, and many of the resulting breakthroughs are much in evidence at the Hunt Heart Center. Exercise tolerance (treadmill) tests are administered in three specially equipped laboratories donated in memory of Melville S. Rose by his wife, Jeannette Rose, a long-time Baylor volunteer who underwent coronary bypass surgery for heart disease on April 2, 1970. Because of a family history of heart-damaging rheumatic fever, Mrs. Rose's primary medical interest has been heart disease, its prevention and treatment.

Other testing procedures at the center include echocardiography, a technique that sends ultra high-frequency sound waves through the heart to reveal lesions in its valves and chambers; vectorcardiography, a "stereo version" of the electrocardiogram that records the electrical stimulus triggering the heartbeat in three dimensions instead of one; phonocardiography, which records pulse, electrocardiogram and heart sounds simultaneously, and the Holter monitor, a portable device that can be worn constantly by a patient to detect irregular heartbeats, fainting spells or latent heart disease.

The second floor of the center houses the largest cardiac catheterization facility in North Texas, where as many as 16 procedures can be performed each day in two surgical suites funded by the Hillcrest Foundation of Dallas. Catheterization is a surgical procedure in which a long, flexible catheter is passed into the heart via a vein or artery to measure pressure and obtain blood samples. In a related procedure known as angiocardiography, opaque dye is injected into the heart through the catheter while high-speed x-ray film records its passage to detect valve damage, blood vessel disorders or other defects that may require open heart surgery. While the entire procedure is usually done in a single operating room, Baylor has expedited the process by using three rooms in each surgical suite. Simultaneously, while one patient is in the operating room, another is being prepared for surgery and still another is having his surgical incision repaired. For each patient, the whole procedure usually takes about an hour and a half, but only about 30 minutes is actually spent in the operating room.

The cardiac rehabilitation unit on the center's third floor, where a scientifically formulated program helps cardiac patients to return to productive life, was made possible through contributions by Mr. and Mrs. I. A. Victor. The Victors provide another example of heart center donors who have a personal interest in the conquest of heart disease. Both have been patients at Baylor so often that they refer to it as their "home away from home," and Victor, a patient of Dr. Hyland's since 1966, knows about the need for rehabilitation himself. "When I was scheduled to take an exercise stress test after my surgery, I was very apprehensive and agreed to do it only if my physician would be right there with me," Victor recalls. "Because he was there, I relaxed and the test went well. That was when the idea of cardiac rehabilitation with medical supervision impressed me."

In the rehabilitative program, patients are supervised by a physician, Dr. Walter Berman, and benefit from the expertise of a rehabilitation team consisting of an exercise physiologist, chaplain-counselor, dietitian, physical therapist and occupational therapist. Lil Stewart, the exercise physiologist, is the supervisor of the unit, which is equipped with stationary bicycle ergometers, motor-driven treadmills and a telemetry system which is used to monitor each patient's heart rate and electrocardiogram during an exercise session.

As the first fully computerized medical facility in the region, the Hunt Heart Center, which is directly connected to the first and second floors of the Hoblitzelle Hospital, also houses a pacemaker clinic where patients can receive periodic checkups. These checkups can be done either in person or by

In 1977, Baylor opened the H. L. and Ruth Ray Hunt Heart Center, which was made possible by a substantial gift from the Hunt Oil Company and the family of H. L. Hunt, above. Among those present at the dedication on September 25, 1977, were Boone Powell, left, Ruth Hunt and her son, Ray Hunt.

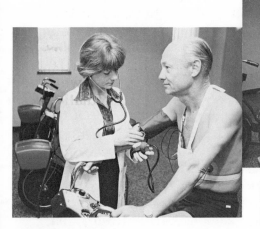

Mr. and Mrs. I. A. Victor, above, were the financial benefactors for the rehabilitation unit of the H. L. and Ruth Ray Hunt Heart Center. At left, Lil Stewart, the unit's exercise physiologist, checks the blood pressure for businessman Jack G. Smith, who was the first coronary bypass surgery patient at Baylor in the 1960s.

Charles Bruton, right photo, at left, unit manager for National Data Communications, Inc., and Howard Chase discuss the installation of the VITAL System, above.

telephone from home via a specially designed transmitter that reproduces the patient's electrocardiogram at the clinic. More than 250 permanent pacemakers, which stimulate the heart through electrical impulses, are inserted each year in Baylor's catheterization laboratories.

Besides its other functions, the center serves as a source for gathering research data to help physicians evaluate various kinds of treatment with large numbers of patients. This capability is the result of a gift from the Harry S. Moss Trust Fund for the establishment of an electronic data base, where information on cardiac diagnostic and treatment procedures is automatically accumulated. An independent oil operator who came to Texas from his native Canada after World War I, Moss, too, had a personal interest in combating heart disease. Moss made numerous contributions to Dallas medical institutions after suffering a heart attack in 1948. When he died in 1970, his will placed a major portion of his estate in a trust fund designated for heart research. His widow, Florence M. Moss, is trustee for the fund.

With the opening of the Hunt Heart Center, Baylor also opened a physical conditioning center, featuring exercise equipment, sauna, whirlpool, steam room and a jogging track on the third floor of the Medical Plaza. The center serves three main groups— post-cardiac patients who have completed rehabilitation, persons wishing to rebuild muscle strength following injury and healthy individuals who wish to build or maintain physical fitness.

Arthritis Center

On February 15, 1977, Baylor's board approved the establishment of a third specialized treatment center—this one for arthritis, the crippling disease of adults that affects seven per cent of all patients coming to the Medical Center for all types of ailments.

While it is not the killer that cancer and heart disease are, arthritis is the nation's number one crippler of working-age Americans, affecting at least 20 million people, including about 250,000 children. In Dallas County alone, it has been estimated that arthritis costs $87 million per year in medical bills and lost wages and causes its victims to miss 31,300 days of work annually. By some other estimates, up to half the nation's total population shows some symptoms of some form of arthritis. Ten cents out of every dollar spent nationally on medical care is spent to fight arthritis— which isn't actually a single disease but up to 100 separate disorders informally categorized under one catch-all term.

To effectively tackle the enormity of the arthritis problem, the Arthritis Center will be staffed by rheumatologists when the facility opens in late 1979, and will integrate a number of other specialties, including orthopedics, surgery, radiology and physical medicine, in the treatment of arthritic patients.

In the past, Baylor has more than kept pace with the many recent advances in the treatment of arthritis. Each of its five staff rheumatologists holds a clinical faculty appointment at Southwestern Medical School. The arthritis treatments administered by these specialists and by the orthopedic surgeons who also serve the Arthritis Center may range from a variety of drugs to complex joint replacement surgery.

A special Arthritis Committee, meanwhile, coordinates efforts between the departments of orthopedics, surgery, radiology, rheumatology and physical medicine at Baylor in order to give arthritis patients the most comprehensive treatment possible. A team of rehabilitation specialists under Dr. E. M. Krusen also combines its talents to help get patients back on their feet after surgery or during drug therapy.

Virginia Chandler, Baylor's director of occupational therapy, lists four major steps in rehabilitating the arthritis patient so that he can return to gainful employment. First, each patient is evaluated to determine the level of normal daily functions he is able to maintain. Then personalized treatment is initiated with the dual purpose of preventing further deformity and rebuilding physical abilities. For this task, the patient has access to a complete workroom equipped with many types of tools and utensils. Next, the patient is advised of any job-related changes considered necessary, told how to alter his work procedures when required and directed to outside agencies for further assistance. Finally, an at-home program of extended treatment and assistance is made available to those who need it.

The labor of rehabilitation can be a fulltime job in itself, according to Georgiann Magnenat, director of Baylor's Hand Rehabilitation Unit, which began operating in March 1976 and now handles about 30 patients each day—some of whom spend 40 hours per week in therapy. The unit offers special exercises, paraffin baths, hot packs and other devices to relieve the arthritic's pain. It is one of only a half-dozen such units in the entire country and is helping establish Baylor as one of the nation's leading centers for the total treatment of arthritis—a position that will be greatly enhanced by the new Arthritis Center.

Computerization

In June, 1977, implementation began at the Medical Center on a new computerized patient care communication system, known as VITAL. Planning for this system had begun 20 years earlier when Baylor served as the site for the first official feasibility studies on the use of computers in hospitals. In those studies, sponsored by the American Hospital Association, Baylor's management identified the potential utilization of computers in the health care setting, and, as a result, all of the systems ultimately developed closely followed those specifications.

254

However, the installation of a computer system at Baylor had to await the development of equipment with much larger data storage capacity and faster means of retrieval, as well as new computer language technology.

Finally, in 1976, the VITAL system, developed by National Data Communications, Inc., was selected for the Medical Center, and a contract was signed with Honeywell, Inc., for its installation. It will require three years to program and install the entire system, although portions of it became operational in the summer of 1977. VITAL's purpose is to facilitate patient care by instant electronic communication of data on patients among the various departments involved in providing services.

In the Medical Center, there are computer terminals with television-like screens in 150 locations. When a patient registers at the admitting office, the initial entry on that patient is made into the computer. Throughout the patient's hospital stay, the data accumulates rapidly and is immediately and continuously available to the nursing unit and to other individuals and departments on a selective and controlled basis.

Physicians' orders are entered at the terminals located at the nursing stations, in the operating rooms and at other strategic points throughout the Medical Center. The orders are transmitted instantaneously to the appropriate diagnostic and therapeutic departments, thereby eliminating thousands of paper requisitions formerly prepared and handled each day. More importantly, if the details of the orders vary from certain predetermined standards and conditions, the computer will not accept them. This capability will be greatly enhanced in 1979-80 when the computer will be designed to monitor the appropriate dosages of medication and the interactions of medications with each other.

In addition, the computer speeds up the

performance of tests and treatments and, as a result, the accuracy and completeness of all aspects of patient care. This is essential at an institution like Baylor where distances between departments are so great and where patients receive services from so many separate specialized sources.

By the 1980s, Baylor's VITAL system will also be capable of producing sophisticated analyses of patient care data for use in medical and administrative research, opening up exciting new opportunities in this field.

XIV

The Age of Specialization

A Complex Science

Seventy-five years ago, as we have seen, medicine was a relatively simple science, one that had more in common with carpentry than with computers—even if there had been such a thing. Basically, there were physicians, and there were surgeons. Surgeons performed operations on whatever part of the anatomy required their attention, and physicians did everything else pertaining to the diagnosis and treatment of disease. In the larger towns, a few practitioners concentrated on a particular area of medicine, such as psychiatry or pediatrics. Here and there was an ob-gyn specialist or an eye, ear, nose and throat man. But for the most part, "Doc Jones" treated everything, from diarrhea to dropsy. In the very biggest cities, there may have been a handful of surgeons with enough training, skill and confidence to tackle thoracic or orthopedic surgery, but most of those in the field limited their efforts to performing appendectomies or amputating limbs.

Today, of course, all of this has changed. Fields that were once considered medical specialties in themselves have since been divided into many different types of specialization. Meanwhile, the diseases that afflict mankind most often—and, therefore, draw the most attention—have also changed drastically. Communicable diseases at which the thrust of medical knowledge was aimed for so long have been all but wiped out by new vaccines, antibiotics and other drugs. Gone from the scene are the scourges of diphtheria, typhoid, smallpox, yellow fever, polio and tuberculosis. In their place have arisen equally dread diseases rooted deep in the molecular structure, the genes, the psyche and the lifestyle of the patient. And even though these new diseases are non-communicable, they, too, have swept the country in epidemic proportions reminiscent of the influenza outbreak of 1918 or the summertime polio nightmares of the 1940s and 50s.

To combat the increasingly complex disorders of the human race, medical science has itself become more and more complex, until today it is less one identifiable science than a whole system of inter-related but separate sciences. The accumulation of medical knowledge has been so great that no one physician, no matter how intelligent or talented, can store it all in his mind. Even the surgeon has had to concentrate on a relatively small area of the body—in many instances on a single organ—in order to keep abreast of the advancements in procedures relating to that area. Specialization, in short, has been the only reasonable route for medical progress to follow.

In the process, hospitals, too, have had to divide their facilities into areas of highly specialized treatments and facilities. These do not stop with the major centers devoted to the most urgent physical problems of the period, such as cancer, heart disease and arthritis, but extend through every physical and organizational level of a giant medical complex like Baylor. Not all these specialties can be discussed here, but no book on Baylor would be complete without a brief look at some of the major ones and the men who have helped to develop them and refine them over the years into the exacting sciences they are today.

Thoracic Surgery

When Dr. Robert Shaw came to Dallas in 1938, fresh from residency training at University Hospital in

Ann Arbor, Michigan, to become the city's first thoracic surgeon, few people even knew what the term meant. Even if they had, the definition of thoracic surgery in the early 1930s was far different from what it is today. It still pertains to the chest—or thorax—but the purpose for which the thoracic surgeon operates now is much broader than what it was then. When Dr. Shaw first came to Baylor, thoracic surgery was confined mainly to patients suffering from tuberculosis and a few other lung disorders. Prior to his arrival, these conditions had been treated primarily at Baylor by two general surgeons, Dr. John V. Goode and Dr. H. Walton Cochran. Lung cancer, which has become so prevalent in the last few decades, was virtually unknown, and surgery for heart defects was beyond contemplation.

Because tuberculosis was highly contagious, hospitals were reluctant even to admit patients with the disease in those days, but Dr. Shaw was instrumental during his early years in Dallas in getting this situation changed, not only at Baylor, but at other local hospitals. But, as Dr. Shaw worked to improve conditions for TB patients, World War II began, interrupting his efforts from January 1942 until September 1945. During the war, he was stationed with the U.S. Army Medical Corps in Europe and was chief surgeon of a thoracic surgery center in Paris, France.

Back in Dallas, during the war years, a new kind of thoracic surgery, relating to the heart, was being performed by Dr. J. Warner Duckett, a general surgeon at Baylor. In the operations, known as patent ductus arteriosis, Dr. Duckett closed an opening between the aorta and the pulmonary artery, a congenital malformation found primarily in children.

By the time Dr. Shaw returned from overseas, Dr. John Chapman had joined the Baylor staff as a pulmonary specialist. Together, they were instrumental in establishing the city's first private hospital ward for tuberculosis patients at Baylor. The 14-bed ward—

un-air-conditioned, obviously, since there was practically no hospital air-conditioning at the time—was in a wing of the old Texas Baptist Memorial Sanitarium building, facing Hall Street. A dedicated nurse named Mary Mebane (her name in now Mary Beard, and she is a nurse in radiation therapy at Baylor) tended the patients there, undertaking a job that few nurses of her day would have risked. In 1949, the ward was moved to another un-air-conditioned area, but that same year, Leslie Sinclair, influential president of the Dallas Petroleum Club, happened to be a patient there. Mounting a massive telephone campaign from his hospital bed, Sinclair managed to raise enough money to have the ward air-conditioned.

During the 1940s, the practice of all types of surgery began to expand rapidly, aided by advances in anesthesiology. Before World War II, anesthesia had been administered through a face mask, but afterward, anesthesiologists used an endotracheal tube developed during wartime. This greatly improved the safety of operations, particularly those involving the chest cavity. Dr. Earl Weir, who became chief of anesthesiology at Baylor after the war, was already using the method when Dr. Shaw returned from service to become the hospital's first chief of thoracic surgery. In July 1946, Dr. Donald L. Paulson, whom Dr. Shaw had met at Brooke General Hospital in San Antonio, joined him in practice in Dallas, as thoracic surgery was beginning to become an increasingly important specialty. Dr. Paulson, who was to succeed Dr. Shaw as chief in 1962, had been chief of the thoracic surgery center at Brooke General Hospital.

An approved resident training program in thoracic surgery was established at Baylor in 1948 and later coordinated with Parkland Memorial Hospital under the auspices of Southwestern Medical School. Several members of the Baylor thoracic surgery staff and many practicing thoracic surgeons in the state were products of this training program.

By the close of the 1940s, patent ductus arteriosis and coarctation, a procedure to correct a congenital deformity causing a narrowing of the aorta, were becoming routine at Baylor. In 1950, Drs. Shaw and Paulson began performing an operation known as mitral commissurotomy, in which the mitral valve connecting the heart's left atrium with the left ventricle was opened after having been severely narrowed by the effects of rheumatic fever. At about the same time, Dr. Duckett began performing another type of surgery, known as Blalock-Taussig or "the blue baby operation," in which a congenital narrowing of the pulmonary artery was bypassed. In 1956, Drs. Shaw and Paulson pioneered an operation for removal of "pancoast tumors" in the upper part of the lung, which brought national and international recognition to the Baylor surgeons. The operation—a lung resection after pre-operative radiation therapy—increased the survival rate from a year to long-term survival in 40 per cent of selected cases. Under Dr. LeRoy J. Kleinsasser, director of Surgical Education, Baylor surgeons and residents also began experimenting in the 1950s with open heart surgical techniques and heart-lung machines that would come into common use within the decade of the Sixties.

The first open heart operation in Dallas took place on August 30, 1957, when Dr. Kleinsasser and Dr. Paul Ellis, who had done his surgical residency at Baylor, operated on a 14-year-old boy from Houston, using hypothermia, a cooling process that allowed the patient to tolerate a brief interruption of the circulatory system. The following April, the same team of surgeons performed the first successful open heart procedure at Baylor, using a heart-lung machine, as they repaired the defective heart of a 17-year-old girl. The first coronary bypass operation at Baylor was performed in 1968 by Dr. Ben Mitchel, now chief of thoracic surgery at the Medical Center.

Another Baylor thoracic surgeon, Dr. Maurice

Adam, did the first pacemaker implant in the Southwest on July 28, 1960, in a procedure that makes today's pacemaker operations seem simple by comparison. At the time, the pacemaker electrodes had to be sewn directly to the surface of the patient's heart. The wires were then brought through the chest wall and attached to an external pacemaker. Today's pacemakers are much smaller and are totally implanted within the chest cavity. Dr. Adam's success in that historic operation 18 years ago is evidenced by the fact that his patient is now the world's second longest survivor with a continuous pacemaker.

Dr. Mitchel vividly recalls the extremely difficult circumstances under which thoracic surgeons had to work, even as recently as the 1960s. "In the early days, we had only one heart-lung pump, and we had to transport it from the experimental lab to the operating room for each operation," he says. "One case was an all-day effort by everybody. We could only do about two open hearts a week, because we didn't have enough time in the operating room to do more than that. Now we have two operating rooms exclusively for thoracic surgery, and we can do as many as five heart operations a day. We also have three heart-lung pumps, one in each operating room and another on standby."

The last few decades also have given rise to large-scale advancements in life support services for Baylor's thoracic surgery patients, especially in the coronary intensive care unit, post-coronary care unit and other intensive care units throughout the Medical Center. If a patient develops an irregular heartbeat, a temporary pacemaker can be inserted to normalize the rate in a special room equipped with a fluoroscope, through which insertion and placement of the pacemaker can be viewed. If a patient has low blood pressure, is in cardiac shock or needs help to prevent further heart damage, an intra-aortic balloon pump can be used to decrease the workload of the patient's own heart and increase the flow of blood to the heart muscle. Or if a patient goes into cardiac arrest, a defibrillator can be used to start his heart beating again. Baylor's Emergency Department has also been equipped with most of the recently developed cardiac monitoring devices, emergency resuscitation equipment and treatment rooms for cardiac patients.

Orthopedics

The history of orthopedics, not only at Baylor but in the entire Southwest, began with Dr. W. B. Carrell, who first encountered orthopedic surgical methods in England during World War I, where he was stationed as an Army doctor. When he returned to Dallas after the war, he established an orthopedic clinic for crippled children with two other local physicians, Dr. P. M. Girard and Dr. Sim Driver. As the first head of orthopedics at Baylor, he was also instrumental in founding the Texas Scottish Rite Hospital for Crippled Children in the 1920s.

The term orthopedics is derived from a Greek word meaning "straight child," and, for many years, it was a specialty devoted primarily to crippled children, because most of the orthopedic problems in adults were considered beyond successful treatment. Many of the children who underwent orthopedic operations were victims of polio, and most of the surgery was performed free, until a federal law enacted under President Franklin D. Roosevelt provided funds to pay surgeons for this work.

In the years since Dr. Carrell's death in 1944, however, orthopedics has evolved into a complete specialty field that can help people of any age group, from childhood through old age, with any type of bone or joint injury. And many conditions that would have defied the skills of even the greatest surgeons of Dr. Carrell's era are now being corrected every day. At Baylor, approximately 3,000 orthopedic operations are performed annually, and orthopedic patients make up just over 12 per cent of all admissions to the Medical Center. Striking breakthroughs in surgical techniques and in the development of new materials have made possible total joint replacements of the hip, knee and elbow, allowing thousands who would have been hopeless cripples doomed to a life of bedridden invalidism a few years ago to walk out of the hospital unaided in a few short days.

One of the most important such breakthroughs is a procedure called Swanson's implant, which is now performed frequently and routinely at Baylor. It involves the implanting of spacers in the patient's hands in such a way that the bones are held apart while an entire new joint is formed to replace an old one hopelessly damaged by arthritis. Pioneered in Dallas by Dr. L. L. Lankford, the technique represents just one of many types of surgery now used to allow arthritis-crippled joints to function again.

Baylor's chiefs of orthopedics have included Dr. Felix Butte, Dr. Marvin Knight (now the team physician for the Dallas Cowboys), Dr. F. Leon Ware and, currently, Dr. B. Clyde Halley. Under their leadership, the department has flourished.

Urology

The father of the modern specialty of urology in the Southwest was Dr. Alfred I. Folsom, who established a general medical practice in Dallas in 1910 at about the same time the new Texas Baptist Memorial Sanitarium was getting into full operation, after receiving his M.D. degree two years earlier from Southwestern Medical College. By 1912, Dr. Folsom had become extremely interested in urology—or the study of "genito-urinary diseases," as it was known at the time—and he began studying at the Mayo Clinic and other centers where the specialty had been established. In those early years, urology usually dealt with the treatment of venereal diseases, as well as disorders of the kidney, bladder and prostate. Since there were no antibiotics to fight infections, the treatment usually consisted of using mild antiseptics to wash out the bladder and irrigate the kidneys. Malignancies of the prostate were sometimes treated surgically but without very good results. "I used to hate to see those patients come," says Dr. Harold O'Brien, who joined Dr. Folsom in practice in 1932. "There was so little we could do then, and now prostate cancer can be easily cured if it's caught early enough."

In the early 1930s, Baylor had only one operating room for cystoscopic studies of the bladder and prostate, which were done on a makeshift examining table. In 1934, however, the hospital acquired an especially-designed cystoscopic table and greatly improved its methods of diagnosis. But because there was no portable x-ray equipment at the time, patients had to be taken out of the operating room on the third floor of what is now the Veal building to the basement to have x-rays made. It was not until the 1940s that portable x-ray machines became available in the operating rooms.

Although surgical treatment for urological diseases was primitive in those years, Dr. Folsom strove to improve existing methods through research and strong training programs for aspiring urologists. Soon after World War II, Dr. Folsom helped to found the American Board of Urology, but a short time later, on October 3, 1946, he was killed in a tragic automobile accident at a time when he was serving both as chief of urology at Baylor and as president of the American Urological Society.

Dr. O'Brien, who had completed his residency in urology at Wisconsin General Hospital in Milwaukee, was appointed to succeed Dr. Folsom as chief of urology at Baylor. On his retirement in 1965, he was succeeded by Dr. Harry M. Spence, who had been a major force in strengthening educational programs in urology in Dallas. Dr. Spence served as chief at Baylor until 1970, at which time Dr. Foster Fuqua assumed the position. In 1977, Dr. William W. Hoffman became chief.

Through their efforts, urology grew from an unknown specialty to a major field of medicine at Baylor, where seven per cent of all current admissions are urology patients and where more than 2,600 urological surgeries are performed each year.

The latest innovation in the field at Baylor came in August 1978 with the opening of a new Urodynamics Laboratory in the Medical Plaza to serve both inpatients and outpatients. Equipped with a four-channel urodynamics testing device, the laboratory is used exclusively to assist urologists in diagnosing various disorders by measuring such vital functions as the flow of urine and the pressure in the bladder. Prior to the development of this equipment, diagnosis for most urological problems depended upon exploratory surgery.

Colon and Rectal Surgery

Dr. Curtice Rosser carried on a grand tradition at Baylor. Like his father, Dr. Charles M. Rosser, whose determined efforts led to the establishment of a medical school in Dallas in 1900 and indirectly to the founding of Texas Baptist Memorial Sanitarium three years later, the younger Dr. Rosser was a pioneer. He was the first physician in Dallas to specialize in what was then called proctology—colon and rectal surgery. In 1947, as chief of colon and rectal surgery at Baylor, he established a residency program in the specialty that made it one of the earliest such programs in the United States.

Because of Dr. Curtice Rosser and the program he set up, the Colon and Rectal Service at Baylor developed rapidly and other eminent proctologists were attracted to the Medical Center. That growth has continued under Dr. Alvin Baldwin, who succeeded Dr. Rosser as chief and served in the position from 1961 to 1970, and Dr. Wallace Bailey, the current chief. With almost 1,200 colon and rectal surgeries performed annually, Baylor is believed to rank second in the nation in such procedures.

One of the major current interests of the department is the use of an automatic suturing instrument for end-to-end anastomosis, a new technique in colon resection which reduces the time required for the surgery by about 45 minutes and appears to decrease the risks involved in this type of operation. Members of the Baylor department are assisting the manufacturer of the instrument in studies designed to further refine the techniques and assess the results.

Neurosurgery

In the 1930s, the developing art of neurosurgery was synonymous, at least insofar as Dallas was concerned, with one man—Dr. Albert P. D'Errico. He came to Baylor in 1932 from University Hospital in New Haven, Connecticut, as the city's first specialized neurosurgeon. Before that, all neurological surgery in Dallas had been done primarily by general surgeons.

Upon his arrival at Baylor, Dr. D'Errico, who had received his M.D. degree from Western Reserve University Medical School in his hometown of Cleveland, was less than impressed with what he found. "The neurosurgical facilities were poor, and the aseptic techniques seriously lacking," he says. As an illustration, he recalls one incident that took place while he was removing a brain tumor. Suddenly, a delivery boy in a white jacket appeared at the open door of the operating room with bottled soft drinks tucked in all his pockets and nonchalantly asked if anyone wanted one. He then handed the drinks to the circulating nurse for those who requested them, made change and left. "I just gulped," Dr. D'Errico remembers.

Because neurosurgery was such a new specialty in Dallas, neither patients nor their families readily realized the serious and delicate nature of brain and spinal operations. On one occasion, Dr. D'Errico had just removed a brain tumor and was gratified to note after the operation was completed that the patient was doing extremely well. When he reported this good news to the man's wife, her response was, "Oh good. Can I take him home now?"

Despite the primitive conditions under which Dr. D'Errico began his practice at Baylor, the specialty began to grow rapidly under his leadership. Over the years, the various testing procedures used to detect brain and spinal lesions improved tremendously, and many conditions were alleviated by neurosurgery as techniques became more reliable and surgical results more predictable.

In the early 1930s, tests to determine the location of lesions in the spinal column consisted mainly of injections of "Lipiodol," an opaque oil, directly into the spine, following which x-rays were made. Unfortunately, the oil was very heavy and was not always as easy to remove as it was to inject. But in the 1940s, "Lipiodol" was replaced by "Pantopaque," a radiopaque substance that was easily removed and served as a much better contrast medium for x-rays. Later, the development of electromyography provided additional valuable information on peripheral nerve involvement with spinal lesions.

Other tests available in the 1930s that were of particular value in localization of intracranial tumors included ventriculograms, in which air was injected directly into the ventricles of the brain; and encephalograms, in which air was injected into the spinal fluid spaces by spinal puncture. By the mid-1930s, cerebral angiography was being developed. It later proved to be useful in locating aneurysms, vascular malformations, vascular occlusions and intracranial tumors. With the early procedures, the carotid artery in the neck was exposed surgically, and a radiopaque substance was injected directly into the artery. X-rays were made during the injection. Later, the radiopaque substance was injected into the artery with a needle. Angiography was well-tolerated by patients, where air studies had sometimes disturbed the intracranial pressure relationships in the brain. By the 1940s, electroencephalography had become available as a diagnostic tool, although it was not entirely reliable from a surgical standpoint, and in the 1950s, an entirely different technique known as brain scanning was introduced. Brain scanning utilized radionuclides, which were injected into a vein and became selectively deposited in abnormal areas of the brain.

In the 1930s, there were few procedures available for the treatment of head injuries or lesions of the brain and spinal cord. The most common treatment for a head wound was the application of iodine to its exposed surface. Bone fragments were removed only when they presented themselves obviously. Dr. D'Errico introduced newer neurosurgical management to Dallas, however, which included irrigation of the wound with normal saline solution and removal of dead tissue. Small bone fragments buried deep within the brain were removed with suction and irrigation, and large fragments were wired in place when possible.

Prior to the discovery of penicillin in the 1940s, brain abscesses and other infections were treated surgically. Brain abscesses were usually the result of extension of infection from the sinuses or middle ear into the brain. The size and location of the abscess could be determined by the injection of a radiopaque material into the abscess cavity. After repeated aspirations, the abscess was removed surgically. Treatment for osteomyelitis of the skull, also an infection, involved extensive removal of bone, usually with repeated operations. With the advent of penicillin, however, brain abscesses, osteomyelitis and other infections have been rarely seen.

Brain tumors, another common problem faced by neurosurgeons of the era, were ordinarily treated with rather discouraging results, but new surgical techniques were constantly being developed with increasing success. In the early years, neurosurgeons attempted complete removal of one type of tumor, known as "medulloblastoma," which occurs primarily in early childhood. This radical surgery usually resulted in an extremely high post-operative mortality rate. However, the procedure was later altered, removing only enough tumor to restore the flow of cerebral spinal fluid through the affected area. This was then followed by x-ray therapy, since the "medulloblastoma" is particularly susceptible to radiation. Because of this change, the post-operative mortality rate dropped markedly. "Cerebellar astrocytoma," another tumor of childhood, is characterized usually by a cyst with an associated tumor nodule. With removal of the nodule and as much of the cyst as possible, many patients could be cured. There was an even higher rate of cure with "hemangioblastoma," another cerebellar tumor also associated with a nodule and cyst formation.

In the early 1940s, Dr. D'Errico reported a series of patients suffering with "meningioma of the cerebellar fossa," a tumor which attaches itself to the large sinuses. With modification of a previous surgical approach in which only a portion of the tumor was excised, complete removal was achieved in all cases in the series. While there were two post-operative fatalities, eight patients survived with little or no disability. This represented a marked improvement over other reports.

During his 43-year tenure at Baylor, Dr. D'Errico operated on more than 1,000 brain tumors. The most common of these was "glioblastoma multiforme," which comprises about 25 per cent of all cases.

Despite many types of treatment used over the years, the survival period for patients with this tumor, is still measured in months. But with modification of treatment other forms of tumors showed more gratifying results. A particular example is the "pinealoma," located in the posterior portion of the third ventricle of the brain. In a 1960 study of 14 cases at Baylor, a ventriculocisternostomy (a bypass to relieve fluid blockage in the brain) was done in all cases with symptoms of obstruction. Complete removal was done in two cases. Twelve cases were treated only with x-ray therapy. In considering the entire group of cases, it was found that the treatment of choice was x-ray therapy with a ventriculocisternostomy for relief of pressure. At the time the study was published, one patient had died six months after surgery when the tumor spread to other locations, but thirteen patients were doing well with no evidence of recurrence.

Since the 1930s, there have been many changes in the treatment of pituitary tumors. The standard intracranial operation has been replaced in many instances by a "transphenoidal" approach, in which the tumors are removed through the nose. Cryogenic destruction (freezing) of the pituitary gland has also been employed in a procedure called "hypophysectomy," which is done for the treatment of certain malignancies of the body. It can also be used for small pituitary tumors.

Through the years, operations for congenital malformations in newborns became increasingly utilized. One such defect, craniostenosis, results when the sutures of the skull become fused, thus restricting the growth of the head. In correcting the defect, a small strip of bone is removed along the involved suture lines, and a strip of polyethylene is sutured to the bone to prevent re-fusion. If the patient is operated on before six months of age, marked improvement is usually accomplished in the growth and shape of the head. Spina bifida, another congenital malformation, was often treated by neurosurgeons. This condition is characterized by a sac, containing nerve root elements and abnormal spinal cord tissue, that overlies a defect in the vertebrae. In such cases, the sac is removed, sparing the nerve elements, and muscle flaps are then used to cover the defect in the spinal column. Another condition, Arnold-Chiari malformation, is usually associated with spina bifida. With the malformation, the medulla of the brain is elongated and extends into the upper part of the neck. This malformation is surrounded by scar tissue, which causes an obstruction of spinal fluid and results in hydrocephalus. Treatment for this condition, reported in 1938 by Dr. D'Errico, consists of removal of bone overlying the lower most part of the skull and the adjacent vertebrae. The scar tissue is then dissected free, and the compression caused by the obstruction is alleviated.

By the 1930s, considerable progress had also been made in pain-relieving techniques. "Retrogasserian section" was fairly well developed for relief of trigeminal neuralgia, a condition characterized by sharp, shooting pains in the face. The technique involves the selective surgical severance of the sensory root, sparing the nerve fibers to the forehead and cornea in the eye. A similar condition, "glossopharyngeal neuralgia," is also relieved by intracranial severance of the nerve. Cordotomy, which brings relief from pain in the lower part of the body, is performed by cutting the "spinothalamic," or pain-carrying, fibers in the spinal cord. Over the years, the procedure was refined by various neurosurgeons and was changed from an open surgical procedure to a closed one known as "stereotaxic cordotomy." With the closed technique, a needle is inserted into the spinothalamic tract with x-ray guidance. By the 1940s, another pain-relieving technique, "intramedullary spinothalamic tractotomy," was utilized, which partially alleviated pain in the neck, when the spinothalamic tract was severed in the medulla of the brain. In 1949, however, Dr. D'Errico reported that by careful extension of the incision in the medulla, complete relief of pain in the neck could be accomplished.

In the mid-1950s, with the advent of hypothermia, surgery on aneurysms, vascular malformations and tumors was greatly improved. With the lowered body temperatures produced by the cooling-down process of hypothermia, cellular metabolism in the body was decreased, allowing the temporary interruption of blood circulation. With this technique, more thorough operations could be done with reduced mortality and disability.

Up until the mid-1940s, Dr. D'Errico was the only neurosurgeon practicing at Baylor, but by the early 1950s, there were five neurosurgeons on the staff. There were also two operating rooms, instead of the original one that had been designated for neurosurgery. And as the number of surgeons and operating rooms grew, the number of patients grew accordingly.

In 1965, when Dr. D'Errico retired as chief of neurosurgery, Dr. Charles M. Wilson assumed the position. Dr. Wilson, a graduate of Tulane Medical School who had done his neurosurgery residency at the University of Michigan at Ann Arbor, had joined Dr. D'Errico in practice in 1950 and had become a member of the Baylor staff at that time. During Dr. Wilson's tenure, diagnostic and surgical techniques have changed dramatically, and the department has continued to grow until there are now 14 neurosurgeons on the Baylor staff, performing more than 700 operations a year.

Today, a neuroradiologist does most of the diagnostic procedures, rather than the neurosurgeon performing the tests himself. The primary method of diagnosis is the use of the EMI brain scanner, purchased in 1974, which can produce a computerized x-ray of the entire head, showing abscesses,

Dr. Abner V. McCall, president of Baylor University, presents an honorary Doctor of Laws Degree to Dr. Milford O. Rouse, an early-day gastroenterologist in Dallas and former president of the AMA.

Dr. Charles L. Austin, who died in April, 1975, organized the first kidney dialysis treatment unit at Baylor in the mid-1960s.

Dr. Donald L. Paulson, thoracic surgeon at Baylor, has received international recognition for his surgical techniques in the treatment of lung cancer.

The late Dr. H. Frank Carman was the first pulmonary medicine specialist in Dallas.

Dr. Ruth Jackson, below, was the first woman to be certified by the American Board of Orthopedic Surgery. She is shown in this 1973 photo with orthopedic residents, Dr. Peter Carter, left; Dr. Joel Q. Peavyhouse and Dr. Douglas L. Gamburg. Dr. Carter, now on the Baylor staff, specializes in hand surgery.

The late Dr. W. B. Carrell was the first orthopedic surgeon in Dallas.

Dr. Albert P. D'Errico was the first well-trained neurosurgeon to come to the Dallas area.

The late Dr. Curtice Rosser, left, first proctologist in Dallas, and Adolph Weinberger, benefactor of the Weinberger Endocrine Laboratory, were honored by the medical staff in 1961.

Dr. LeRoy J. Kleinsasser, above, performed the first open heart surgery in Dallas with the late Dr. Paul Ellis.

The late Dr. J. Warner Duckett, a general surgeon, performed the first heart operations in Dallas.

Dr. Robert Shaw, below, was the first thoracic surgeon in Dallas.

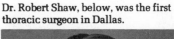

The late Dr. Ted Mills was the first plastic surgeon in Dallas.

collections of pus, tumors and the size of the brain's ventricles. Angiography, which is now done by injecting a radiopaque substance through a catheter into the femoral artery in the groin, is still used to supplement the scanner, which does not always show certain blood vessel conditions. In addition, pain-relieving techniques are usually performed by percutaneous (with a needle) radiofrequency currents, rather than by surgery.

The most significant advance in neurosurgical techniques in recent years has been the development of microsurgery. With improvements in optical design, unknown in the 1930s, binocular magnification, improved lighting with high intensity "cold" light, and extremely fine, delicate micro-instruments, a whole new era of neurosurgical procedures has opened up. Operations considered impossible or too hazardous in the 1930s are becoming routine, and older established operations are being done with less morbidity and mortality.

The revival of older abandoned procedures includes "transphenoidal hypophysectomy," the direct approach to pineal tumors, other tumors in the third ventricle, and "medulloblastomas" (in which some permanent cures have been obtained from a previously hopeless condition).

The operating microscope has given new impetus to the transphenoidal operations on the pituitary, so that now very small tumors (detected only by their hormonal effects) can be removed without destroying the entire gland which is itself about the size of a Boston baked bean.

Aneurysm surgery has been greatly improved with the use of the microscope. Small, but important arteries, almost invisible to the naked eye, can be spared. Adjacent structures can be seen with clarity and detail, allowing more precise placement of clips on the "neck" of the aneurysm. Even the clips are better.

276

An additional bonus of the operating microscope is the ability to "televise" the magnified field, projecting the image in a natural color on a screen, or "monitor," in the operating room. For the first time, the nurse, assistant, consultant or student can see exactly what is going on while the operation is in progress.

In addition to the miscrosurgery, micro-vascular surgery is gaining in recognition, as small arteries of the brain are given new circulation in certain stroke patients, by direct connection to extra cranial arteries, much like the "jump-graft" surgery of the heart, where new blood vessels bypass obstructions in the coronary arteries.

Many of the improvements in neurosurgical techniques are the results of the improved technology of engineering, pharmacological, biochemical, electronic, metallurgical, and other related fields. For example, the development of a siliconized rubber compound, well tolerated by body tissues, has opened avenues in the development of superior shunting devices which have made possible great improvements in ventricular shunts, with better results and simpler procedures. Fiber-optic lighting, battery operated power drills, electronic monitoring and telemetry, bipolar electrosurgical hemostasis, implantable platinum electrodes, transcutaneous nerve stimulators, pressure transducers are but a few of the technological developments available to the ever expanding field of neurosurgery at Baylor University Medical Center.

Plastic Surgery

The foremost pioneer in the then-new field of plastic surgery in Dallas was Dr. James Theodore "Ted" Mills, who came to the city in 1932 after receiving his M.D. degree from the University of Minnesota, interning at the Washington Boulevard Hospital in

Chicago and training with the renowned Dr. Ferris Smith in Grand Rapids, Michigan. In 1937, he became head of plastic surgery at Baylor and served in that post until 1965.

In the late 1930s, Dr. Mills also served as a diplomate of the American Board of Plastic Surgery, being certified as one of the founders of the organization. He had also become a member of the American Association of Plastic Surgeons in 1934, when that group was only three years old, and later served as its president in 1948. In addition, he was one of the earliest members of the American Society of Plastic and Reconstructive Surgeons, serving as its president in 1952-53.

During his years at Baylor, he became an outstanding national leader in his field, serving as an associate editor of *Plastic and Reconstructive Surgery* and as chairman of the Division of Plastic Surgery and a professor of plastic surgery at Southwestern Medical School. In 1962, he received a special honorary citation from the American Society of Plastic and Reconstructive Surgeons, and in 1973, just a year before his death, he was honored by the State Department of Health for his work as chief technical adviser on the problems of crippled children in Texas. He also received a citation for meritorious service as an officer in the U.S. Naval Reserve during World War II.

In 1965, upon Dr. Mills' retirement, he was succeeded as chief of plastic surgery at Baylor by Dr. Dean C. Kipp, who had received his M.D. degree from Kansas University in 1943 and served a preceptorship in plastic surgery under Dr. Mills from 1949 to 1951. At Baylor, he carried on and expanded upon the tradition established by Dr. Mills. As one associate put it: "It was Dr. Mills who gave birth to plastic surgery in North Texas, and Dr. Kipp who nurtured it into a multispecialty field."

The plastic surgery performed routinely today was undreamed of when Dr. Mills first came to Dallas.

During his career, the primary operations were for congenital anomalies such as cleft palate. But today's procedures include craniofacial surgery, microvascular surgery and major head and neck reconstruction. There are now nine plastic surgeons on the Baylor staff, performing a combined total of about 1,000 operations annually, most of them reconstructive procedures.

Otolaryngology

The best-known otolaryngologists at Baylor during the 1920s were Dr. Lyle M. Sellers and Dr. Edward H. Cary, (who also practiced ophthalmology as did many physicians of the period.) Dr. Sellers became chief of the department at Baylor in 1946 and served in the position until 1962. Dr. Oscar Marchman Sr., for whom the Marchman Award of the Dallas Southern Clinical Society is named and who joined the Baylor staff in the 1930s, was another well-known otolaryngologist in the early days of the specialty.

In the beginning, otolaryngologists concentrated their efforts primarily on treating ear infections. But after World War II, surgical techniques for correction of ear problems began to evolve. "We still get rid of infections, but we can also rebuild ear structures to improve hearing through new surgical techniques," says Dr. Ludwig Michael, who joined Dr. Sellers in practice in 1949 and who serves today as chief of the department at Baylor.

One of the major advancements in otolaryngology at Baylor came in 1956 with the purchase of an operating microscope, which made possible delicate operations dealing with fine ear structures and diminished the risk of infections. This and other developments have made surgical techniques for the restoration of hearing increasingly sophisticated and successful. One of the newest developments in the field is represented by a fully equipped audiology lab in the Baylor Medical Plaza, used for testing hearing and vestibular functions of patients complaining of dizziness, as well as for evaluating the effectiveness of hearing aids.

Ophthalmology

Dr. Edward H. Cary, who won fame in many fields of endeavor during his colorful career, was also the most famous eye surgeon in early-day Dallas. It was he who performed the very first surgical procedure at the Texas Baptist Memorial Sanitarium in 1909, and that procedure was an eye operation. Because of Dr. Cary, Baylor has enjoyed a strong reputation in ophthalmology from the very beginning.

In about 1928, Dr. Kelly Cox became head of ophthalmology at Baylor, and he, along with Dr. Speight Jenkins and Dr. Maxwell Thomas, carried on a very active teaching program in the ophthalmology clinic, as well as on the wards of the hospital. A portion of their duties consisted of training all the medical students and residents in how to do proper eye examinations and how to use the ophthalmoscope to look into the eyes. Many practicing ophthalmologists in Dallas today had their primary training under these men. In about 1941, Dr. Lester H. Quinn became head of Baylor's ophthalmology services and was followed in the position by Dr. Tom McCrory, an associate of Dr. Thomas, in 1965.

Dr. Ken Foree III serves today as Baylor's chief of ophthalmology, having been named to the post four years ago. Under his direction, the department upholds its long-standing reputation for excellence. Although the department decreased in size with the migration of many physicians to the suburbs in the 1950s and 1960s, it is now growing again. Approximately 500 surgeries performed during 1978 almost tripled the number performed five years earlier, and the ophthalmology staff has increased to a present strength of 25.

As with ear surgeries, the introduction of the operating microscope has also made an important difference in ophthalmology, and three such microscopes are now available to Baylor surgeons. Surgical techniques also have improved for both cataract surgery and corneal transplants, and the facilities for such operations were greatly enhanced with the construction of two specialized operating rooms for ophthalmology on the seventh floor of the Collins Hospital.

Dr. Foree, who received his M.D. degree from Southwestern Medical School and served his residency at New York Eye and Ear Infirmary in New York City, is a native Dallasite with a life-long association with Baylor. His grandmother, Mrs. Kenneth Foree, was the first president of the Baylor Auxiliary, and Dr. Foree himself was born at Baylor.

Among the staff that serves with him are two ophthalmologists who specialize in retinal detachments.

Oral Surgery

Because of its close association over the years with Baylor College of Dentistry, the Medical Center has a long history in the treatment of oral and dental disorders.

Dr. D. Lamar Byrd serves as chief of the Department of Oral Surgery at Baylor and as professor and chairman of the Department of Oral and Maxillofacial Surgery at the dental college—posts he has held since 1951. The first well-trained oral surgeon to practice in the Dallas area, Dr. Byrd received his graduate degree in dentistry from the Northwestern University Dental School in Chicago and served residencies in oral surgery at Jackson Memorial Hospital in Miami and at Charity Hospital in New Orleans. He established the Parkland Memorial Hospital Oral Surgery program and later established the residency program in oral surgery at Baylor.

Under Dr. Byrd, a team approach has been developed in the treatment of all types of oral, dental and facial injuries and deformities. With this system, general surgeons, oral surgeons, dentists, orthodontists and maxillofacial prosthodontists work together for the reconstructive benefits of the patient.

The cooperative arrangement between the Medical Center and the dental college gives Baylor unusually extensive dental capabilities.

Nephrology

In 1976, Baylor expanded its nephrology (kidney disease) service for patients needing kidney dialysis from two to four beds, established a specialized nephrology laboratory, formalized a nephrology rotation as part of the internal medicine residency program with one or two residents in training at all times, and established an educational program for fellows in this vital specialty. These advancements in a field that has been steadily developing at Baylor for more than a decade were made under Dr. Martin G. White, who became director of nephrology in 1975, after serving as chief of the hemodialysis unit at Dallas' Veterans Administration Hospital.

The nephrology and hemodialysis program at Baylor was started in the mid-1960s by Dr. Charles Austin and Dr. Al Roberts. In hemodialysis, the blood of a victim of kidney failure is cleansed by chemical osmosis in a machine, equipped with a system of porous membranes which separates the blood from the chemicals. The first hemodialysis treatment at Baylor was done in 1964 in a one-bed unit on the third floor of the Veal building. In the beginning, Dr. Austin or Dr. Roberts would personally handle all the details of the treatment, with some assistance from Sybil Hunter, the only dialysis nurse then on the

Baylor staff. But as the service became more routine, three part-time registered nurses administered the treatment under the supervision of the physicians. At that time, the nurses had to mix the fluids used to bathe the artificial kidneys during the treatments, change the fluids every two hours, and also bag the blood that was needed to prime the artificial kidney machine. Preparation time for a treatment ranged from eight to nine hours—longer than the time the patient actually spent on the machine. Later, the preparation time was reduced markedly by automatic features and disposable parts for the machine.

By 1967, the dialysis unit had been moved to the medical and surgical intensive care unit on the third floor of the Truett Hospital and increased to two beds. Shortly thereafter, the nurses who had been employed only part-time in the unit became full-time dialysis staff members. Today Baylor has two full-time nephrologists on its staff, plus four full-time nurses. Its four artificial kidney machines are used to perform more than 1,200 treatments annually—almost double the number being done when Dr. White assumed directorship of the service.

Gastroenterology

Specialists in gastroenterology, which deals with diagnosis and treatment of diseases of the digestive tract, have been present on the Baylor staff for many years. In fact, until the early 1930s, there were only four physicians practicing this specialty in the entire City of Dallas, and all four were Baylor staff members. Dr. H. G. Walcott was the first local full-time gastroenterologist, with a practice dating back to the mid-1920s.

In 1928, Dr. Walcott hired a young graduate of Baylor Medical College who had just completed his internship at the Army hospital at Fort Sam Houston in San Antonio. His name was Dr. Milford O. Rouse, and he worked with Dr. Walcott for $250 per month to learn the specialty because there were no residency programs in gastroenterology in the whole State of Texas. Dr. Rouse, who also became a member of the Baylor staff in 1928, went on to become one of the most distinguished men of medicine in the history of Dallas and one of two Texans ever to serve as president of the American Medical Association. After nearly five decades of service to Baylor, Dr. Rouse retired in July 1976 because of ill health.*

Although physicians like Dr. Rouse, Dr. Walcott, Dr. Cecil Patterson and Dr. G. E. Brereton had compiled outstanding records in gastroenterology prior to that time, it was not until the early 1970s that today's highly specialized laboratory and testing procedures for many digestive diseases came into existence at Baylor. Rapid changes began to take place with the arrival in January 1971 of Dr. Daniel E. Polter as the first full-time gastroenterologist on the Baylor staff. Dr. Polter, who had been in private practice with Dr. Patterson, developed and later expanded a "GI" laboratory, the first facility of its kind in a private hospital in Dallas, in the Veal building. This lab gave Baylor the capability to conduct numerous new tests, including laparoscopy for the diagnosis of liver disease, intra-abdominal tumors and infections; colonoscopy for detection of intestinal bleeding due to polyps and malignancies; transhepatic cholangiography to establish the site and cause of bile duct obstructions; endoscopic retrograde cholangio-pancreatography (ERCP) to aid in the diagnosis of various pancreatic and bile duct disorders, and esophageal

---

*Dr. Milford O. Rouse died in April 1978, a few months before this book was published, but his interest in the book and his willingness to be interviewed, despite failing health, on important historical details pertaining to the Medical Center were invaluable contributions that were deeply appreciated by the author. Prior to his death, Dr. Rouse endowed a lectureship in digestive diseases and nutrition at Baylor.

284

motility, used to detect the cause of swallowing disorders and chest pain.

In 1978, further advancements were made in the department with the merger of the Medical Center's hyperalimentation and IV services, both of which utilize intravenous procedures to provide for infusion of nutrients, vitamins and minerals into the patient's bloodstream. Hyperalimentation can provide up to 5,000 calories of nourishment per day when administered through a large centrally located vein to a patient who cannot take food by mouth for long periods of time due to various diseases or after extensive surgery.

Baylor's Gastroenterology Department is now staffed by three gastroenterologists with Dr. Polter as director. Growth of the department is illustrated by the fact that, when the GI lab first went into operation in 1971, only 50 to 60 tests were run each month. Today, some 4,300 testing procedures are conducted annually.

Pulmonary Medicine

In 1928, after completing his residency at the Texas Tuberculosis Sanitarium in San Angelo, Dr. H. Frank Carman returned to Baylor, where he had served an earlier internship and residency, to become the first pulmonary medicine specialist in Dallas. Later, Dr. J. O. Armstrong and Dr. John Chapman, also pulmonary medicine specialists, joined the Baylor staff.

While these men were instrumental in creating a strong practice in pulmonary medicine at Baylor, and in helping change public attitudes toward tuberculosis patients, there was no formal pulmonary medicine service at Baylor until October 1966. At that time, Dr. Charles E. Jarrett left his private practice in Brunswick, Georgia, to become Baylor's first full-time director of pulmonary medicine and respiratory therapy. By 1970, the combined departments had become known as Pulmonary Services, and their growth since then has been so great that it was necessary to name separate full-time medical directors for respiratory therapy and the pulmonary laboratory.

The growth in Pulmonary Services coincided with the increase in the number of open heart surgeries at Baylor. These operations rely on heart pumps to oxygenate the patient's blood, and it is critically important that a means be available to measure oxygen, carbon dioxide and acid base levels in the blood. These procedures are the responsibility of the pulmonary laboratory. To understand the growing need for such services, it is necessary only to look at the figures for the past few years at Baylor. In 1970, only 2,700 procedures were performed in the pulmonary laboratory. By 1976, that number had climbed to 13,700.

The original pulmonary laboratory at Baylor was started in 1964 under a part-time director, Dr. George Schools, and the facilities were located in the cardiac laboratory. The "cardiopulmonary" lab occupied two nine-by-twelve rooms in the Veal building. In 1971, the lab was moved to the second floor of the Truett Hospital, as was the Respiratory Therapy Department, where the two services occupy 2,500 square feet of space.

Pulmonary Services now has three pulmonary specialists, 13 technical personnel in the pulmonary laboratory and 80 respiratory therapists. Under Dr. Jarrett's leadership, a full-scale educational program has been initiated in Pulmonary Services, which includes the training of laboratory technicians, respiratory therapists and medical students. A fellowship in pulmonary medicine also has been established.

Endocrinology

When Dr. Zaven Chakmakjian was in training at

the University of Southern California School of Medicine in Los Angeles in the mid-1960s, endocrinology—the diagnosis and treatment of hormonal disorders—was just beginning to evolve from animal research into a science that could be applied to human beings. In 1967, when Dr. Chakmakjian arrived at Baylor to become the first full-time endocrinologist on the staff and director of the Rose and Henry A. Weinberger Endocrine Laboratory, there were only a few tests available for endocrine disorders. Today, a staff of seven medical technologists works with the Medical Center's two endocrinologists to conduct 35 to 40 different tests. The machines utilized are complex, highly sophisticated equipment capable of analyzing a wide range of hormonal malfunctions. The results can alert a physician to many different physical disorders, ranging from a hyperactive thyroid to a pituitary tumor. An average of 2,000 tests are done monthly, and existing testing procedures are being constantly refined, even as new ones are being developed.

Originally, the laboratory was designed to do basic research and developmental studies, but in 1972 it was made a part of Baylor's overall laboratory system, and Dr. Chakmakjian was given dual appointments in internal medicine, the specialty under which endocrinology is a subspecialty, and pathology, the department that oversees all the laboratories. At that point, the endocrine lab began to grow, and today it ranks as the largest facility of its kind in North Texas. To accommodate its phenomenal growth, a second endocrinologist was added to the staff in 1977.

Among the patients who benefit from the endocrinology services are those with under-active or over-active thyroid, endocrine hypertension, calcium disorders, diabetes, hirsutism (excessive body hair resulting from an overabundance of male hormone in females), couples troubled with infertility, women with menstrual problems and hypo-pituitary dwarfs.

The endocrine section is currently conducting two separate projects in the area for hypo-pituitary dwarfs, using a growth hormone supplied by the National Pituitary Agency. For more than two years, the laboratory has also been in charge of measuring hormone receptors in females with breast cancer to determine if hormone manipulation will aid in treatment. Recently, the laboratory also began measuring thyroid hormone in all Baylor newborns in a move to detect the one newborn in every 5,000 with low thyroid hormone, a condition that can lead to mental retardation. Through routine testing, however, the hormone can be supplemented at birth and the condition reversed.

Neurology

In July 1977, a four-bed neurologic cerebral vascular intensive care unit was established on the fourth floor of the Truett Hospital for patients with strokes and other disorders caused by abnormalities of the blood vessels leading to and from the brain.

The unit's opening was another milestone in the progress that had begun at Baylor in 1973, when Dr. Sheff D. Olinger left his private practice to become the Medical Center's first full-time director of neurology and head of the EEG (electroencephalogram) Laboratory. It was Dr. Olinger who formally organized the Neurology Department and consolidated the stroke and neurology units at Baylor. Under his supervision, the number of beds for neurologic patients has gradually increased from 32 to 47, and five other neurologists have been added to the staff.

Although recognized as a medical subspecialty since 1935, neurology had not grown as fast in the South and Southwest as in other parts of the country until recently because of what Dr. Olinger calls "a lack of tradition." Before Dr. Olinger's arrival at Baylor, the EEG Laboratory was under the direction of a neuropsychiatrist, Dr. Paul Levin. Dr. Levin and Dr. Stephen Weisz, also a neuropsychiatrist, served as consultants at Baylor during the 1930s and 1940s. However, most diagnosis, as well as the treatment of neurological patients at Baylor, was handled primarily by the Department of Neurosurgery. When Dr. Olinger came to Dallas in 1959 after completing his residency at the University of Michigan, there was only one neurologist on the faculty of Southwestern Medical School and one other physician in private practice in Dallas who limited his practice to neurology. By comparison, there are 17 neurologists on the medical school faculty today and a total of 30 practicing throughout the city.

The number of EEG tests administered at Baylor has increased from 70 to 300 per month since 1973, and another 85 tests are conducted each month in an outpatient EEG lab established two years ago in the Medical Plaza. Future plans for the Neurology Department call for development of specialized centers for treatment of convulsive disorders and chronic and migraine headaches.

Family Practice

In the early days of this century, before the age of medical specialization began, almost every physician was a "family doctor" or general practitioner. But the very progress and sophistication that triggered the growth of the specialties and sub-specialties also ate away steadily at the ranks of the family practitioners. As time went by and medical specialization became increasingly popular, few new physicians wanted to go into family practice anymore. As a result, the number of residency programs in family practice decreased, and, for a time, the nation faced a critical shortage of family practitioners.

That was the situation in 1952, when Dr. Perry E. Gross, now chief of Baylor's Department of Family

Practice, decided to buck the trend and go into family practice—even though he had completed residencies in both psychiatry and internal medicine.

In 1952, a Department of General Practice was established at Baylor, with Dr. John Minnett as chief. By 1955, the department had about a dozen physicians and was steadily increasing its ranks. In the 1960s, the name was changed to the Department of Family Practice. And by 1974, when Dr. Gross became chief of the department, renewed emphasis was being placed on the role of the family practitioner all across the country—a fact that caused the number of family practitioners at Baylor to increase even more.

Today, as the realization grows that proper medical care for the American family, particularly in inner cities, smaller towns and rural areas, depends upon building and maintaining family practice as a vital "specialty" in its own right, more and more residency programs are being opened up.

Baylor's former chiefs of family practice include E. R. Cox, Doyle Ferguson and Wright K. Smith.

Other Contributions

In August 1975, Dr. B. Roy Simpson, a world-renowned anesthesiologist and professor of anesthetics at the London Hospital Medical College in London, England, came to Baylor as full-time chief of anesthesiology and medical director of anesthesia services. Along the way, new specialty fields are continually being added, both in medical and nonmedical areas at Baylor, and renowned specialists from other areas of the country—and even overseas—are joining the ever-growing Baylor "family."

It has not been Baylor's physicians alone who have pioneered in many areas of patient care and services. Credit is also due to the competence and loyalty of its thousands of employes, many of whom

290

have served for decades in vital roles within the Medical Center. Three employes, Velma Ferguson, R.N., director of nurse anesthesia; Argetta Parnell, chief admitting officer; and Lewis S. Smith, director of pharmacy, received 40-year service pins before retiring. Six current employes have each compiled more than 35 years of service—Raymond Arellano, chief admitting orderly; Geraldine Warsteane, L.V.N., of the Truett nursing service; Eva Thomas, R.N., supervisor of the employe health clinic; Roy Gentry, laundry supervisor; Peck Shirley, physical medicine orderly; and Mary Beard, R.N., radiation therapy supervisor. Three other employes, John W. Smith, director of finance; Louise Bane of the accounting office; and Myrtle Roenau, a radiation therapist, received 35-year pins prior to their retirement. No less than 33 other Baylor employes have been recognized for 30 or more years of service.*

Many employes at Baylor are also acknowledged leaders in their own specialty fields and have won recognition for themselves and Baylor at the national, regional and state levels. Robert C. Paul has served as president of both the American Society of Hospital Engineers and the Texas Society of Hospital Engineers, and the annual award for outstanding hospital engineers in Texas is named in his honor. Former Public Relations Director Marjorie Saunders was president of the American Society of Hospital Public Relations Directors, and numerous staff members have headed statewide organizations in their specialty fields.

In addition to its regular staff members, Baylor's Volunteer Service Corps has played an indispensible role in assisting hospital patients over the past 24 years. Volunteers now serve in nearly 30 different areas of the Medical Center, and the corps includes 350 active volunteers who have contributed some

*See Appendix H

three quarters of a million hours of service to Baylor and its patients.

Along that invisible line where the present merges with the future and today meets tomorrow, other developments are constantly taking place within the massive conglomeration of human endeavor, scientific and technological marvels, brick, steel, glass and concrete that comprises Baylor University Medical Center. Even as this book goes to press, another cavernous 1,000-car parking garage is being completed to double the number of covered parking spaces within the conplex. So there is no convenient place to pause and draw a line between what has already happened, what is happening at this precise moment, and what will be happening in the weeks and months ahead—not even for the authors of books. As Baylor enters the last quarter of its first century, the growth process continues unabated on all fronts.

Indeed, much has changed in the 75 years since 1903, but one thing has not. The challenge of the future remains constant.

XV

The Years Ahead

Charting the Course

As Baylor University Medical Center looks toward yet another new decade filled with more new challenges, responsibilities and opportunities, it is well prepared to meet the demands of the future. Whatever surprises the "Enigmatic Eighties" may hold in store, Baylor will be equipped to cope with them using a dynamic combination of new tools and crisis-tested, time-proven leadership.

No single individual or one small group of individuals can be credited with Baylor's incredible growth over the past 75 years from a tiny, struggling hospital to one of the world's outstanding centers of medical achievement. During that time, scores of people from all walks of life have played indispensible roles in the unfolding drama of Baylor University Medical Center. While it is impossible to single out each individual or group that has contributed to Baylor's advancement, a few deserve special recognition for their roles.

From the beginning, the Baptists of Texas have given their unfailing support to Baylor University Medical Center, and that support today continues through the Baptist General Convention of Texas, under the executive directorship of Dr. James H. Landes, and its Human Welfare Coordinating Board, directed by Dr. James Basden; and a number of Baptist ministers who have brought leadership to the Medical Center board, including Drs. W. A. Criswell, Travis S. Berry, M. B. Carroll, Marshall Craig, Charles Cockrell,

Bruce McIver, Wallace Bassett, James Draper and others.

Since 1920, when Baylor University at Waco and Baylor Hospital were united under the same charter, the two institutions have worked in a partnership that has brought recognition to both the university and the Medical Center. The bonds of that partnership are strengthened today by Dr. Abner V. McCall, president of the university and chief executive officer, and Dr. Herbert H. Reynolds, the university's executive vice president and chief operating officer.

And the University of Texas Southwestern Medical School (a part of the UT Health Science Center at Dallas), which evolved out of a controversy that caused Baylor College of Medicine to leave Dallas, has developed in recent years into one of Baylor Medical Center's strongest allies. Presently, a number of residency programs are conducted jointly with Southwestern; many members of Baylor's medical staff hold joint clinical appointments on the Southwestern faculty; and the health science center and Baylor work jointly in the presentation of post-graduate education programs at the A. Webb Roberts Center for Continuing Education in the Health Sciences. These developments, and the strengthening of relationships between the two institutions, have been primarily due to the influence of one man—Dr. Charles C. Sprague, president of the health science center, who has committed himself to having his institution and the hospitals of Dallas work cooperatively together.

Baylor's Leadership

Decade after decade, there have been those key figures who rose to take up the endless task of progress. The 1980s should be no different in that respect. Indeed, a vital part of that progress in the years to come will be the very cultivation of such leaders.

But today, at this vantage-point in history, the term "leadership" at Baylor University Medical Center is synonymous with two men—Boone Powell, who continues to serve as vice president of Baylor University and chairman of the Medical Center's Executive Committee, and David H. Hitt, now executive director of the Medical Center. These two men have set the pace of Baylor's progress over the past two decades or more, and their unique brand of leadership will set the course and point the way through the troubled and tranquil seas ahead. Rarely, if ever, in the history of hospital administration, has a management partnership brought together such a wide range of talents, skills and creative drives in two individuals who are significantly different. But instead of allowing their differing management approaches to confuse and confound, they have used them to complement each other and to forge a spirit of cooperative effort at the Medical Center today.

In his 26 years at Baylor, David Hitt has demonstrated the outstanding management abilities and the broad grasp of the intricate health care field that has gained him wide respect in the hospital industry nationally and has brought significant recognition to Baylor nationwide. His activities have also served to keep the Medical Center in touch with the rapidly changing health care field in advance.

Hitt is a man who has come to grips with and enjoys the enormity of the job before him and realizes that he must move at a strenuous pace in order to coordinate all the complex issues that fall under his jurisdiction and to pursue his many other interests. "He has the utmost patience," says one Baylor employe. "He never says, 'You made a mistake.' It's always, 'I think we can correct this,' or 'I think we can find a better way to do this.' " He has no concept of an eight-hour day or a 40-hour week; he just works until he gets the job done. Frequently, this means evenings, weekends, even holidays, because the demands of being available to people during office hours usually limit the time necessary for matters requiring concentrated study. In addition to his administrative duties, Hitt also maintains a rigorous schedule of community activities, as well as travel and speaking engagements. Because of his national reputation as an expert on health policy and governmental interaction with hospitals, he is in constant demand as a strategist and spokesman for the hospital industry.

Through the years, Hitt has concentrated on building a flexible organization for accommodating Baylor's present needs and continued expansion. Quality of care, relationships among groups, organization of new services, economic operation and numerous other essentials of the institution depend upon the coordination and constant attention to both the present and future. Countless large and small components interlock to form the pattern of day-to-day activities in the massive Medical Center complex that encompasses nine city blocks and 4,000 employes. In Hitt's opinion, Baylor's success requires a strong management organization that is able to keep pace with the Medical Center's growth in size and intricacy and the vast number of regulatory and other externally-imposed complexities which now affect its operations without loss of momentum and effectiveness. The focal point of these concepts is to maintain organizational flexibility and decentralized decision-making and to strengthen the management abilities of individual managers, preparing them for increased responsibilities and promotion as the Medical Center expands in size and scope.

In his position as associate executive director of the Medical Center, Howard Chase heads a team of associate directors and administrative assistants that has charge of Baylor's centralized departments and programs (diagnostic, therapeutic and administrative services, the physical plant, and subsidiary corpora-

296

At Baylor University Medical Center, future planning has been the key to successful and meaningful growth. Boone Powell, right, and David H. Hitt engage in a planning session that will help guide Baylor into the decade of the Eighties.

tions). He holds a Master's Degree in Hospital Administration from the University of Minnesota, is a fellow of the American College of Hospital Administrators and a director of the Dallas Chapter of the American Red Cross. Chase is also president of the Church University Insurance Company, Baylor's liability insurance subsidiary, and is Baylor's representative on the Board of Directors of the Voluntary Hospitals of America, an organization consisting of 30 hospitals over the nation formed for group purchasing and other cooperative activities to achieve cost savings on supplies and services.

Bob M. Inge joined the Baylor staff as associate executive director in September 1977, providing general direction and coordination of the administrators of Truett, Jonsson, Hoblitzelle and Collins Hospitals and of the executives working with such medical staff activities as medical education, surgery and anesthesia, as well as the Medical Center's public relations program. A certified public accountant who holds degrees from Wake Forest University and the University of Arizona, Inge received his doctorate degree in business administration from Harvard University. Before joining the Medical Center's management team, he was professor and director of the U.S. Army-Baylor University program in health care administration and assistant dean of the Baylor University Graduate School.

Other key management figures at the Medical Center include these associate directors: L. Gerald Bryant, who has general administrative responsibility for the departments of Accounting Services and Management Development; Glen R. Clark, who provides general administrative direction for the departments of Personnel Services, Laboratories, Radiology, Physical Medicine, Chaplaincy Service and Pastoral Care; William S. Carter, who is responsible for the departments of Business Services, Data Processing, Engineering Services and all construction and also serves as president of three Medical Center subsidiaries, Baylor Medical Plaza, Inc., Baylor Medical Plaza Services Corporation, and Gaston Construction Company; Ralph E. Cross Jr., who provides general administrative direction for the Hunt Heart Center and for the departments of Emergency Services, Pharmacy, Medical Records, Materiel Services, Property Services and Photography and Audio Visual Services; Stephen D. Trowbridge, who is responsible for the Sammons Cancer Center and the departments of Neurology, Gastroenterology, Pulmonary Services and Central Food Service; and Robert A. Hille, who provides administrative direction for the Operating Room and Anesthesia Services and all medical education units.

Also included in the management team are George J. Tsamis, administrative assistant for systems in charge of administrative research studies and management statistical and report systems; W. Joe Allen, Truett Hospital administrator; John D. Hicks, Jonsson Hospital administrator; John Carver, Collins Hospital administrator; J. Larry Read, Hoblitzelle Hospital administrator; Leonard J. Garron, assistant director; and Wilbur B. Smith, evening administrator.

These highly skilled management professionals not only oversee hundreds of daily hospital functions, but also help to map out Baylor's overall strategy for meeting the demands of the future.

The Future Needs

Many of Baylor's future needs are clearly evident to everyone familiar with its facilities. In the 28 years since the Truett Hospital was completed, numerous beds have been added to the Medical Center, and a multitude of new services have been established. However, many departments have not been proportionately expanded in size. Through the years, the space for surgery, laboratories, radiology, kitchens,

299

and the laundry has steadily compacted until these rapidly growing departments are badly overcrowded. Some need new equipment, which can be provided only when there is more room. For example, most of the rooms in which surgery is performed are the same size as they were in the 1950s. Although the operating rooms were considered quite large when they were originally constructed, the space in those facilities is now inadequate due to the amount of new surgical equipment utilized and the large numbers of personnel required for major surgical cases. The need for more patient rooms and new scientific services for outpatients is also certain to create increasingly severe space shortages in years ahead.

The solution to such overcrowding at the Medical Center, while still some years away, would need to come in the form of another new hospital to house the operating rooms, post-anesthesia recovery units and related facilities, Baylor officials say. This, in turn, would allow the present operating room spaces to be used for expanded laboratories and other services.

The Truett Hospital should be renovated, they add, to provide additional patient bathrooms and to modernize the whole structure internally. This would mean reducing the number of beds in Truett from 435 to about 300, and these lost beds would have to be replaced in a new hospital. By that time, additional beds will also be needed for growing numbers of patients, especially as new medical specialties evolve, and for the patients coming to the Emergency Services Department. Already, one-fifth of all patients who come to Baylor's Emergency Department are admitted to the hospital—a figure that grows steadily with each passing year.

In addition, the Medical Center will need to relocate the Hunt Heart Center, now located in the Wadley Tower of the Medical Plaza, officials project, so that more physicians' offices can be built in the space that the Heart Center now occupies. At present,

Board Chairmen

These men have served as chairmen of the Baylor University Medical Center Board of Trustees. Not pictured are R. C. Buckner (1903-1908), C. C. Slaughter (1908-1911), J. P. Crouch (1911-date unknown), Hal E. White (date unknown-1931) and Earl B. Smyth (1931-1938).

W. Dewey Presley
1973-present
1965-1972

Omar Harvey
1972-1973

Cecil M. Higginbotham
1964-1965

Clare H. Zachry
1963-1964

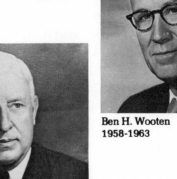

Ben H. Wooten
1958-1963

G. H. Penland
1955-1958

Charles R. Moore
1943-1955

301

16 of the 20 floors available for physicians' offices are already filled. Because of the growing emphasis on ambulatory outpatient care, Baylor also expects the medical staff to request more facilities for this purpose.

In the interim, Baylor is making preliminary plans in hopes of building a new service facility to house a laundry, food production area, storerooms, maintenance area and space for other services that can be located at greater distances from patient care areas. Removal of these services will vacate space for the expansion of the Department of Emergency Services, central supply and other facilities.

These projections are based on solid, factual information, and the needs foreseen are the practical, down-to-earth requirements for running a burgeoning health care amalgam that must continue to progress. Nobody knows that better than Boone Powell, who glimpses the future of Baylor University Medical Center in visions of jutting towers of glass and steel and broad expanses of brick and concrete—and the funds it takes to make such visions become realities. Boone Powell sees the Medical Center of today, and of the future, as one grand and glorious whole.

In his own office, Powell unrolls a big map of East Dallas and spreads it out on the table in front of him. Carefully marked on the map are the locations of many existing and proposed developments that will change the face and character of the area around the Medical Center in years to come—developer Dave Fox's new inner-city housing development for middle-class homeowners; the recently designated historic districts of Swiss Avenue and Munger Place, where some of the city's finest homes are being restored to their former opulence; the again-fashionable Lakewood area; various major thoroughfare development proposals—and, of course, the sprawling Medical Center itself. Powell, as much as any individual in Dallas, has been a moving force in the urban revitalization that began in East Dallas early in the 1970s, but the area still has not come nearly as far as Powell wants it to come.

As he talks and points to the map, the here-and-now seems to fade, and Powell is leading his listener away on a tour of the future—a place where he spends a lot of his time. "There will be major development along these streets," he says, pointing to the area adjacent to Fox's new homesites. "And there will be a tree-lined boulevard here," he adds, pointing to a proposed route for a scenic traffic link between downtown and Fair Park. "Just imagine what that will do to the area." As he paints his futuristic picture, his positive tone and his optimistic outlook are strangely infectious. His listener can almost participate in his vision, almost see it all happening just as he projects it. For a moment, it is possible to visualize the East Dallas of the future and to feel a surge of eager anticipation. It is this ability to share his visions with others that has been instrumental in convincing so many others to share their wealth with Baylor.

Boone Powell brings a sense of reality to the term "dreamer." He is one of those rare persons who can turn what might seem a fantasy into a workable plan, and who has the foresight (and the ability to scheme a little, too, if necessary) to make dreams come true. As one associate says of him: "Mr. Powell can actually see the future while it is still in the future, and prepare for it."

A simple man who believes in hard work and who loves Baylor on an emotional level that most people are incapable of reaching, Powell is the undisputed "Papa Bear" of the Dallas campus. Powell himself credits his wife of 43 years for giving him the kind of personal support that has made his successful leadership at Baylor possible. Ruth Powell, although often in the background, has been another very real and very important member of the Baylor team. In addition, she has served the Medical Center in many

303

volunteer capacities, as an active member of its Woman's Auxiliary, a contributor of floral arrangements to hospital waiting rooms and suites, a talented musician who has entertained at scores of staff social gatherings, and a gracious hostess to guests of the Medical Center.

In his own personal version of urban renewal, Powell has demolished dozens of buildings and erected dozens of others. As a fund-raiser without equal, he has seen to it that an appropriate share of Dallas' great wealth found its way to the city's largest medical facility. "He has a total belief in Baylor and what it stands for," says another associate. "That's what he sees when he asks someone for money. He sees himself helping Baylor to fulfill its destiny. He knows his strengths and for the things he can't do himself, he picks people who can and places complete trust in them. He has his own way of organizing things. He'll often act on a hunch or intuition, and a lot of people who operate that way are terrible failures, but he has an uncanny ability to make it all come out right and to keep everybody working together. One of his favorite expressions is, 'Let your brains think about an idea, then let your heart make the decision.' "

His abilities and accomplishments earned Powell the Distinguished Service Award of the American Hospital Association in 1977. The citation accompanying the award praised Powell for his "courage . . . vision . . . and immense talent." It also included a quotation from one of his admiring colleagues: "Boone Powell and Baylor University Medical Center are virtually synonymous. When reference is made to one, the image of the other is automatic." Finally, the citation graphically captured Powell's overall philosophy by saying: "He believes that hospital executives should look outward to the community and, in turn, the community should look to its hospitals as a source of leadership."

Powell's own words today strongly emphasize

Boone Powell has been an executive officer for Baylor University Medical Center for almost 33 years. "The average length of tenure for a hospital administrator is three years," he quips, "so I've spent the last 30 on borrowed time."

In April 1952, Powell was "chief wrangler" for a courtesy round-up at the Medical Center.

For Christmas 1957, Powell was presented this lengthy Christmas card from the entire staff at the Medical Center.

In August 1964, Powell was honored at a luncheon after he was named president-elect of the American College of Hospital Administrators. Clare Zachry, Baylor trustee, accompanies Powell.

In 1978, Powell, who serves as president of the new Baylor University Medical Center Foundation, engages in a planning session with R. Glen Smiley, the foundation's executive vice president.

Dr. Kenneth Randolph, dean of the Baylor College of Dentistry, presents Powell with a distinguished service award in November 1971.

this belief. "We are making a continuous effort to improve and upgrade not only our immediate environment, but to help in the revitalization of all of East Dallas, from downtown outward through Lakewood," he says. "Even though much progress has been made, we still aren't where we want to be. We want to acquire any additional land we feel we need for growth and expansion, and are currently negotiating on some key pieces of property. We want land that will enhance our environment."

As part of his planning for the 1980s, Powell must take into consideration a significant restructuring which he foresees in the system of health care delivery in this country. "Preventive medicine is the number one goal now," he says, "and a lot of programs will be necessary to educate the public in this direction. Hospitals will play a primary role in that education. The emphasis will be on doing everything you can for patients outside the hospital, and on admitting them only when it is absolutely necessary."

No matter how vast it may become, a hospital never outgrows the need for a cooperative interrelationship with the community around it, Powell believes. "Anything that happens on this side of the city affects us," he says. "We have been committed to the inner city ever since the Truett Hospital was built, and every time we've added a building our commitment has become even greater. At one time, we thought about establishing satellite hospitals, but we never did it. Our primary role is to serve as a major medical referral center, and we know we can serve that purpose better in one spot."

Throughout the years, Powell has remained proud of the fact that Baylor has managed to survive—and to prosper—without the federal funds that many hospitals have received in recent years. Powell says, "All our construction has been done without tax money. We have maintained a position of leadership by meeting the health care needs of the people of this

306

community, and they have responded generously with their support—and that's a good gauge for the future."

New Times, New Tools

One of the most important new "tools" for continuing and broadening that community support is the Baylor University Medical Center Foundation, established in 1978 as a "vehicle for development of understanding and support . . . necessary to meet the demands of the ever-changing world of health science" and as a "medium for involvement of outstanding community leaders in the work of the Medical Center in a mutually beneficial manner." Herman W. Lay serves as chairman of the board of the foundation; Powell is its president, and R. Glen Smiley is its executive vice president and chief operating officer. Ultimately, the foundation's board of directors will include 100 members, one-third of whom will be Baylor physicians. The remaining two-thirds will be composed of lay people representing a wide range of business and professional fields and all religious denominations. Each board member is expected to be involved on a working committee within the Medical Center.

In setting forth the objectives of the foundation and the reasons for its creation, its original board issued the following statement: "As more and more restrictions are placed on hospitals and with the prospect of national health insurance looming large in the future, it becomes more apparent that to assure continued quality, Baylor will have to place an increasing emphasis on obtaining private philanthropic support. Doing so will require that we broaden our base of support and provide a meaningful involvement to persons who are now only familiar with us by reputation."

"The foundation brings us to a new era," says

Smiley. "The foundation will, in large part, determine the future of the Medical Center, because philanthropic dollars enabled Baylor to be what it is today, and will allow it to become greater in the years ahead."

Symbolic of the type of concerned community leaders who have deeply involved themselves with the work of the foundation during its brief history is its board chairman, Herman Lay. A native of Charlotte, North Carolina, Lay came to Dallas in 1962 after his Atlanta-based firm, H. W. Lay and Company, merged with the Dallas-based Frito Company to form Frito-Lay. Now a board member and chairman of the executive committee of the parent Pepsico, Inc., Lay became interested in medicine through working with the American Cancer Society, both in Atlanta and Dallas. During this association, he not only worked in local campaigns, but served on the society's national board. His interest in Baylor grew out of an acquaintance with Dewey Presley, the Medical Center's board chairman. Lay subsequently served a nine-year term as a member of the Baylor board, ending in January 1978, and, over the years, he made many financial contributions to the Medical Center, including a $350,000 gift for expansion of the Radiology Department. "My work with Baylor was a natural evolution," Lay says. He realizes, however, that without the foundation, many other business leaders might not experience this same kind of "evolution." The foundation, he emphasizes, will not only provide further financial support, but also serve as an important vehicle for getting people acquainted with Baylor.

Printed in white letters inside the blue front cover of a brochure explaining the purpose of the foundation is a simple slogan that sums it all up neatly in nine short words:

"THE FUTURE BELONGS TO THOSE WHO PREPARE FOR IT."

After three-quarters of a century of tumult,

trauma, tragedy and triumph, Baylor University Medical Center is prepared and eager to claim that future.

Regardless of how glorious and golden our yesterdays may have been, or how charged with urgency the drama of today, all must eventually stand aside for the relentless march of tomorrow. And so, in the final analysis, there is really no place to end this story. It is a story that has no end, a story that will go on and on, as long as there are men and women with the wisdom, the energy and the vision to continue writing it.

The first 75 years of Baylor-in-Dallas are history. The next 75 years are just beginning.

Appendix

Appendix A

ARTICLES OF INCORPORATION
Original Charter
Texas Baptist Memorial Sanitarium
October 16, 1903

Know all men by these presents, that the undersigned citizens of Texas, and residing in the City of Dallas, do hereby form and incorporate ourselves into a voluntary association and corporation, for the purposes hereinafter mentioned, and to that end and for that purpose we subscribe the following:

Charter

Art. I. The name of this corporation is and shall be The Texas Baptist Memorial Sanitarium.

Art. II. Its business is to be transacted in the City of Dallas, Dallas County, Texas.

Art. III. This corporation shall exist for the term of fifty years.

Art. IV. The corporation is organized for the purpose of supporting an educational, benevolent and charitable undertaking, viz, a hospital and sanitarium, to be conducted on the broadest humanitarian principles, uncontrolled by politics, uninfluenced by sectional ambition or strife, and free from all invidious distinction or preference as to political parties or as to religious sects or creeds. This institution shall be open to all reputable physicians and surgeons, and to all reputable schools.

Art. V. The income from the holdings, earnings and endowment of this institution shall be expended on charity patients, on current necessary expenses of the institution, and for its enlargement and general betterment. Such incomes shall not be diverted to the financial benefit of the incorporators of this institution, nor to any of its directors at this or at any future time.

Art. VI. Title to all property of every kind shall be in the incorporated name of the institution, and shall be under the control and management of the Board of Directors.

Art. VII. It shall be the privilege of all patients to choose their own spiritual advisers, and such advisers shall be received with courtesy. Religious liberty shall ever be preserved.

Art. VIII. The Board of Directors shall adopt and publish necessary by-laws, which shall always be in harmony with the articles of the charter.

Art. IX. The affairs and business of this corporation shall be controlled and managed by its Board of Directors, which shall consist of thirteen members, who must be members in good standing of regular Baptist churches. The following named persons shall constitute the Board of Directors for the first year.

R. C. Buckner, Pres., who lives in Dallas, Dallas County, Texas
Geo. W. Truett, Secy., who lives in Dallas, Dallas County, Texas
C. C. Slaughter, Treas., who lives in Dallas, Dallas County, Texas
A. B. Flanary, who lives in Dallas, Dallas County, Texas
J. B. Gambrell, who lives in Dallas, Dallas County, Texas
G. W. McDaniel, who lives in Dallas, Dallas County, Texas
E. T. Lewis, who lives in Dallas, Dallas County, Texas
A. N. Hall, who lives in Dallas, Dallas County, Texas
Geo. W. Carroll, who lives in Beaumont, Jefferson County, Texas
G. H. Connell, who lives in Ft. Worth, Tarrant County, Texas
F. W. Johnson, who lives in Pecos, Reeves County, Texas
F. L. Carroll, who lives in Waco, McLennan County, Texas
J. P. Crouch, who lives in McKinney, Collin County, Texas

Art. X. Temporary vacancies in the Board of Directors may be filled by the remaining members of the board, and such persons so elected shall serve until the next succeeding meeting for the annual election of directors.

Art. XI. Members of the Board of Directors may be represented by proxies, duly authorized thereunto in writing, and such proxies may be counted in declaring a quorum.

Art. XII. The corporation has no capital stock, since it is organized for benevolent and charitable purposes only. Its present assets consist only of rights and credits estimated of the value of thirty-five thousand dollars, exclusive of any holdings or properties that may be secured as endowments.

Art. XIII. In connection with and as accessory to its hospital and sanitarium work, a school for trained nurses may be conducted, and diplomas issued to such as may show themselves of moral worth and exemplary conduct, and as possessing that degree of attainment and skill creditable to nurses of the very best modern sanitariums, all of which shall be passed on, and rules to govern which adopted by the Board of Directors.

In testimony of which, we hereunto affix our signatures, this the 14th day of October, 1903.

R. C. Buckner
Geo. W. Truett
E. T. Lewis

Appendix B

315

Charles L. Cockrell . . . . 1955 James G. Harris 1967
John S. Tanner . . . . 1956 Herman Lay 1969
Noble Hurley . . . . 1959 C. T. Beckham 1969
M. B. Carroll . . . . 1959 James D. Springfield 1970
Cecil Higginbotham . . . . . . 1959 Gordon K. Teal 1970
Wre Sutherland . . . . 1960 Travis S. Berry 1972
Harold G. Basden . . . . 1961 W. W. Clements 1972
Claude Williams . . . . 1961 George Cowden 1972
Donald Bowles . . . . 1962 Tim A. Paulsel 1974
Ray Parker . . . . 1963 Mrs. Jack Anderson 1974
W. Dewey Presley . . . . 1963 James T. Draper Jr. 1974
Bruce McIver . . . . 1964 Jack G. Folmar 1975
Carl B. Casey . . . . 1965 Ben H. Williams 1975
James L. Erwin . . . . 1965 Jarman Bass 1976
Charles E. Watson . . . . 1966 Kelly McCann 1976
Lester Collins Jr. . . . . 1967 Kenneth Vaughn 1976
Omar Harvey . . . . 1967 James C. Cantrell 1976
George Anson . . . . 1967 E. Alvin Wendlandt 1977

Appendix C

CHIEFS OF SERVICE

SERVICE	CHIEF	DATE
ANESTHESIOLOGY	Earl F. Weir, M.D.	1947-1954
	Raymond F. Courtin, M.D.	1955-1965
	Joe B. Wood, M.D.	1966-1974
	George E. Emmett, M.D.	1975
	B. Roy Simpson, M.D.	1975-Present
COLON AND RECTAL	Curtice Rosser, M.D.	1947-1960
SURGERY	Alvin Baldwin, M.D.	1961-1970
(Proctology)	Wallace Bailey, M.D.	1971-Present
DENTISTRY	Glen R. Hillin, D.D.S.	1951-1964
(Dental Surgery)	D. Lamar Byrd, D.D.S.	1965-Present
FAMILY PRACTICE	John Minnett, M.D.	1952-1955
	E. R. Cox, M.D.	1955-1965
	Doyle Ferguson, M.D.	1966-1967
	Wright Smith, M.D.	1967-1970
	E. R. Cox, M.D.	1971-1973
	Perry E. Gross, M.D.	1974-Present
GENERAL SURGERY	H. Walton Cochran, M.D.	1947-1950
	J. W. Duckett, M.D.	1951-1967
	Robert S. Sparkman, M.D.	1968 (Co-Chief)
	Jesse Thompson, M.D.	1968 (Co-Chief)
	Everard Cox, M.D.	1969
	Robert S. Sparkman, M.D.	1969-Present
INTERNAL MEDICINE	Henry M. Winans, M.D.	1947-1955
	Paul Thomas, M.D.	1956-1957
	Ralph Tompsett, M.D.	1957-Present
NEUROSURGERY	Albert P. D'Errico, M.D.	1947-1964
	Charles M. Wilson, M.D.	1965-Present
OB-GYN	W. K. Strother, M.D.	1947-1968
	Oran V. Prejean, M.D.	1968-1970 (Co-Chief)
	William P. Devereux, M.D.	1968-1970 (Co-Chief)
	Reuben H. Adams, M.D.	1970-Present
ONCOLOGY	Marvin J. Stone, M.D.	1976-Present
OPHTHALMOLOGY	Lester H. Quinn, M.D.	1947-1964
	Tom M. McCrory, M.D.	1965-1974
	Kenneth Foree III, M.D.	1975-Present

317

SERVICE	CHIEF	DATE
ORTHOPEDIC SURGERY	Felix L. Butte, M.D.	1947-1956
	Marvin P. Knight, M.D.	1957-1968
	F. Leon Ware, M.D.	1969-1977
	B. Clyde Halley, M.D.	1978-Present
OTOLARYNGOLOGY	Lyle M. Sellers, M.D.	1947-1963
	Ludwig A. Michael, M.D.	1964-1968
	Marvin G. Shepard, M.D.	1969-1974
	Ludwig A. Michael, M.D.	1975-Present
PATHOLOGY	J. M. Hill, M.D.	1947-1959
	George J. Race, M.D.	1959-Present
PEDIATRICS	Robert L. Moore, M.D.	1947-1967
	Floyd Norman, M.D.	1968-1970
	Percy E. Luecke Jr., M.D.	1970-Present
PHYSICAL MEDICINE & REHABILITATION	Edward Krusen, M.D.	1950-Present
PLASTIC SURGERY	James T. Mills, M.D.	1947-1964
	Dean C. Kipp, M.D.	1965-Present
PSYCHIATRY (Neuropsychiatry)	Guy F. Witt, M.D.	1947-1955
	P. C. Talkington, M.D.	1955-1968
	James K. Peden, M.D.	1969-Present
RADIOLOGY	Frank M. Windrow, M.D.	1947-1948
	J. E. Miller, M.D.	1949-1965
	A. D. Sears, M.D.	1966-Present
THORACIC SURGERY	Robert Shaw, M.D.	1949-1961
	Donald L. Paulson, M.D.	1962-1976
	Ben F. Mitchel, M.D.	1977-Present
UROLOGY	H. A. O'Brien, M.D.	1947-1965
	Harry Spence, M. D.	1966-1970
	Foster Fuqua, M.D.	1971-1977
	William W. Hoffman, M.D.	1977-Present

Appendix D

Appendix E

ADMINISTRATORS
1903-1978

E. T. Lewis 1903-1904
B. J. Roberts 1909-1911
J. B. Franklin 1912-1923
E. E. King 1923-1929
Bryce Twitty 1930-1939
Dr. Geo. M. Hilliard 1940-1942
C. D. Pierce 1942-1943
Lawrence Payne 1943-1948
Boone Powell
    Assistant Administrator 1945-1948
    Executive Director 1948-1975
    Director 1975-1977
    Chairman of the Executive Committee 1977-present
David H. Hitt
    Assistant Administrator 1952-1957
    Associate Director 1957-1970
    Associate Executive Director 1970-1975
    Executive Director 1975-present

Appendix F

Boone Powell	Director of Baylor University Medical Center and Vice President of Baylor University in Dallas
David H. Hitt	Executive Director
Howard M. Chase	Associate Executive Director
Bob M. Inge	Associate Executive Director
L. Gerald Bryant	Associate Director—Planning & Budgeting
William S. Carter	Associate Director
R. Glen Clark	Associate Director
Ralph E. Cross Jr.	Associate Director
Robert A. Hille	Associate Director
R. Glen Smiley	Associate Director
Stephen D. Trowbridge	Associate Director
W. Joe Allen	Administrator, Truett Hospital
John D. Hicks	Administrator, Jonsson Hospital
J. Larry Read	Administrator, Hoblitzelle Hospital
John W. Carver Jr.	Administrator, Collins Hospital
Wilbur B. Smith	Evening Administrator
Leonard J. Garron	Assistant Director
George J. Tsamis	Administrative Assistant—Systems
Robert B. Cook Jr.	Administrative Assistant—Legal Affairs
John L. Hess, C.P.A.	Controller
J. Douglas Howell, C.P.A.	Administrative Assistant—Finance
George J. Race, M.D., Ph.D.	Dean, A. Webb Roberts Center for Continuing Education
Marvin J. Stone, M.D.	Director, Charles A. Sammons Cancer Center
John W. Hyland, M.D.	Director, H. L. and Ruth Ray Hunt Heart Center
George E. Plugge Jr.	Director, Accounting Services
B. Roy Simpson, M.D.	Medical Director, Anesthesia Services
Juanita Webster, R.N., C.R.N.A.	Director, Nurse Anesthesia
Allan D. Sutton	Director, Business Services
Denise Davis, Ph.D.	Director, Central Food Services
Clare Allen, R.D.	Director, Truett Dietary Services
Charlene Giromini, R.D.	Director, Collins Dietary Services
Linda Kratzer, R.D.	Director, Jonsson Dietary Services
Jane Webber, R.D.	Director, Hoblitzelle Dietary Services
Chaplain B. F. Bennett	Director, Chaplaincy Service
John S. Sims	Director, Data Processing Services
Leonard M. Riggs, M.D.	Director, Emergency Services
Robert C. Paul	Director, Engineering Services

Daniel E. Polter, M.D.	Director, Gastroenterology
Tom S. Mouton	Director, Industrial Engineering Services
George J. Race, M.D., Ph.D.	Director, Laboratories
Dennis G. Folds	Director, Management Development Services
Claude L. Hooker	Director, Materiel Services
Ralph Tompsett, M.D.	Director, Medical Education
Marilyn Green, R.R.A.	Director, Medical Records Services
Dolores Carruth, M.D.	Director, Neonatology
Sheff D. Olinger, M.D.	Director, Neurology
Julia Ball, R.N.	Director, Hoblitzelle Nursing Services
Betty Lipman, R.N.	Director, Collins Nursing Services
Suzzette Screeton, R.N.	Director, Truett Nursing Services
Shirley Shofner, R.N.	Director, Jonsson Nursing Services
Reuben H. Adams, M.D.	Director, Obstetrics and Gynecology
Patricia Brydon, R.N.	Director, Operating Room Services
Chaplain Joseph E. Gross, Th.D.	Director, Pastoral Care
E. Elvis Bates	Director, Personnel Services
Charles R. Henry, R. Ph.	Director, Pharmacy Services
Jack R. Tatum	Director, Photography & Audio-Visual Aids
Edward M. Krusen, M.D.	Director, Physical Medicine & Rehabilitation
Bobby K. Stevenson	Director, Property Services
Lois Robinson	Director, Public Relations
Charles E. Jarrett, M.D.	Director, Pulmonary Services
A. D. Sears, M.D.	Director, Radiology-Diagnostic Roentgenology & Irradiation Therapy
Ann C. Milnor, A.C.S.W.	Director, Social Services
Robert S. Sparkman, M.D.	Director, Surgical Education
Louine Murdock	Director, Volunteer Services

322

Appendix G

These employes of Baylor University Medical Center have received awards for 30 or more years of service.

DATE HONORED	EMPLOYE	DEPARTMENT	YEARS OF SERVICE
1961	Velma Ferguson, R.N., C.R.N.A.	Anesthesia	40
1965	Argetta Parnell	Admitting	40
1968	Lewis S. Smith, R. Ph.	Pharmacy	40
1967	Louise Bane	Accounting	35
1968	John W. Smith	Accounting	35
1974	Raymond Arellano	Admitting	35
1975	Geraldine Warsteane, L.V.N.	Truett Nursing	35
1976	Eva Thomas, R.N.	Health Clinic	35
1976	Roy Gentry	Laundry	35
1977	Myrtle Roenau	Radiation Oncology	35
1977	Peck Shirley	Physical Medicine	35
1978	Mary Beard, R.N.	Radiation Oncology	35
1957	Nadine Grant	Elevator Service	30
1957	Sally K. Mooney	Holliday Hall	30
1958	Annie Belle Black	Accounting	30
1960	Sallie Moore, R.N., C.R.N.A.	Anesthesia	30
1960	Opal Sampley	Telephone Service	30
1962	Sylvia Davenport, R.N.	Truett Nursing	30
1963	Paul Willingham	Power Plant	30
1967	Grace Farley, R.N.	Inhalation Therapy	30
1968	Flo Baise	Laundry	30
1971	Hurene Walker	Building & Grounds	30
1971	James Pearl	Engineering	30
1972	Mildred Laird	Business Services	30
1973	Frances Hernandez	Laundry	30
1974	Iris Decker, R.N., C.R.N.A.	Anesthesia	30
1974	Lucille Stampley, R.N., C.R.N.A.	Anesthesia	30
1974	Linnea Carlson, R.N.	Central Service	30
1974	Elva Ruth Wylie	Personnel	30
1975	Boone Powell	Administration	30
1975	Marjorie Saunders	Public Relations	30
1975	Lillian Holcombe, L.V.N.	Hoblitzelle Nursing	30
1975	Ruby Jones	Hoblitzelle Nursing	30
1975	Frances Varner, R.N.	Hoblitzelle Nursing	30
1976	Odie Cole	Engineering	30
1976	Johnny Sills	Laboratories	30
1976	Mable Morrow	Property Service	30

DATE HONORED	EMPLOYE	DEPARTMENT	YEARS OF SERVICE
1977	Elmeader Leach, L.V.N.	Hoblitzelle Nursing	30
1977	Edwina Rentscheler, P.G.P.N.	Jonsson Nursing	30
1977	Wanda Hartoon, R.N.	Truett Nursing	30
1977	Charles R. Henry, R. Ph.	Pharmacy	30
1978	Annie Jenkins	Laboratories	30
1978	Vernell Walker	Hoblitzelle Nursing	30
1978	Effie Littleton, L.V.N.	Truett Nursing	30
1978	Lester Hinson	Operating Room	30
1978	Julio Lopez	Surgical Research	30

Appendix H

ENDOWED LECTURESHIPS

These endowed lectureships, visiting professorships and seminars are offered at the A. Webb Roberts Center for Continuing Education in the Health Sciences at Baylor University Medical Center.

Lila Mae and Arthur E. Thomas Nursing Institute

Charles R. Moore Lectureship in Orthopedic Surgery

Dennard-Carroll Memorial Lectureship in Oncology

M. Kenneth Gilbert Seminar in Radiology and X-Ray Technology

Hattie Louise Slaughter Browning Seminar in Physical Medicine, Physical Therapy and Occupational Therapy

Religion in Medicine Endowment Fund

Pathology Visiting Professorship

Walter R. and Lillian McBee Visiting Professorship in Internal Medicine

Breast Cancer Education and Research Endowment Fund

Mrs. Milford O. Rouse Nursing Institute

Dr. Milford O. Rouse Lectureship in Digestive Diseases and Nutrition

Carl and Thelma Casey Visiting Professorship in Ophthalmology

Albert P. D'Errico, M.D., Visiting Professorship in Neurosurgery

Martha Lou and Cecil M. Higginbotham Seminar in Anesthesiology

Ruth Jackson, M.D., Seminar in Orthopedic Surgery

Frank H. Kidd Jr., M.D., Visiting Professorship in General Surgery

James T. Mills, M.D., Lectureship in Plastic Surgery

Mrs. Charles R. Moore Lectureship in General Surgery

Oliver-O'Dwyer Nursing Institute

Charles and Elizabeth Prothro Lectureship in General Surgery

Boone Powell Visiting Professorship in General Surgery

Boone Powell Education and Research Endowment Fund

Charles A. Sammons Cancer Center Symposium

Thelma Franklin McCann Endowed Nursing Institute

Charles Austin, M.D., Memorial Lectureship

Jo. C. Alexander and Karl B. King Visiting Professorship in Urological Surgery

Annual Lectureship in Vascular Surgery

G. Raworth Williams, M.D., Urological Education Endowment Fund

Cecil Shelton Visiting Professorship in General Surgery

Appendix I

BAYLOR UNIVERSITY MEDICAL CENTER
A STATISTICAL COMPARISON
1952-1978

	1952-53	1977-78
Admissions		
Adults and Children	28,333	42,476
Births	6,987	3,955
Patient Days		
Private Rooms	73,202	162,153
Semi-Private	87,776	170,738
Wards	12,831	31
Intensive Care	0	15,181
Coronary Care	0	3,752
Nurseries	25,591	17,130
Surgical Cases		
Minor	6,864	9,513
Major	8,545	14,136
Emergency Room Patients	9,116	40,613
Laboratory Tests	273,473	2,483,390
Electroencephalograms	0	2,413
Pharmacy-Prescriptions	221,336	933,999
Radiographic Examinations	24,406	130,486
Radiation & Radium Treatments	9,808	49,819
Physical Medicine Treatments	93,439	208,262
Cardiac Catheterizations	0	1,896
Nuclear Medicine Examinations	0	18,898
Electrocardiograms	4,603	42,911
Other Non-Invasive Cardiac Tests	0	7,042
Pulmonary Laboratory Tests	0	140,313
Respiratory Therapy	Unknown	1,011,687

Index

328

333

334

218, 226, 243, 253, 260, 278,
281, 289, 294

Spanish Flu Epidemic — 71

Sparkman, Robert S. — 118, 210,
213, 216, 217

Speer, Robert — 172, 173, 174

Spence, Harry M. — 265, 266

Springer, Frances L. — 96

St. Paul Hospital — 197

St. Paul Sanitarium — 9, 10, 18,
127

Sprague, Charles C. — 211, 294

Standifer, C. H. — 55

Stanley, Thomas E. Architects
and Engineers — 203, 228

State Anatomical Board — 47

State Board of Medical
Examiners — 47

State Dental College — 59, 64

Steinbach, Herbert — 198, 200

Steinmann, Charles — 9

Stemmons, John — 185

Stewart, Lil - 250, 251

Stocks, Chester L. — 143, 220

Stone, Marvin J. — 242, 243

Storey, Robert G. — 99

Strother, W. K., Jr. — 116, 141,
148, 226

Students' Army Training
Corps — 55

Surgical Education — 213

Surgical Oncology, Division
of — 241, 242, 245

T

Talkington, Perry — 207

Tate, Martha - 96

Taylor, Anne — 162

Taylor, Isaac — 192

Teague, Madge — 96

Terrill, James J. — 206

Texas Area Five Health Systems
Agency — 236

Texas Baptist Memorial
Sanitarium — 2, 3, 6, 26, 28,
29, 31, 36, 38, 40, 46, 49, 50,
54, 55, 56, 58, 59, 60, 114,
139, 149, 172, 196, 206, 222,
260, 264, 266, 280

Texas Children's Hospital — 223

Texas City Disaster — 117, 120

Texas Health Facilities
Commission — 236

Texas Hospital Association — 158

Texas Instruments — 187

Texas Medical Association — 7,
8, 69, 195

Texas Research
Foundation — 193

Texas Scottish Rite
Hospital — 263

Thomas, Arthur E. — 126

Thomas, Eva — 290

Thomas, Jameson &
Merrill — 148

Thomas, Maxwell — 280

Thomas, Paul J. — 156, 211, 214

Thomas, W. H. — 69

Thommason, G. W. — 95

Thompson, Jesse — 217

Thompson, Pansy Jo — 96

Thoracic Surgery, Department
of — 217, 258

Thornton, R. L., Sr. — 142, 147

Thralls, Dorothy — 96

Thruston, Stephen D. — 10, 28

Tillery, G. Weldon — 175

Timberlawn Psychiatric
Hospital — 206, 208, 218

Tissue Committee — 118

Titterington, J. B. — 8, 12

Tompsett, Ralph — 156, 211,
213, 214, 215

Torson, Bob — 133

Towers, John L. — 143

Travis, Mrs. O. F. — 158

Trowbridge, Stephen — 299

Truett, George W. — 24, 25, 26,
29, 30, 31, 37, 40, 51, 53, 111,
113, 115, 123, 125, 129

Truett Hospital — 2, 5, 76, 115,
120, 122, 123, 128, 129, 130,
134, 135, 140, 144, 173, 174,
184, 189, 190, 197, 283, 288,
298, 299, 300

Truett Memorial Tower — 122,
126, 127

Truman, Harry — 156

Tsamis, George J. — 181, 299

Tumor Register — 246

Turner, Mrs. M. V. — 158

12 to 20 Club — 149

Twitty, Bryce — 69, 71, 72, 73,
74, 76, 78

Tyne, Michael — 226

U

Ultrasound Scanning — 200

336